VBA For Dummies, 2nd Edition

Cheat Sheet

Keyboard Shortcuts in the Visual Basic Editor

Displaying Windows

To Do This	Press
Display the Code window for the selected form or control	F7
Display the form corresponding to the active Code window	Shift+F7
Move to the next Code or UserForm window	Ctrl+Tab
Activate the Object Browser window	F2
Active the Properties window	F4
Activate the Immediate window	Ctrl+G
Activate the Call Stack window while a program is running	Ctrl+L

Working with Code

To Do This	Press
Jump to the definition of the item	Shift+F2
Display the Find dialog box	Ctrl+F
Find Next (find the next occurrence of the Find text)	F3
Find Previous	Shift+F3
Replace	Ctrl+H
Jump to the line previously edited	Ctrl+Shift+F2
Undo	Ctrl+Z
List properties/methods	Ctrl+J
List constants	Ctrl+Shift+J
Display Quick Info about the variable or object at the insertion point	Ctrl+I
Display parameter information for the function at the insertion point	Ctrl+Shift+I
Complete the word you're typing automatically	Ctrl+spacebar

Working with Properties

To Do This	Press
In the Property window, move to the next property in the list that begins with a particular letter	Ctrl+Shift+ <letter>

Running Programs

To Do This	Press
Run the procedure or UserForm in the active window	F5
Pause code execution and enter break mode	Ctrl+Break

Debugging

To Do This	Press
Execute code one line at a time (*step* through code)	F8
Execute statements one line at a time without stepping into procedure calls	Shift+F8
Run, stopping at the line containing the insertion point	Ctrl+F8
Specify (*set*) the next statement to be executed	Ctrl+F9 (after placing the insertion in the target statement)
Run the error handler code or return the error to the calling procedure	Alt+F5
Step into the error handler or return the error to the calling procedure	Alt+F8
Toggle the breakpoint in the code line with the insertion point	F9
Clear all breakpoints	Ctrl+Shift+F9
Add a watch for the item at the insertion point	Shift+F9

W9-CPF-323

VBA For Dummies, 2nd Edition

VBA Data Types

Use the keywords in the Data Type column to declare variables in Dim statements and to specify the data types of arguments in function declarations:

Data Type	What It Stores	Range of Permitted Values
Boolean	Logical true or false	True (-1) or False (0)
Byte	Small whole number	0 to 255
Integer	Smallish whole number	-32,768 to 32,767
Long	Large whole number	-2,147,483,648 to 2,147,483,647
Single	Single-precision floating-point value	-3.402823E38 to -1.401298E-45 for negative values; 1.401298E-45 to 3.402823E38 for positive values
Double	Double-precision floating-point value	1.79769313486232E308 to-4.94065645841247E-324 for negative values; 4.94065645841247E-324 to 1.79769313486232E308 for positive values
Currency	Large, precise number; 19 significant digits, including four fixed decimal places	-922,337,203,685,477.5808 to 922,337,203,685,477.5807
Decimal	Even larger, more precise numbers with 29 significant digits and up to 28 decimal places	+/-79,228,162,514,264,337,593,543,950,335 with no decimal point; +/-7.9228162514264337593543950335 with 28 places to the right of the decimal
Date	Dates and times	January 1, 100 to December 31, 9999
Object	VBA object	Any object reference
String (variable-length)	Sequence of text characters of variable length	Size of a variable-length string variable can range from 0 to approximately 2 billion characters
String (fixed-length)	Sequence of a specified number of text characters	Size of a fixed length string variable can range from 1 to approximately 65,400 characters
Variant	Any valid data	Same as for the type of data stored in the variant, as shown above in this table
User-defined (requires the Type statement)	Group of variables used together as a unit	The range of each variable in the group corresponds to its data type, as shown above in this table

...For Dummies®: Bestselling Book Series for Beginners

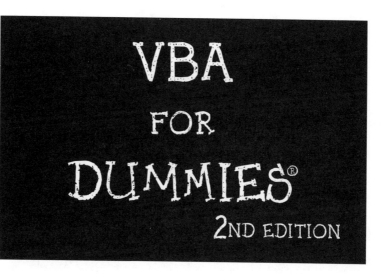

VBA FOR DUMMIES®
2ND EDITION

by Steve Cummings

IDG Books Worldwide, Inc.
An International Data Group Company

Foster City, CA ◆ Chicago, IL ◆ Indianapolis, IN ◆ New York, NY

VBA For Dummies®, 2nd Edition

Published by
IDG Books Worldwide, Inc.
An International Data Group Company
919 E. Hillsdale Blvd.
Suite 400
Foster City, CA 94404
www.idgbooks.com (IDG Books Worldwide Web site)
www.dummies.com (Dummies Press Web site)

Library of Congress Catalog Card No.: 99-64906

ISBN: 0-7645-0567-X

Printed in the United States of America

10 9 8 7 6 5 4

2O/RR/QY/ZZ/IN

Distributed in the United States by IDG Books Worldwide, Inc.

Distributed by CDG Books Canada Inc. for Canada; by Transworld Publishers Limited in the United Kingdom; by IDG Norge Books for Norway; by IDG Sweden Books for Sweden; by IDG Books Australia Publishing Corporation Pty. Ltd. for Australia and New Zealand; by TransQuest Publishers Pte Ltd. for Singapore, Malaysia, Thailand, Indonesia, and Hong Kong; by Gotop Information Inc. for Taiwan; by ICG Muse, Inc. for Japan; by Norma Comunicaciones S.A. for Colombia; by Intersoft for South Africa; by Eyrolles for France; by International Thomson Publishing for Germany, Austria and Switzerland; by Distribuidora Cuspide for Argentina; by Livraria Cultura for Brazil; by Ediciones ZETA S.C.R. Ltda. for Peru; by WS Computer Publishing Corporation, Inc., for the Philippines; by Contemporanea de Ediciones for Venezuela; by Express Computer Distributors for the Caribbean and West Indies; by Micronesia Media Distributor, Inc. for Micronesia; by Grupo Editorial Norma S.A. for Guatemala; by Chips Computadoras S.A. de C.V. for Mexico; by Editorial Norma de Panama S.A. for Panama; by American Bookshops for Finland. Authorized Sales Agent: Anthony Rudkin Associates for the Middle East and North Africa.

For general information on IDG Books Worldwide's books in the U.S., please call our Consumer Customer Service department at 800-762-2974. For reseller information, including discounts and premium sales, please call our Reseller Customer Service department at 800-434-3422.

For information on where to purchase IDG Books Worldwide's books outside the U.S., please contact our International Sales department at 317-596-5530 or fax 317-596-5692.

For consumer information on foreign language translations, please contact our Customer Service department at 1-800-434-3422, fax 317-596-5692, or e-mail rights@idgbooks.com.

For information on licensing foreign or domestic rights, please phone +1-650-655-3109.

For sales inquiries and special prices for bulk quantities, please contact our Sales department at 650-655-3200 or write to the address above.

For information on using IDG Books Worldwide's books in the classroom or for ordering examination copies, please contact our Educational Sales department at 800-434-2086 or fax 317-596-5499.

For press review copies, author interviews, or other publicity information, please contact our Public Relations department at 650-655-3000 or fax 650-655-3299.

For authorization to photocopy items for corporate, personal, or educational use, please contact Copyright Clearance Center, 222 Rosewood Drive, Danvers, MA 01923, or fax 978-750-4470.

About the Author

Steve Cummings has been programming computers for over 20 years in languages as diverse as Assembler, Cobol, and C++, as well as VBA and Visual Basic. He is author or co-author of over ten computer books, including *Office 97 Secrets* (published by IDG Books Worldwide, Inc.). He has written hundreds of articles and columns — many on programming topics — for major computer magazines, including *PC World, Macworld, PC Magazine, PC/Computing,* and *PC Week.*

ABOUT IDG BOOKS WORLDWIDE

Welcome to the world of IDG Books Worldwide.

IDG Books Worldwide, Inc., is a subsidiary of International Data Group, the world's largest publisher of computer-related information and the leading global provider of information services on information technology. IDG was founded more than 30 years ago by Patrick J. McGovern and now employs more than 9,000 people worldwide. IDG publishes more than 290 computer publications in over 75 countries. More than 90 million people read one or more IDG publications each month.

Launched in 1990, IDG Books Worldwide is today the #1 publisher of best-selling computer books in the United States. We are proud to have received eight awards from the Computer Press Association in recognition of editorial excellence and three from Computer Currents' First Annual Readers' Choice Awards. Our best-selling ...For Dummies® series has more than 50 million copies in print with translations in 31 languages. IDG Books Worldwide, through a joint venture with IDG's Hi-Tech Beijing, became the first U.S. publisher to publish a computer book in the People's Republic of China. In record time, IDG Books Worldwide has become the first choice for millions of readers around the world who want to learn how to better manage their businesses.

Our mission is simple: Every one of our books is designed to bring extra value and skill-building instructions to the reader. Our books are written by experts who understand and care about our readers. The knowledge base of our editorial staff comes from years of experience in publishing, education, and journalism — experience we use to produce books to carry us into the new millennium. In short, we care about books, so we attract the best people. We devote special attention to details such as audience, interior design, use of icons, and illustrations. And because we use an efficient process of authoring, editing, and desktop publishing our books electronically, we can spend more time ensuring superior content and less time on the technicalities of making books.

You can count on our commitment to deliver high-quality books at competitive prices on topics you want to read about. At IDG Books Worldwide, we continue in the IDG tradition of delivering quality for more than 30 years. You'll find no better book on a subject than one from IDG Books Worldwide.

John Kilcullen
Chairman and CEO
IDG Books Worldwide, Inc.

Steven Berkowitz
President and Publisher
IDG Books Worldwide, Inc.

WINNER

*Eighth Annual
Computer Press
Awards 1992*

WINNER

*Ninth Annual
Computer Press
Awards 1993*

WINNER

*Tenth Annual
Computer Press
Awards 1994*

WINNER

*Eleventh Annual
Computer Press
Awards 1995*

IDG is the world's leading IT media, research and exposition company. Founded in 1964, IDG had 1997 revenues of $2.05 billion and has more than 9,000 employees worldwide. IDG offers the widest range of media options that reach IT buyers in 75 countries representing 95% of worldwide IT spending. IDG's diverse product and services portfolio spans six key areas including print publishing, online publishing, expositions and conferences, market research, education and training, and global marketing services. More than 90 million people read one or more of IDG's 290 magazines and newspapers, including IDG's leading global brands — Computerworld, PC World, Network World, Macworld and the Channel World family of publications. IDG Books Worldwide is one of the fastest-growing computer book publishers in the world, with more than 700 titles in 36 languages. The "...For Dummies®" series alone has more than 50 million copies in print. IDG offers online users the largest network of technology-specific Web sites around the world through IDG.net (http://www.idg.net), which comprises more than 225 targeted Web sites in 55 countries worldwide. International Data Corporation (IDC) is the world's largest provider of information technology data, analysis and consulting, with research centers in over 41 countries and more than 400 research analysts worldwide. IDG World Expo is a leading producer of more than 168 globally branded conferences and expositions in 35 countries including E3 (Electronic Entertainment Expo), Macworld Expo, ComNet, Windows World Expo, ICE (Internet Commerce Expo), Agenda, DEMO, and Spotlight. IDG's training subsidiary, ExecuTrain, is the world's largest computer training company, with more than 230 locations worldwide and 785 training courses. IDG Marketing Services helps industry-leading IT companies build international brand recognition by developing global integrated marketing programs via IDG's print, online and exposition products worldwide. Further information about the company can be found at www.idg.com.
1/24/99

Dedication

For Ellie and Rufus

Publisher's Acknowledgments

We're proud of this book; please register your comments through our IDG Books Worldwide Online Registration Form located at http://my2cents.dummies.com.

Some of the people who helped bring this book to market include the following:

Acquisitions, Editorial, and Media Development

Project Editor: Jade L. Williams
(Previous Edition: Kelly Oliver)

Acquisitions Editor: Gregory Croy

Copy Editor: James Russell
(Previous Edition: Christa J. Carroll)

Technical Editor: Eric Butow

Media Development Editor: Marita Ellixson

Associate Permissions Editor:
Carmen Krikorian

Media Development Coordinator:
Megan Roney

Editorial Manager: Leah Cameron

Media Development Manager:
Heather Heath Dismore

Editorial Assistant: Beth Parlon

Production

Project Coordinator: Regina Snyder

Layout and Graphics: Angela F. Hunckler,
David McKelvey, Brent Savage,
Jacque Schneider, Janet Seib,
Michael A. Sullivan, Mary Jo Weis

Proofreaders: Vickie Broyles,
Christine Pingleton, Marianne Santy,
Rebecca Senninger

Indexer: Ty Koontz

Special Help
Diana Conover

General and Administrative

IDG Books Worldwide, Inc.: John Kilcullen, CEO; Steven Berkowitz, President and Publisher

IDG Books Technology Publishing Group: Richard Swadley, Senior Vice President and Publisher; Walter Bruce III, Vice President and Associate Publisher; Steven Sayre, Associate Publisher; Joseph Wikert, Associate Publisher; Mary Bednarek, Branded Product Development Director; Mary Corder, Editorial Director

IDG Books Consumer Publishing Group: Roland Elgey, Senior Vice President and Publisher; Kathleen A. Welton, Vice President and Publisher; Kevin Thornton, Acquisitions Manager; Kristin A. Cocks, Editorial Director

IDG Books Internet Publishing Group: Brenda McLaughlin, Senior Vice President and Publisher; Diane Graves Steele, Vice President and Associate Publisher; Sofia Marchant, Online Marketing Manager

IDG Books Production for Dummies Press: Michael R. Britton, Vice President of Production; Debbie Stailey, Associate Director of Production; Cindy L. Phipps, Manager of Project Coordination, Production Proofreading, and Indexing; Shelley Lea, Supervisor of Graphics and Design; Debbie J. Gates, Production Systems Specialist; Robert Springer, Supervisor of Proofreading; Laura Carpenter, Production Control Manager; Tony Augsburger, Supervisor of Reprints and Bluelines

◆

The publisher would like to give special thanks to Patrick J. McGovern,
without whom this book would not have been possible.

◆

Contents at a Glance

Cartoons at a Glance

By Rich Tennant

page 367

page 313

page 7

page 81

page 115

Fax: 978-546-7747 • E-mail: the5wave@tiac.net

Table of Contents

Introduction

● ●

Yes, this really is the book you need when you're starting out with VBA. With *VBA For Dummies,* 2nd Edition, you find out all the key concepts and skills you must have to write hot VBA (Visual Basic for Applications) programs that do genuinely useful things — and you discover all this stuff painlessly.

The approach in this book is casual and on the lighthearted side because goodness knows we have too many ponderous tomes in this world already. I explain everything in plain English, dumping the buzzword jargon overboard whenever possible. Now and then I throw in a bad joke, just to give you something to moan about.

On the other hand, I haven't dumbed-down or oversimplified the thornier topics. Jokes aside, this is a real reference book — it covers the essential VBA topics in enough depth that you'll actually want to refer to it later.

What the Book Covers

As you may know, VBA is the programming language built into many software applications, including everything from Microsoft Office, Microsoft Project, Visio, and AutoCAD to a host of specialized software in areas such as manufacturing, accounting, and help desk.

VBA For Dummies, 2nd Edition takes on all the essential aspects of VBA programming. You find complete information on topics such as:

- ✔ Taking charge of the VBA visual programming tools
- ✔ Recording and modifying macros
- ✔ Running VBA programs from within your applications
- ✔ Laying out lovely dialog boxes and other windows
- ✔ Working with objects, the key to tapping the power of VBA applications

I Shouldn't Make Any Assumptions . . .

But I have. I assume that you're not really a dummy at all — that instead, you already know how to use Windows quite comfortably. If you don't know how to work the mouse, make choices from menus, or click buttons on the screen, you should read one of the *Windows For Dummies* books (separate titles are available for Windows 95, Windows 98, and Windows NT from IDG Books Worldwide, Inc.) before you start on this book. To use VBA, you need at least one application that comes with the VBA software development environment built in. Again, applications that qualify include the mainstream Microsoft Office business software, along with a growing number of non-Microsoft products. Among many possibilities, any of the following Windows 95/Windows 98 or Windows NT applications will do just fine:

- Any Microsoft Office application, including Word, Excel, PowerPoint, Access, Outlook, or FrontPage
- Microsoft Project
- Corel WordPerfect Office 2000
- Micrografx iGrafx series of business graphics applications
- Visio versions 4.5 and 5
- AutoCAD Release 14 or AutoCAD 2000 for Windows
- Autodesk World
- TurboCAD Professional
- M.Y.O.B Accounting Software
- Great Plains accounting software (certain products include VBA)
- OmniTrader, a securities trading analysis and management tool
- EdgeworX, a sophisticated Web page design tool

Divide and Conquer

The skills and theoretical concepts you need to program with VBA form a seamless whole, an organic synthesis, an interdependent web like the circle of life. . . . Even so, I couldn't write about everything all at once, so I broke up the material into five big sections, each of which contains two or more chapters.

Part I: VBA Boot Camp

After just one chapter of dull theoretical stuff at the very beginning of the book, three quick chapters get you up and running with VBA. You find out how to record macros to avoid programming whenever possible and how to run your own VBA programs within your applications. You even get to write a complete working program.

Part II: Mastering the VBA Development Environment

The Visual Basic Editor is the face VBA presents to you on the screen — it's where you write your programs, construct the windows they display, and test your creations to see what makes them stop working. After you read through this part, you'll have a complete grasp of the rich set of tools at your disposal in the Visual Basic Editor.

Part III: The Main Course in VBA Programming

Here is the heart of the book. In chapter after lovingly written chapter, I spread out before you the secrets of the VBA realm. The first chapter in the section catalogues the components of a VBA program and details their structures so that you know what to type where. Next comes a practicum on the proper ways to name things in VBA and make your code presentable. Chapters on working with variables and objects to skillfully manipulate information follow in turn. I then take you on a tour of VBA's abundant built-in commands so that you won't have to reinvent the fission reactor. Other chapters explore techniques for controlling what happens while your program runs and for locating and correcting at least some of the bugs your program is bound to have.

Part IV: Designing Active Forms

Compared to some other Windows programming tools, VBA is less dependent on "forms" — its term for dialog boxes and other windows. That's because your programs don't need to have their own windows. Instead, you can run them from the user interface of the application program you're working with, or from within the VBA development environment itself. Nevertheless, VBA has a complete set of tools for form layout. You can create highly sophisticated windows studded with buttons, switches, and boxes for your users to play with. In this part, you find out how.

Part V: The Part of Tens

Two chapters on miscellaneous topics complete your tour of the VBA experience. First, I introduce a slew of advanced programming topics. The coverage isn't extremely deep, of course, but it's not overly shallow either — it's enough to get you started with actually using the capabilities. Next comes a catalogue of other VBA resources, including both information and software products. Turn here to enrich your knowledge of VBA programming and to fill your programmer's kit with software tools.

How to Use the Examples

VBA For Dummies, 2nd Edition is peppered with examples of code that illustrate the concepts I try to get across. Code samples are indicated in monospaced type, either in a separate block, like this

```
WhatEverItIs.Color = "Chartreuse"
```

or, within ordinary paragraph text, like this: `Debug.Print`.

To keep the bulk down, these samples are often just fragments that you can't run by themselves. VBA statements only run when they are inside a procedure, and many of the examples don't include the statements that define the procedure. The point is, if you want to really run the samples in your own copy of VBA, you're going to have to enclose them inside a procedure (and in some cases add additional code, as explained in the text). On the CD-ROM, these source code examples do appear as complete procedures so you can import them into a project and run them without any further work.

Because VBA statements (individual units of programming code) often run quite long, they tend not to fit within the book's margins. In general, I use the VBA line continuation character, the underscore (_), to indicate where a single statement is broken up over two lines.

What's on the CD-ROM

I claim that typing code builds moral fiber, but I realize that argument may not impress some of you. Therefore, I've gallantly included the code for the longer examples in the text on the CD-ROM stuck to the back cover of this book. See the "About the CD-ROM" appendix for information on how to use this stuff.

In addition, I collected on the CD a variety of shareware, trial, and demonstration versions of various software products that you may find useful in VBA programming. They too are mentioned in more depth in the appendix.

Icons Used in This Book

By now, you've probably seen more than a few books that use icons in the margin to help you key in on important information. I settled on only four icons for this book, so the icons themselves won't need their own guidebook.

The Remember icon marks any kind of information that I thought needed emphasis — either because it's an easier way to accomplish something or because the important stuff comes a few paragraphs after the last heading, and I was worried you might skip over it.

Finding out how to program in VBA is fun and easy, sure, if you're comparing it to physical chemistry or Sanskrit. But there's no question that it's more technically complex than working with Windows or ordinary software. In other words, the paragraphs I mark with the Technical Stuff icon aren't that much more technical than the other material. The icon does improve the book's design though, don't you think?

Ka-boom!

I mark the longer code examples with this icon just to reassure you that you won't have to retype them if you want to try them out in real life. If the icon is missing, don't worry — many of the shorter examples are on the disk, too, but I didn't want to crowd the book with icons.

The VBA For Dummies Web Site

I'm planning a Web page to accompany this book at the following address:

`www.seldenhouse.com/vba`

The site will include:

- Updates and corrections to the text
- Additional material that didn't fit in the book
- Downloadable source code as I get my hands on it
- Links to other VBA sites, including the relevant pages for specific VBA applications

Don't expect fancy page layout or lots of entertaining graphics — I'll concentrate on posting useful information instead. Please let me know if you come across any tips or solutions that other people should know about, or if you have suggestions for links to other sites.

Part I
VBA Boot Camp

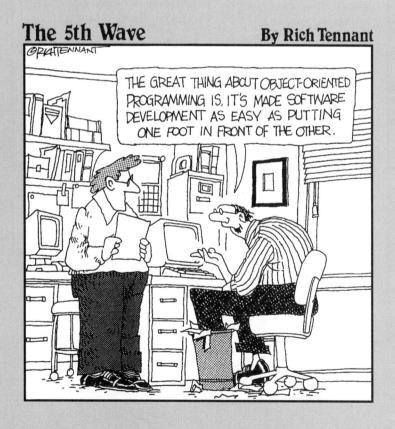

The 5th Wave   By Rich Tennant

THE GREAT THING ABOUT OBJECT-ORIENTED PROGRAMMING IS, IT'S MADE SOFTWARE DEVELOPMENT AS EASY AS PUTTING ONE FOOT IN FRONT OF THE OTHER.

In this part . . .

Chapter 1 introduces all the basic concepts that underlie the VBA programming experience. These ideas really are vital, I promise — until you understand them, serious work with VBA will be painful at best. But from then on, *VBA For Dummies,* 2nd Edition gets fiercely practical. Chapters 2 through 4 introduce the mechanics of recording macros, writing VBA code, and running your programs, including macros. After acquainting yourself with their pages, you'll own the fundamental skills for bringing VBA programs to life in your applications. You still won't know what to put in those programs, but that's why this book has fourteen or so more chapters.

Chapter 1

Don't Sweat the Technical Stuff — And It's All Technical Stuff

These days, software programs intended for professional use are overflowing with interesting, clever, and powerful features. But no matter how sophisticated the software, chances are that you can find something in it that needs improvement.

That's where VBA comes in. If the design of your software is too constricting, VBA can help you let out the waistline for a fit that's quite comfortable — and perfectly tailored to your curves and bulges.

Why Bother with VBA?

You shouldn't take a whack at VBA just to sound impressive at parties. Instead, you should get up close and personal with VBA if you want to personalize your software programs for yourself or other people.

After all, a computer is useless to you unless it does what *you* want. Visual Basic for Applications — that's what *VBA* stands for — is a set of programming tools for developing your own software. As the name suggests, VBA is designed for customizing existing applications. An *application,* of course, is a full-scale computer program that does practical work, such as a word processor or database, as opposed to a *utility,* which helps your computer system run smoothly.

With VBA, you can tweak the way an application looks and works, or even add entirely new features. Here are some of the situations where VBA may be the right solution:

✔ A feature you rely on heavily is buried deep in a dialog box somewhere. Why not place that command on a toolbar button so you can activate it with one click of the mouse? And wouldn't it be slick to have the button appear only when you actually need that command?

✔ You often repeat the same series of commands. Wouldn't you like to have the program memorize those steps so that you can launch the whole sequence with one command?

✔ Your software just isn't equipped with a feature or two you really need. Why not add the missing commands yourself?

VBA enables you to make any of these modifications, and more — you can even build complete, custom programs of your own using VBA. The section "More about What You Can Do with VBA" later in this chapter explores the possibilities in more detail.

Want another reason to get on board the VBA express? Try this one: VBA is fast becoming a standard in the software industry. After you've figured out VBA, you can put it to use in any application that is equipped with VBA. (However, for each VBA application you work with, you also need to master its special VBA jargon. For details, see "VBA, a standard — sort of" section later in this chapter.)

And if you know VBA, you're automatically an expert at Visual Basic. Another Microsoft product, Visual Basic is one of the most popular software development tools on the planet and is used to create everything from simple shareware utilities to complex, major-league applications.

By the way, one other advantage of the VBA standard is that you need to install only one copy of the special support files that VBA requires for all the applications that use VBA. In a standard installation, the VBA DLLs (Dynamic Link Libraries) and related files are located in the folder \Program Files\ Common Files\Microsoft Shared\VBA.

VBA Is the Steering Wheel, but You Still Need the Car

Okay, so VBA is great for customizing applications. There's only one catch, however — VBA must be built into the application you're trying to modify. (In this book, I use the term *VBA applications* for applications that have VBA capability built in. I refer to the software *you* create with VBA as *VBA programs*.)

Microsoft — you've heard of that company, right? — created VBA and builds it into its flagship applications. In both Office 97 and Office 2000, Word, Excel, Access, and PowerPoint are all equipped with VBA. In Outlook, the remaining member of the Microsoft Office suite, you use a simplified version of VBA called VBScript to add custom functionality to forms. Outlook 2000, unlike previous versions, provides full-fledged VBA for customizing Outlook itself. VBA is also built into FrontPage 2000, Microsoft's Web page authoring and Web site management tool (included with some versions of Office 2000), and into Microsoft Project 98.

Non-Microsoft VBA applications

Microsoft also licenses its VBA technology to many other software developers. Here's a sampling of the non-Microsoft VBA applications now available:

- ✔ **Visio:** A popular business graphics package.

- ✔ **Corel WordPerfect Office 2000:** A competitor to Microsoft Office, the Corel WordPerfect suite includes word processing, spreadsheet, database, and presentations applications.

- ✔ **Corel Draw 9**: The most popular PC graphics package, Corel Draw and its suite-mates let you create and edit both "draw"-style illustrations and "paint"-style graphics, and use them in print or Web page layouts.

- ✔ **AutoCAD:** A hugely successful Computer Aided Design application — several other programs from the same publisher are also VBA applications.

- ✔ **M.Y.O.B. Accounting:** A complete accounting package for small businesses.

- ✔ **Micrografx iGrafx series:** Business graphics applications for laying out flowcharts, organization charts and the like, and for modeling business operations graphically. A demo of iGrafx Professional, complete with VBA 6, is included on the CD-ROM that accompanies this book.

- ✔ **OmniTrader:** A securities tracking and analysis application.

You can buy applications that include programming tools that are similar to but different from VBA. Although you can customize these applications in much the same way as you can VBA applications, VBA programs don't run in these non-VBA applications.

The range of VBA applications

Applications of just about every type are more powerful when you can customize them easily. For this reason, you should see VBA popping up in all kinds of software, from the mainstream to the highly specialized.

You never stand alone with VBA

In contrast to most other programming languages, including Visual Basic, VBA doesn't enable you to create independent, *stand-alone* programs. In other words, you can't start a VBA program by double-clicking it in a My Computer window. Entering the program name in the Run command on the Start menu doesn't work, either.

Instead, a VBA program can run only within a full-scale software application such as Microsoft Word, Visio, or AutoCAD. After you start the application, you can then run any VBA program designed for that application. You can

even set things up so that a VBA program is triggered to run automatically as soon as you start the application. You just can't run the VBA program on its own.

A VBA program capitalizes on the functionality that's under the hood of the application, tapping that power for its own purposes. If you'll excuse a biological metaphor, a VBA program and the application it runs in have a symbiotic relationship. Both parties benefit: The VBA program needs the application to run at all, and the application gains customizations and new features from the VBA program.

With millions and millions of copies of Microsoft Office in circulation, the Office applications are about as mainstream as you can get. I already mentioned some non-Microsoft VBA applications with broad appeal (such as WordPerfect, Visio, and AutoCAD).

However, many other VBA applications are designed for very narrow, highly specialized markets. One example is manufacturing control applications, the kind that run robotic production lines. Another is help desk applications, which are used by a company's technical support staff to help customers or other employees solve problems. VBA has also found a home in software for sales force automation, civil engineering, telephony, data warehousing, document management, financial services, and the legal and healthcare industries.

VBA has also been licensed by a number of corporations that aren't in the business of selling software. These companies are developing their own in-house applications designed from the ground up for the specific needs of each firm. Even so, they're building in VBA so that their applications can be further customized and extended with a minimum of hassle.

Programming with VBA

In essence, programming a computer means simply telling it what to do. When you create a computer program, you give the computer a particular set of steps to follow. For example, you may tell the computer to

✔ Bring up a window full of interesting buttons and menus.

✔ Summon a box asking you to type in your birth date.

✔ Click a Calculate Age button that figures your age based on the birth date you typed in.

In days gone by, creating a program meant that you had to write out all the instructions of the program yourself. Because computers don't understand human languages, programmers had to type in the program *code* — the list of these commands — using the terminology of a special programming language.

VBA eliminates the need to type code to define the way your program looks on the screen. Unfortunately, though, coding is still required in programs of any complexity. *Part* of VBA is a programming language. Here's an example of some VBA code:

```
Sub SelectNextQuestion()
   If SelectionStrategy = Randomly Then
      AskRandomQuestion
   Else If CurrentQuestion = TotalQuestions Then
      CurrentQuestion = 1
   Else
      CurrentQuestion = CurrentQuestion + 1
   End If
End Sub
```

If you read this code carefully, you may be able to guess what it's supposed to do. One of the best things about the VBA language is that it has a lot in common with ordinary English. But it's still a foreign language, so don't worry if it looks like gibberish. One of the major goals of this book is to make you comfortable writing VBA code.

What's so visual about Visual Basic for Applications?

Fortunately, VBA eliminates a lot of the drudgery of typing code. For one thing, you can record the commands you use in your application as a starting point for a new program.

For another, VBA lets you design the parts of your program that appear on the screen — the dialog boxes, buttons, check boxes, and so on — by drawing them with the mouse or picking options from dialog boxes. This capability is what makes VBA a visual programming tool. With VBA, you can slap together the on-screen structure of your program in no time flat. In contrast, you may take hours, days, maybe years if you have to type in the program code needed to define these same elements and display them on the screen.

Unfortunately, VBA can't guess what you want your program to *do.* You still have to type the code that defines the function of each button, check box, and so on in your program. Even if your program has no buttons or check boxes, you still have to write code for the steps it should follow when it runs.

The main events

In VBA, an *event* is something that happens while your program is running, in order to change what the program does. The obvious example is clicking the mouse button. When the user of your program clicks a button labeled Calculate Age, that action is an event. Likewise, each time the user presses a key on the keyboard, double-clicks the mouse button, or simply moves the mouse, an event occurs.

Of course, your program can't respond to these events by telepathy. *Au contraire,* you have to write an *event procedure,* a special snippet of VBA code, for each event that you want your program to recognize. You need one event procedure to respond to clicks on the Calculate Age button, but another if you want the program to do something when the mouse just points to the button without clicking. Of course, if you have another button labeled Lie about Age, you have to supply yet another event procedure for clicks on that button. Chapter 16 covers writing event procedures in fastidious detail.

The programming cycle

No matter what programming tool you use, you can boil down the process of creating any new software program into a series of five simple steps.

1. **Design.**

   Decide what the program is supposed to do, how it should look on the screen, and how it should interact with other software.

2. **Implement.**

   To get the results you planned for in Step 1, construct the windows and other elements the program will display on the screen, and then type the necessary code. This part is fun.

3. **Test.**

   Run the program to see whether it looks right and does what you want. It won't.

4. **Debug.**

   Hunt through the code until you find out what's wrong, and then correct it (like all good programming tools, VBA gives you special features to help with the debugging process).

5. Keep testing.

Repeat Steps 3 and 4 until you are too tired or hungry to go on.

Fortunately, you don't have to memorize these steps — they become second nature as soon as you start VBA programming in earnest.

More about What You Can Do with VBA

In the section in this chapter called "Why Bother with VBA?" I mention the different ways you can customize your software using VBA. It's time to explore these in greater depth, just so you know what's possible with VBA.

Before you get carried away with your customization plans, keep the following in mind: How much you can accomplish with VBA depends on the application with which you're working. Some programs let you redefine every element of the user interface and every built-in command, and they give you a wealth of building blocks with which you can construct your own new features. In other applications, you're much more limited.

Customizing the user interface

One obvious way you can put VBA to work is in changing an application's user interface to match your work habits and suit your sense of personal style. (Just in case you're new to the term, *user interface* means the way the program looks on the screen, how the mouse and keyboard work, and any other means the program provides for you — the user — and the software to communicate.) In many applications, VBA permits you to alter the user interface elements as you see fit. With a few lines of code, you can add, delete, or rearrange the buttons on the toolbars, create new toolbars, redefine the keyboard layout, or modify the menu structure. Figure 1-1 shows Microsoft Word with a user interface modification courtesy of VBA.

Of course, you don't use a blowtorch when a match will do — and VBA is often overkill for simple user interface customizations. Many of today's applications allow you to customize the user interface without any programming at all, via drag-and-drop or dialog boxes.

Still, VBA can come in handy even with these applications. For one thing, even highly customizable applications may not let you change certain parts of the interface without VBA (see Chapter 5). Most importantly, however, VBA allows you to orchestrate automatic changes in the user interface — changes that occur while the application is running, based on what you're currently doing with the program.

Figure 1-1:
You need VBA to work on Microsoft Word documents with a completely clean screen — with no toolbars at all.

Suppose that when you're working on amounts greater than $1,000,000 you always use the same three toolbars. You can create a VBA program that displays all three toolbars at the same time and then hides them all when you no longer need them.

So far, I'm talking about customizing the VBA application's user interface, not creating a user interface for your VBA program itself. Although many VBA programs are automatons that require no interaction with you to complete their work, times definitely occur when you have to create your own windows and dialog boxes (these are generically called *forms* in VBA).

Adding new features

VBA really comes into its own when you use it to extend the functionality of your application. Suppose that you want red stars in the computer illustrations you draw on the first Monday of each month, but you want blue hearts every other Tuesday. Can you really expect the designer of your graphics program to anticipate your taste in graphical doo-dads? Using building-block functions provided by the application's designers, you can assemble little VBA programs that do special tricks like this.

At its simplest, a VBA program just triggers a series of commands in sequence, performing exactly the same steps each time you run it. Even at this level, however, the VBA program saves you time, compared to activating each of the commands yourself, one by one.

As a simple example, Microsoft Word lacks a command for saving a selected block of text into a separate file. To accomplish this task, you must copy the selected text to the Clipboard, start a new document, paste in the Clipboard text, and finally save and close the new document. With VBA, however, you can write a little program that carries out all these steps automatically — providing Word users with a feature that most word processors have had since the days of CP/M (an operating system used in many of the earliest personal computers). The VBA code for this program looks like this:

```
Public Sub CopyBlockToFile()
Selection.Range.Copy  ' copies the selection to
                      ' the Clipboard
Documents.Add  ' creates a new document
Selection.Range.Paste '  pastes the Clipboard into
                      ' the new document
Dialogs(wdDialogFileSaveAs).Show '  displays the
                      ' Save As dialog box
ActiveDocument.Close  '  closes the new document
End Sub
```

Because VBA is a full programming language, however, a VBA program doesn't have to follow exactly the same steps in exactly the same order each time it runs. Instead, your program can react to the conditions it finds at the time. Here are examples of how this feature can work:

✔ A VBA program can respond to what the application is doing or to current settings of the whole system at the time it runs. In the Word example above, for instance, you may decide that the program should save a new document only if some text is *already* selected — otherwise, it should scratch its head and pat its tummy simultaneously. Likewise, you may want your special program to do one thing in the morning but do something else in the afternoon.

✔ A VBA program can take action depending on information contained in the current document, in another document created by the same application, or even in documents from other applications.

✔ A VBA program can respond to information supplied by the user when the program runs (see Figure 1-2). With VBA, you can easily build dialog boxes that allow the user to select from pre-fab options or to enter text or numbers from scratch.

✔ A VBA program can change its behavior based on the current sign of the zodiac or the phase of the moon. (Unfortunately, you must write the code needed to translate the date and time into the correct astrological sign or moon phase.)

Figure 1-2:
You can create dialog boxes like this one whenever your program needs information from the user.

As to *how* your VBA programs can be made to react to changing conditions, I cover that topic in depth in later chapters.

Creating advanced custom programs

Creating VBA programs that add individual features to your existing applications is well within the reach of anyone who can say their times tables or read cereal boxes while eating. You should know, though, that you're not limited to making minor additions and modifications to existing software. Actually, VBA gives you the tools to create complete and very sophisticated programs that rival the power of off-the-shelf applications.

Most of the time, custom programs created with VBA take advantage of the features of the underlying VBA application (in fact, custom programs created with VBA can even access the functionality of *multiple* VBA applications). To the user, however, a custom program can appear as a distinct entity, with its own set of windows, buttons, and menus.

Creating a full-scale custom program is an ambitious project. This book gives you most of the skills you need, and even includes a scratch-the-surface introduction to accessing multiple VBA applications in a single program (see Chapter 17 for that).

By the way, VBA doesn't force you to use the application's features. If you want, you can just ignore those capabilities and build an entirely unrelated program of your own. The trouble is that you would still need to run the VBA application each time you want to run your custom program, a step that wouldn't be necessary with Visual Basic. (You run into another catch, too — see the "Why VBA is usually slower than Visual Basic" section later in this chapter.)

Not Your Mama's BASIC

You could say that VBA is a direct descendant from the original BASIC programming language. Well, you could say so, but that would be like saying that people came from amoebas — a lot has happened since then.

The original version of the BASIC language was created in the 1960s in hopes of making programming easier for ordinary folks. BASIC stands for Beginner's All-purpose Symbolic Instruction Code. Compared to other programming languages such as C++ or FORTRAN, the commands of the BASIC language are more like English; they're easier to understand and remember.

Many of the special-purpose "words" used in the VBA programming language were part of the original BASIC and had similar functions. Likewise for VBA's "grammar" — some of the rules for which words go together, and in which order, originated with BASIC.

Still, the VBA language has evolved far beyond the early versions of BASIC. Many of the VBA commands, and the rules for fitting them together, just weren't part of the original BASIC. Simply put, the VBA language can do more than plain old BASIC — a whole lot more — especially when it comes to displaying interesting shapes on the screen and interacting with other software.

Besides, VBA isn't just a programming language. It includes a complete software *integrated development environment* (IDE) with all kinds of special-purpose windows that help you design and test your programs (see the section "The VBA integrated development environment"). Then, too, VBA has something BASIC never even dreamed of — it lets you design a sophisticated user interface without typing any program code. As you've seen, that feature is what makes VBA a *visual* software development tool.

The VBA integrated development environment

All your work with VBA takes place in an *IDE* (integrated development environment). This term may sound cold and intimidating, but don't let it scare you off — think of an IDE as a cozy home base where you can do all your programming chores in comfort.

The IDE that comes with VBA is called the *Visual Basic Editor.* The Visual Basic Editor constitutes a top-level application window with one menu and toolbar system, in which you have access to an assortment of subsidiary windows providing all the tools you need to create your programs. Figure 1-3 shows the Visio version of the Visual Basic Editor, but it looks the same in every VBA application.

Microsoft Visual Basic - C:\My Documents\VisioVBA.vsd

File Edit View Insert Format Debug Run Tools Window Help

Project - VisioVBA

CustomSpinners
LifeOptionsReview
Manycontrols
QuotationForm
UserForm4
Modules
PopUpQuotation
PracticalProcedures

Properties - CommandButton1

CommandButton1 CommandButton

Alphabetic Categorized

(Name)   CommandButton1
Accelerator
AutoSize   False
BackColor   &H0000FFFF&
BackStyle   1 - fmBackStyleOpaque
Cancel   False
Caption
ControlTipText
Default   False
Enabled   True
Font   Tahoma
ForeColor   &H80000012&
Height   56.25
HelpContextID   0
Left   153.35

C:\My Documents\VisioVBA.vsd - PopUpQuotation (Code)

(General)   VizioDizio

    PauseTime = 2   ' Set duration. 600 = 10 minutes
    Start = Timer   ' Set start time.
    Do While Timer < Start + PauseTime
        DoEvents   ' Yield to other processes.
    Loop
    QuotationForm.Show

End Sub
Sub VisioVBAtest()
' try to add button to Visio
Dim uiObj As Visio.UIObject

Object Browser

<All Libraries>

control

Search Results

Library   Class
MSForms   Control
MSForms   Controls
VisioVBA   Manycontrols
MSForms   Frame

Classes   Members of 'Control'
Connect   Cancel
Connects   ControlSource

Toolbox

Controls

C:\My Documents\VisioVBA.vsd - CustomSp

Fantasy Sweepstakes

Select desired payout

$100,000,000

Figure 1-3:
The Visual
Basic Editor
as it
appears
in Visio.

Not *all* VBA applications come with the Visual Basic Editor (more on this in
the "VBA dialects" section later in this chapter).

I delve deeply into the Visual Basic Editor in Part III. For now, this partial list
of its accouterments should give you a sense of the tools it gives you:

- A place for designing the *forms* (windows and dialog boxes) used in
  your programs

- A palette from which you can pick the buttons, check boxes, and other
  controls you want to add to your forms (see the "Controls — ActiveX and
  otherwise" section later in this chapter)

- A window for telling VBA how you want your forms and the controls on
  them to look and act

- Windows for typing and editing VBA code so that you can make your
  program do something useful

- Windows that display the current values of the program's *variables* —
  the numbers and text that it stores and changes — as the program runs
  (these are a big help when you're tracking down bugs)

Macros and VBA

One of the most common uses for VBA is consolidating a set of your application's commands. If you repeatedly use the same commands in the same sequence, storing this sequence as a VBA program makes sense. You can then activate the whole sequence with a single command — the one that fires up the VBA program you created for this purpose.

The easiest way to make this type of VBA program is simply to record the sequence of commands. Most VBA applications come with a *macro recorder*. It works something like a tape recorder. As soon as you start the macro recorder, it records all the commands you use in your application. After you stop the recorder, it converts those recorded commands into equivalent lines of VBA code. The resulting VBA program is called a *macro*. Chapter 3 covers the ins and outs of recording macros.

Aside from how you create a macro, no difference exists — none at all — between a macro that you record and a VBA program that you type in as VBA code. You can edit the macro code, adding or deleting items at will, just as if you had typed in the code yourself.

Controls — ActiveX and otherwise

In any Windows program, the *controls* are the doohickeys on your screen that you can click or type into to get a certain action from the program. Familiar controls include push-button-type buttons on toolbars and in dialog boxes, radio buttons and check boxes for picking from predetermined options, and text boxes in which you can type or edit entries. Figure 1-4 shows a dialog box with lots of sample controls.

VBA comes with these and all the other standard types of Windows controls. They work like plug-in components. To add a control to one of your forms (a window or dialog box), you just click the control in the Toolbox, a special toolbar shown in Figure 1-5, and then plop the control down on the form.

Because of something called *ActiveX,* you're not limited to the controls that come with VBA. Developed by Microsoft, ActiveX defines a standard by which software developers create interchangeable controls that can be plugged into your programs as you see fit. The controls that come with VBA are ActiveX controls, but many, many others are available. ActiveX controls work in C++ and Java programs, too, as well as in VBA. Anyway, to be able to use a new ActiveX control on your VBA forms, all you have to do is install it onto the Toolbox (see Chapter 17 for instructions). After it's there, it works just like the controls that come with VBA.

Radio buttons (option buttons) ⌐ Check boxes

Text box
List box
Tab strip

Figure 1-4:
A dialog
box full of
controls.

└Combo box | Spin buttons

Frame   Label   Command button

Figure 1-5:
The VBA
Toolbox
offers a
palette of
controls for
your forms.

Anybody who wants to can create these special-purpose software widgets for their own use — or for sale to programmers like you. With the huge market for Windows software, you can easily see why lots of ActiveX controls are available. You can find enhanced versions of the standard controls, as well as new types of controls, such as dials, meters, clocks, calendars, and many more. If VBA doesn't come with a control that you need, you can probably buy one that does the job. Figure 1-6 gives you an idea of the possibilities.

Figure 1-6:
This form is
filled with
ActiveX
controls that
don't come
with VBA.

For some of these third-party ActiveX controls, the main selling point is looks. These controls more or less duplicate the functions of standard controls, but with a snazzier façade. Suppose that you are creating a space adventure game and you want to let players set the speed of their Astro-Cruisers. I know, I know, no one is going to use VBA to program a space adventure game. But just imagine — instead of a pair of drab spinner buttons, wouldn't you rather give them big, bright red rocket ship icons?

In many cases, though, add-on ActiveX controls do things the standard controls can't. For example, you can buy controls that create small spreadsheet grids on your forms. Chapter 19 reviews some of the most popular and useful third-party ActiveX controls.

If you're really ambitious you can create your own ActiveX controls. You need a copy of the Professional or Enterprise versions of Visual Basic 5.0 or 6.0.

Object-oriented programming with VBA

Visual Basic has evolved into a (nearly) full-fledged *object-oriented* programming language. Although working with objects poses challenges for the VBA novice, the rewards are well worth your efforts. Chapter 10 takes up the nuts and bolts of programming with objects, but you deserve a brief introduction here.

So what's an object?

Objects are vital features of the VBA landscape. Through them, you have access to the functionality of the underlying VBA application you're working in. Eventually, you may go on to access objects from other compatible applications and even build your own objects (see Chapter 17).

From a practical standpoint, an object is simply a named item that has

- **Properties:** settings you can check and change
- **Methods:** actions the object can perform when your program asks it to
- **Events:** things that happen to the object, to which it can respond by automatically taking a predetermined action

Something is an object if it possesses both data and the code that acts on that data. An object *encapsulates* the data and the related code.

Objects as components of VBA applications

The easiest way to start thinking about objects is to see them as parts of your VBA application and its documents. A shape in a Visio drawing is an object, as is each *connect* (line) that joins two shapes. So is each layer to which shapes can be assigned, and so is each page where the layers reside. And so is the document itself, to which all the pages, layers, shapes, and connects belong.

Similarly, Excel objects include the cells in which you enter data or formulas, named ranges of cells, the charts that grace many worksheets, individual worksheets, and complete workbooks. And in most VBA applications, the toolbars and menus, and the buttons and menu choices they contain, are objects as well. VBA objects exist in a hierarchy in which one type of object contains objects of other types. These object hierarchies are called *object models*.

VBA is a standard — sort of

One of the big selling points of VBA is that it's a *standard* — it works the same in every VBA application. If you figure out how to build programs with VBA in, say, Microsoft Word, all those skills should transfer directly to Visio, AutoCAD, or any other VBA application.

A lot of truth is in this claim. The Visual Basic Editor and all its parts are identical in all VBA applications (all that include the Visual Basic Editor, anyway). The way the Visual Basic Editor works is also the same. This fact holds, for example, for the visual process of creating forms (again, forms are the custom windows and dialog boxes you make for your programs). In fact, you can create a form in one VBA application and use it later in a different application. To be honest, though, form design is the easy part of VBA.

When it comes to the programming language at the core of VBA, things aren't quite so consistent. On the one hand, the basics of the language are always identical. For example, you always use the special keyword Dim to define a new variable (remember, a variable is a parking place where the program stores a number, bit of text, or some other item that may change while the program runs). In any VBA application, the statement:

```
Dim MyVariable as Integer
```

creates a variable called MyVariable and defines it as an integer — rather than text or a number with decimal points.

Likewise, you use the same techniques to set up the sub-units of your program that perform specific tasks *(procedures* and *functions)*, regardless of which VBA application you're working in.

Apart from such essentials, however, many VBA programming commands are unique to the application you're using. What I mean is that you can have a lot of learning to do when you switch from programming in one VBA application to another — even though VBA is supposed to be standardized.

Of course, a graphics application such as Visio would logically have different commands from a word-processing application such as Word. Unfortunately, though, different VBA applications often use different commands even for features they have in common.

Commands for customizing menus and toolbars are a good example of this discrepancy. Would you believe that, even Word, Excel, and PowerPoint — all kissing cousins in the Microsoft Office family — require different VBA commands for customizing certain elements? Oh, well, it ain't a perfect world.

Technically, the VBA language itself is the same in all VBA applications. It seems to vary because each application has its own unique set of *objects,* with its own methods (commands) and properties (characteristics). You can find out more about objects, methods, and properties in Chapter 2.

VBA 5 versus VBA 6

This book covers the two most recent renditions of VBA, versions 5 and 6. VBA 5 came out with Microsoft Office 97, and most non-Microsoft applications are still based on this version. VBA 6 is the version used in the Office 2000 applications, and is also available in Micrografx' iGrafx products and in Corel WordPerfect 2000 and Corel Draw 9.

The differences between the two versions aren't dramatic, and you can move back and forth between the two versions without missing a beat. Still, you should know what the most important changes are, as follows:

✔ VBA 5 provides online Help using the older WinHelp program, while VBA 6 relies on Microsoft's new HTML Help technology for the same purpose (many people actually prefer WinHelp).

✔ VBA 6 enhances the core VBA language with 13 new functions, most of which are used for manipulating text or formatting values. Chapter 11 covers built-in VBA functions and identifies those that are available only in VBA 6.

✔ VBA 6 forms can be modeless, whereas all forms in VBA 5 are modal. I won't try to define these terms now — they're covered fully in Chapter 15.

Several other enhancements in VBA 6 benefit advanced developers and are beyond the scope of this book.

Other VBA dialects

Most VBA applications come with all the bells and whistles — the macro recorder, the full version of the Visual Basic Editor, and the complete VBA programming language. Such Cadillac VBA applications include Visio, WordPerfect, AutoCAD, and, of course, the big guns from Microsoft — Word, Excel, Access, and PowerPoint.

Microsoft Access diverges from mainstream VBA applications a bit. Access doesn't have a macro recorder — Access macros must be coded by hand, and for that matter, they aren't VBA macros. Access forms (custom dialog boxes) aren't interchangeable with those of other VBA applications. And while Access 2000 includes the Visual Basic Editor, Access 97 does not. Instead, you get independent windows for typing VBA code, debugging, and designing forms.

VBScript is a pared-down version of VBA used in some applications, including Microsoft's Internet Explorer and Outlook. VBScript-based applications don't come with the Visual Basic Editor, and the programming language itself isn't as complete. Still, it's pretty powerful. IDG Books Worldwide, Inc. has a whole book on VBScript programming for Internet Explorer; it's called *VBScript For Dummies,* 2nd Edition, by John Walkenbach.

Why VBA is usually slower than Visual Basic

Besides the fact that you can't create separate, stand-alone applications in VBA, one other big difference exists between it and Visual Basic proper: VBA programs are slower, at least some of the time.

The reason for this difference is simple. A VBA program has to be *compiled* at least once during each session with the corresponding VBA application. Compiling is the process of converting the *program code* (that you can read) into *machine code* (the instructions that the computer actually executes when the program runs). A *compiler* is a software program that converts human-readable code into instructions the computer can follow.

After a standard Visual Basic program has been compiled, it is stored on the computer's hard drive in an executable form that can always run at the computer's full speed, as soon as the program has been loaded into memory. VBA programs, by contrast, are stored as VBA code. When you give the order to run a VBA program, the following steps occur:

1. **The program is compiled.**

   This step is the bottleneck. As the VBA compiler does its work, you hear your hard drive drumming, but nothing seems to be happening.

2. **The compiled version is stored in the computer's memory.**

3. **Finally! The program runs.**

Step 2 limits the damage. As long as the compiled version of a VBA program remains stored in memory, it can run at full speed as many times as you need it. After you exit the VBA application, however, the compiled program disappears into the ether. It has to be compiled again the next time you run the application. Unfortunately, a compiled VBA program may also lose its temporary home in memory even before you exit the application. This eviction can happen when the program is idle and when the memory is needed for some other purpose, such as running a bunch of other applications.

For the tasks that VBA specializes in — working with the objects of a VBA application — a program written in VBA actually runs faster than the same program written in Visual Basic.

Chapter 2

Don't Program When You Can Record a Macro

- -

In This Chapter

▶ Recording macros — sequences of commands — so you can use them again and again

▶ Starting the macro recorder

▶ Figuring out how to record macros so they work the way they're supposed to work

▶ Viewing and modifying macro code in the Visual Basic Editor

- -

*I*f you don't have to write program code, why bother? If all you want to do is automate a set of your application's commands, record them as a *macro*. Read on to find out how macros can help you minimize the amount of code you write.

Understanding How Macros Work

Some VBA applications — specifically, Microsoft Word, Excel, and PowerPoint — include a *macro recorder,* which operates something like a tape recorder. When you turn on the macro recorder, it records every command you use in your application from that point on, until you click the Stop button. After the macro has been recorded, you can play it back whenever you need to use that same sequence of commands again.

By the way, the word *macro* means big. The implication is that you're collecting a bunch of small commands into one bigger command. Actually, your macros can be as little and modest as you like — if you have too much time on your hands, you can record a useless macro that includes only one command.

In VBA applications that *don't* include the macro recorder, the term *macro* may refer to any VBA programs, the kind that you create by programming. In Visio 4.5 and 5.0, for example, creating a macro starts a new program in the Visual Basic Editor. On the other hand, in at least one major VBA application — Access — macros have nothing directly to do with VBA. In Access, although you can create macros that trigger sequences of commands, Access macros aren't automatically stored as VBA code (see the sidebar "Macros are not rows of Macintosh computers" later in this chapter). All versions of Access lack a macro recorder, so you have to select commands you want to store in a macro using a special dialog box.

When to record macros

Macros save time and make you less grumpy. Really. The computer can play back a command sequence much, much more quickly than you can click the corresponding buttons or menu choices. The computer doesn't make any mistakes, either. And your mood becomes better because people hate doing the same thing more than two or three times in a row.

So . . . train yourself to notice whenever you repeatedly use the same sequence of commands in your application, over and over again. As soon as you become aware that you're in a repeating pattern, record the commands as a macro right away. Better yet, when you know ahead of time that you're going to be reusing a series of commands, you can record the macro the first time you carry out the commands. From then on, use the macro instead.

Macros are not rows of Macintosh computers

A *macro* is actually just another term for a VBA program. While the macro recorder is running, it converts each command you use in the application into a corresponding line of VBA code. The finished macro is stored as a single VBA *procedure*. Procedures, as Chapter 8 makes plain, are units of VBA code you can run by name. (To get squeaky-clean technically correct, a macro is a *Sub procedure* that takes no arguments. Are you sure that you wanted to know that?)

One other technical point: Microsoft Access has macros and it has VBA, but Access macros *aren't* VBA programs. You construct an Access macro by selecting a series of commands in a special dialog box. To muddy the waters further, however, I must tell you that an Access macro can trigger an Access VBA procedure. Oh, dear.

Macros feel good, but they lead to the hard stuff

Although they are plenty useful in their own right, recorded macros are also a great way to ease into VBA programming. After you record a few macros, you soon start hankering after ways to make them more flexible. With just a little VBA programming, you can build rudimentary intelligence into a macro, allowing it to alter its behavior depending on what's going on at the time. See "Modifying Macros — the Easy Way to Write Code" later in this chapter.

Planning a Macro

After you've skipped this boring section and plunged right in to record a few macros, you may be ready to listen to some conservative advice. Here it is: To save yourself headaches, devote a few moments to planning your macros before you start recording them.

As soon as you have a vague sense of what you want a macro to accomplish, you are tempted to fire up the recorder and start piling on the commands. The trouble is that the recorder faithfully records every command you issue, including all your mistakes. Eight or nine times out of ten, you make some.

Of course, you can always delete a bungled macro and start from scratch. But you may as well save yourself that trouble, and plan. Think through the steps the macro should perform, practice them to see that they do in fact get the job done, and *then* record the macro.

As you plan your macro, take into account any special conditions that must be in effect for the macro to work properly. Plan to include in the macro the commands needed to re-create these conditions.

As a simple example, imagine that you're working with Microsoft Word. Say that you want your macro to insert the date at the very beginning of a document. You could easily assume that the text insertion point (cursor) will already be at the top of the current document whenever you run the macro. Don't be so confident. Even if the insertion point is in the right place when you record the macro, the first command you record should be the one that moves to the top of the document. That way, the macro will work properly no matter where the insertion point happens to be.

Recording Macros

Fortunately, the mechanics of recording a macro are as easy as falling into bed. I detail the steps for you, anyway.

Starting the macro recorder

You can start the macro recorder with either of the following methods:

- ✔ Choose <u>T</u>ools⇨<u>M</u>acro⇨Record New Macro. If you're using Office 2000, the Macro menu item may not appear until you click the down-arrow button at the bottom of the Tools menu.

- ✔ Click the Record Macro toolbar button, if your application has one. In Microsoft Office, the Record Macro button is on the Visual Basic toolbar.

Either way, the Record Macro dialog box appears. Figure 2-1 shows the Record Macro dialog box from Microsoft Excel (it looks different in different applications).

Naming the baby

Trying to be helpful, the Record Macro dialog box suggests a lovely and very distinctive name for your new macro, Macro1 (or Macro2, or Macro3). Offering polite thanks, you quickly erase the suggestion and type in a name of your own.

A macro's name should, of course, be descriptive of its function. However, you have to live within some rules. Class, repeat after me:

- ✔ **Macro names must start with a letter, not a number.** Numbers are okay after the first character, though.

- ✔ **A macro name can't contain spaces.** You have to use mixed-case capitalization to indicate separate words, as in

  ```
  EraseEntireHardDrive
  ```

- ✔ **Punctuation marks are off limits, too.** Exceptions exist, but you can safely ignore punctuation marks. If you do use punctuation marks, VBA returns an "Invalid procedure name" dialog box.

Chapter 8 covers VBA's naming rules in detail.

Figure 2-1:
Excel's
Record
Macro
dialog box.

Making other choices in the Record Macro dialog box

Other choices you can make in the Record Macro dialog box depend on the application. Here are some examples:

✔ You may be able to enter a lengthier description for the macro.

✔ You may be able to tell your application where to store the macro. Often, you can choose between placing it in the current document or in a document template.

✔ You may be able to assign the macro to a toolbar button or keyboard shortcut. If this option is available in your application, by all means, use it! See the next section for details.

Button, button, who's got the button?

Some VBA applications let you assign a new macro to a toolbar button or keyboard shortcut at the time you record the macro. Take advantage of this opportunity — the most convenient way to play back a macro is to trigger it using a button or the keyboard.

If your application permits this option, you should be able to see it on the Record Macro dialog box. In Excel, for example, the Record Macro dialog box has a Shortcut Key field. Here, you can type a key combination, such as Ctrl+M, that fires off the macro (go back and look at Figure 2-1 again). The Word version of the Record Macro dialog box (see Figure 2-2) has buttons that let you assign a new macro to a toolbar button or a keyboard shortcut. If you click one of these buttons, you're taken to another dialog box where you make the assignment.

If you do assign the new macro to a keyboard shortcut, do yourself a favor and write down the shortcut now. Until you memorize the shortcut, stick a little note on your desk or computer screen as a reminder.

Figure 2-2:
Word's
Record
Macro
dialog box.

Starting the macro recorder

Clicking OK in the Record Macro dialog box starts the recorder. You know that it starts because the Stop Recording toolbar appears (see Figure 2-3). The mouse pointer changes, too, becoming a little cassette tape graphic.

Figure 2-3:
The little
Stop
Recording
toolbar.

Recording commands

After you start the macro recorder, you don't have to do anything special to record commands into your new macro. Just use the application's commands as you would normally. Everything you do — whether picking commands from a toolbar or menu, formatting a graphic, or typing text — is stored in the macro.

Oh, yes, the macro recorder faithfully records all the mistakes you make, too. You can correct them by re-recording the macro, or by editing its VBA code in the Visual Basic Editor (see "Editing macro code in the Visual Basic Editor" later in this chapter).

Stopping and pausing the macro recorder

After you carry out all the commands you want to record, stop the macro recorder by clicking the Stop Recording button on the toolbar of the same name, shown in Figure 2-3. The macro recorder finishes its business by storing all the recorded commands as a VBA program. (If you don't believe me, you can look at the resulting program code — see "Editing macro code in the Visual Basic Editor" later in this chapter.)

In Word, you can pause the recorder during the process of recording a macro. If you need to use a command that shouldn't be part of the macro, click the Pause Recording button (also on the Stop Recording toolbar). The recorder goes into hibernation, ignoring any commands you use for the time being.

When the macro recorder is paused, the Pause Recording button looks pressed in, as shown in Figure 2-4. Officially, the button is now known as the Resume Recorder button. When you're ready to pick up the macro where you left off, click it to continue recording your macro.

Figure 2-4:
Word's Stop
Recording
toolbar.

Running macros

The whole point of recording a macro is so that you can play it back — or *run it,* if you prefer. Watching a long macro do a bunch of tedious work automatically for you is one of life's little pleasures. (For reasons I explain shortly, save your document before running any macro that makes significant modifications to its content.)

Because macros are VBA programs, all the techniques you can use to run the VBA programs you code yourself work with recorded macros. A method that always works is to open the Macros dialog box (Alt+F8), select the macro, and click Run — see Figure 2-5. I cover this and other techniques for running VBA programs fully in Chapter 4.

A recorded macro has no intelligence — it can't modify its behavior to suit current conditions. When you run a macro, it tries to execute the recorded commands even if they aren't applicable to what's going on in your application at the time. For example, if your macro assumes that you're at the beginning of a document, but you run it when you're at the end of a document, the macro probably won't do anything. If you trigger a text-related macro while you're drawing graphics, it may destroy hours of painstaking artwork. My advice: Save your document just before running a macro of any complexity, and be ready with the Undo command (Ctrl+Z).

Figure 2-5:
The Macro
dialog box
(titled
Macros in
many VBA
applica-
tions).

Modifying Macros — The Easy Way to Write Code

Don't think that the macro recorder will gather electronic dust after you master writing VBA code. In fact, you may use it even more often. After all, most fancy VBA programs rely heavily on the objects, methods, and properties found in your application. Instead of typing the corresponding commands yourself, why not record them as a macro?

Remember, the macro recorder converts the commands you record into corresponding statements in the VBA language. You can take the code from a recorded macro as a starting point for your program, tacking on your own VBA statements as required. At least for the recorded commands, you don't have to worry about remembering the proper VBA statements or making typing errors.

As a bonus, this technique also gives you the easiest way to assign your program to a toolbar button or keyboard shortcut. Of course, this only applies if your application allows you to make such assignments when you record macros (see the "Button, button, who's got the button?" section earlier in this chapter).

Editing macro code in the Visual Basic Editor

After you've recorded a macro, you can easily enough edit the resulting VBA program (or just look at those lines of code). Here's how to proceed:

1. **Choose <u>T</u>ools⇨<u>M</u>acro⇨Macros or press Alt+F8 to display the Macro dialog box (see Figure 2-5).**

2. **Select the macro you want to run in the list under Macro Name.**

   The macro you just recorded is *not* selected automatically, so you may have to scroll through the list to find it.

3. **Click the <u>E</u>dit button.**

You are whisked to the Visual Basic Editor with the chosen macro's code available for editing. Figure 2-6 shows an example.

Making easy macro modifications

This chapter isn't the place to lay out detailed techniques for modifying macros in the Visual Basic Editor. After all, the techniques are the same as the ones you use to create VBA programs from scratch, which is the subject of most of this book.

Still, I'm not jumping the gun to suggest a few simple and commonly useful modifications you can make to your macros. These ideas require a minimum of programming, but can make your macros a lot more powerful. Try the following:

- ✓ **Repeat the commands in the macro a set number of times.** You may know in advance that you'll want to run through the entire sequence — or one specific command — exactly 11 times. All you have to do is add a For...Next loop to the code. So what's a For...Next loop, you ask? It's one of the elements of the VBA programming language, and I discuss it in Chapter 12.

- ✓ **Repeat the macro commands, but determine the number of repetitions when you run the macro.** If you're a little more ambitious, you can add to your recorded macro both a For...Next loop and an InputBox. This is a little dialog box that asks for a typed response, in this case the number of repetitions you want. I cover the use of the InputBox in Chapter 11.

- ✓ **Choose the text used by the macro for a given step.** A macro that always inserts the same text into your documents isn't very flexible. By adding an InputBox to the recorded macro, you can tell it what text to insert each time you run the macro. Again, see Chapter 11 for details on the InputBox.

- ✓ **Check for a selection before starting the macro.** Your macro may not work right unless some text, a graphic, or another object is selected. You can use a VBA If...End If sequence to make sure that the proper type of item is selected, and if not, to cancel the macro. Chapter 12 has the skinny on the If...End If statement.

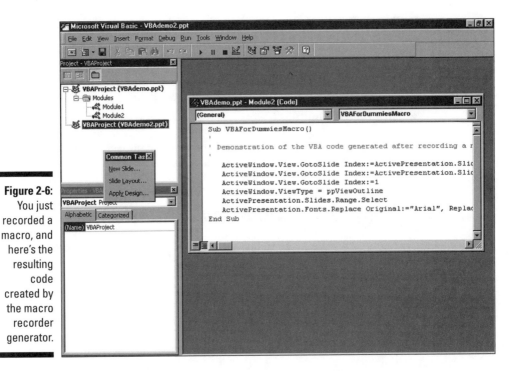

Figure 2-6:
You just
recorded a
macro, and
here's the
resulting
code
created by
the macro
recorder
generator.

As soon as you realize how easily you can get dramatic gains in macro power
by writing a little VBA code, you'll start looking forward to programming.
When that happens, it's only a matter of time before you become a compe-
tent VBA programmer without any great effort.

Chapter 3

Basic VBA Programming

· ·

In This Chapter

▶ Starting the Visual Basic Editor

▶ Working with the VBA Help system

▶ Programming in VBA — a quick and dirty guide

· ·

*M*acros are fine, so far as they go, but you can accomplish much more with custom VBA programs. This chapter serves as your crash-course introduction to VBA programming proper. After introducing the Visual Basic Editor and the VBA Help system, I lead you through the process of building a simple VBA program. With these basics under your belt, you'll have a solid foundation for undertaking all the other complicated stuff in the rest of the book.

Starting the Visual Basic Editor

The Visual Basic Editor is command central for all your work in VBA. It's where you need to be whenever you're designing VBA forms, writing VBA code, or testing and debugging your VBA programs. Chapters 5 and 6 make you an expert on the Visual Basic Editor. For now, you just need to know how to get the Editor onto your screen.

If you've done any nosing around in the code created by the macro recorder, you already know one way to start the Visual Basic Editor — by selecting a macro in the Macros dialog box and clicking Edit. You can, of course, start the Visual Basic Editor directly. In most VBA applications, either of the following methods works:

 ✔ Choose Tools⇨Macro⇨Visual Basic Editor.

 ✔ Press Alt+F11. After some chattering of the hard drive, the Visual Basic Editor appears on your screen. It should bear at least passing resemblance to the picture shown in Figure 3-1.

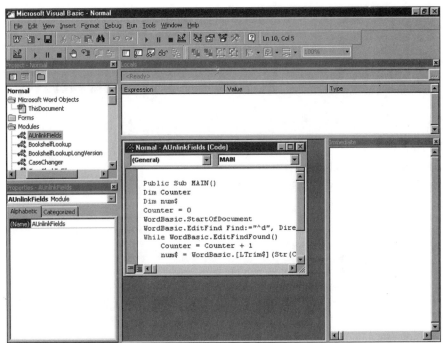

Figure 3-1:
The Visual
Basic Editor.

One-click access to the Visual Basic Editor

If your application has a toolbar button for the Visual Basic Editor, you can also activate the Visual Basic Editor by clicking the button. In the Microsoft Office VBA applications (Word, Excel, and PowerPoint), this button is on the Visual Basic toolbar, shown in Figure 3-2. The collection of buttons is slightly different, depending on which application you're using.

Figure 3-2:
The Visual
Basic
toolbar as
it appears
in Word.

Here's what all the buttons on this toolbar are for, starting at the left side:

✔ The first two buttons are for running and recording macros, respectively.

✔ The middle button activates the Visual Basic Editor. If you use the Visual Basic Editor frequently but don't need the other buttons, copy this button to another toolbar. To copy the button in Office applications, hold down Alt as you drag it into place.

✔ The button showing a hammer and a wrench displays the Control Toolbox, a palette of controls very similar to the VBA Toolbox. In Office, you can place VBA controls into documents themselves, not just on VBA forms.

✔ The button with the ruler, triangle, and pencil switches the document to design mode, in which you can edit VBA controls on the document.

A peek into the Visual Basic Editor

Your first few trips to the Visual Basic Editor can be confusing. The menus and toolbars at the top of the screen are familiar, of course, but what about all those windows? Keeping track of them is tough because they can be arranged and combined in infinite varieties (when you first start the Visual Basic Editor, the windows you see and their location can vary wildly, depending on how the Editor is set up). And if you're not already a programmer, the windows have unfamiliar names and functions.

Chapter 6 is designed to give you a comfortable command of all the windows. For now, Table 3-1 gives a quick summary of their names and functions.

Table 3-1	Names and Functions
Window Type	*What You Use It For*
Project Explorer window	Navigating and managing the components of a VBA project
Code window	Displaying, adding, and editing VBA code
UserForm window	Designing custom forms (windows and dialog boxes)
Toolbox	Adding controls such as text boxes and buttons to your forms (and, in many VBA applications, to your documents)
Properties window	Specifying individual attributes of the selected form or control
Watch window	Keeping track of the values of selected variables in your program

(continued)

Table 3-1 *(continued)*

Window Type	What You Use It For
Locals window	Keeping track of the values of variables in the current procedure
Immediate window	Running individual lines of code for immediate results
Object Browser window	Exploring the objects available to your programs

At this point, focus your attention on the Code window, where you write VBA code, and the UserForm window, where you design your own windows and forms visually. You can see examples of Code and UserForm windows in Figures 3-3 and 3-4. Notice that the type of window appears in each window's title bar.

Figure 3-3: Write VBA code in Code windows such as this one.

Figure 3-4: An example of a UserForm window with a custom dialog box under construction.

Initially, you may see more than one Code or UserForm window — or none at all. It doesn't matter because, after a quick tour of the VBA Help system, you need new windows for the sample program you are about to create.

I Need Help!

These days, almost all software comes laden with self-explanatory menu choices, toolbar buttons with cute little icons that show you exactly what the buttons do, and pop-up tips that spell out the buttons' functions in writing. So who needs on-screen Help anymore? Well, you do, if you're trying to write VBA code.

To begin with, you need help with the Visual Basic Editor itself. Although the Editor's menus and toolbars work like those in any ordinary application, many of the specific commands they offer are unfamiliar at first. Likewise, the Editor barrages you with eight or nine different types of windows, and sorting them all out takes time.

Of course, you'll adapt to the Editor's user interface soon enough. Still, even the most seasoned programmer needs help when it comes to the details of the VBA language itself. With hundreds of objects, methods, properties, key-words, and whatnot to keep track of, you can expect to depend heavily on the VBA Help files.

Microsoft publishes a printed VBA reference manual, but it doesn't come with most VBA applications. The manual *is* included with the Developer's Edition of Office, however.

411 for VBA — or is it 911?

VBA Help screens look different depending on whether you're using VBA 5 or VBA 6. VBA 5's Help system is built on the tried-and-true WinHelp software engine, which dates back to Windows 3.1. In contrast, VBA 6's Help engine is HTML Help, the new Microsoft standard. Introduced with Windows 98, HTML Help looks and works more like a Web browser than does WinHelp. Unfortunately, the versions of HTML Help I've tried to date behave erratically at times, and the software lacks some useful WinHelp features, such as the ability to control whether the Help window remains on top when another window is active.

To open the main VBA Help system, choose Help⇨Contents and Index (in VBA 5) or Help⇨Microsoft Visual Basic Help (in VBA 6). The resulting Help window describes VBA in general. In the case of VBA 5, it may also let you access information about the VBA application you're working with. Figures 3-5 and 3-6 show WinHelp and HTML Help windows for VBA 5 and 6, respectively.

Figure 3-5:
Help for
VBA 5,
brought to
you by the
WinHelp
program.

Figure 3-6:
VBA 6 users
get help in
this HTML
Help
window.

Getting Help for your VBA application

It's sad but true — the Visual Basic Editor doesn't provide a direct command for opening the Help files pertaining to your VBA application. Don't look for such a command because you won't find it. When you want to browse programming information about your application, not about VBA in general, the only sure-fire solution is a three-step process, as follows:

1. **Open the Object Browser by pressing F2 or choosing** <u>V</u>iew⇨<u>O</u>bject **Browser (see Chapter 6 for the skinny on the Object Browser).**

2. **Use the drop-down list at the top left of the Object Browser to select your VBA application by name.**

3. **Highlight an item in the Classes pane at the left of the Object Browser — any item should do.**

4. **Press F1, or click the button with the question mark on it at the top of the Object Browser to open the Help system.**

   You should see the topic pertaining to the item you selected in the Object Browser, but you can now use the Contents tab to browse the entire Help system for your application.

Searching the Help haystack

The VBA Help system works according to the Windows standard. In both WinHelp and HTML Help you can:

✔ Use the Contents tab to see an outline of the available Help information arranged like chapters in a book.

✔ Use the Index tab to search for information in an alphabetical list of key-words assembled by the Help system's designers.

Most often, you can also use the Find tab (in WinHelp) or Search tab to search for almost any word that appears in the entire Help system. In the VBA Help system for Office 2000, however, the Search tab is replaced by one called Answer Wizard. This is supposed to locate Help topics in response to complete questions you type, but it works fine when you type in just a word or two and click <u>S</u>earch.

Context-sensitive Help

In the Visual Basic Editor, F1 is *context-sensitive* — it brings up a Help topic specific to what you're doing at the moment. What you see depends on the type of window currently active in the Editor — and sometimes, on what's going on in the window.

This feature really comes in handy when you're writing code or designing a form. In the Code window, the F1 key responds to the term at the current location of the insertion point, or cursor (that blinking line that indicates where you can type or edit text). Don't fret if you've forgotten how to use a VBA statement such as For...Next, or if you don't know which properties or methods are available for an object. Just place the insertion point in the relevant term and press F1. Figure 3-7 gives an example of what you may see.

F1 can likewise give you Help with the picayune details of form design. In the UserForm window, you can display a Help topic for any control on the form (at the risk of repeating myself, *controls* are items such as buttons, check boxes, and frames). Just click the control to select it, and then press F1. For Help on any specific *property* of a control, select the control, click the relevant line in the Properties window, and then press F1.

The F1 key works as follows in other windows:

- ✔ With the Project Explorer and UserForm windows, pressing F1 displays a Help topic briefly describing that window. This works in the UserForm window only if no control is selected.

- ✔ With the Watch, Locals, and Immediate windows, pressing F1 takes you to a Help screen containing a set of *jumps,* underlined text that you can click to take you to topics on each of these windows. I have no idea why the appropriate topic doesn't appear automatically with these windows.

- ✔ In the Object Browser window, when you select a class or one of its members and press F1, a Help topic on that item appears.

Understanding what's special about VBA Help topics

As you use VBA Help, watch closely for jumps or buttons that display other relevant items in the Help system. Train yourself to use them! The typical VBA Help topic, such as the one shown in Figure 3-8, offers a wealth of these hotspots. If the topic you're reading doesn't have the information you're looking for, you may find it in the related items. Besides, exploring the jumps is a great way to discover VBA programming sort of organically.

Steal that code! Scavenging from the VBA Help system

Be sure to take advantage of the many example code fragments scattered throughout the VBA Help system. You can often find pre-built code that will, with minor modifications, accomplish just the task you're working on. To use Help examples in your own code, select the relevant lines with the mouse, right-click the selection, and choose Copy. Then switch to a Code window in the Visual Basic Editor and click the Paste toolbar button or press Ctrl+V.

Figure 3-7:
Getting Help for the Add method in Visio. If you squint, you can probably make out that the insertion point is within the Add term in the Code window.

Figure 3-8:
Like most VBA Help topics, this one from Visio offers a series of jumps to other Help terms.

Table 3-2 lists jumps you're likely to see.

Table 3-2	Jumping Buttons
Jump or Button	*How to Use It*
`See also`	Click these jumps to see information on related topics.
`Example`	If you see a button or jump labeled `Example`, by all means click it! The examples are vital to understanding muddy or incomplete explanations in the Help file proper. Also, you can copy the example to your own VBA program and modify it there to suit your own needs (see the sidebar "Steal that code! Scavenging from the VBA Help system" in this section).
`Methods`, `Properties`, and `Events`	You see these jumps if the current Help topic covers an object. Click them to explore the methods, properties, and events you can use with that object.
`Applies to`	This jump is available when the current Help topic relates to a property, method, or event. Click to see which objects you can use the item with.

Installing all the Help files . . .

Depending on your application software and the way you installed it, you may or may not have a complete set of VBA Help files on your hard drive. Because the Help files are crucial for any serious work in VBA, be sure that you correct any deficiencies.

With Office, for example, the Setup program installs some, but not all, of the VBA Help files. Most people use the Typical option when they run the Setup program to install Office on their computers. True, this I-don't-want-to-get-my-hands-dirty approach is easy, but it omits many important VBA Help files. If you went this route, run Setup again and choose a Custom install. Go through each Office application in turn, selecting the Help and Sample Files item for each one. When you then click the Change Option button, a dialog box similar to the one shown in Figure 3-9 appears. Here, check the box labeled Online Help for Visual Basic.

In Office 97, even if you used the Custom or Complete options to install Office, you still don't have Outlook's VBA Help files on your hard drive. To install Visual Basic help for Outlook, you must copy the Outlook Help file yourself from the valupack\morehelp folder on the Office CD to the folder where Office 97 is installed. The file you want is called Vbaoutl8.hlp.

Figure 3-9:
Check the
box labeled
Online Help
for Visual
Basic to
install
VBA Help.

Creating a VBA Program

Now that you have a passing acquaintance with the Visual Basic Editor and
the VBA Help system, you're ready for your first foray into the frontier of programming. In Chapter 1, I explain that the programming process consists of a
few basic steps. In a book as fastidious as this one, I could never toss out that
orderly approach for the sake of quick thrills. You have to do the drill.

Step 1: Designing the sample program

Because I don't know which VBA application you're working with, I'm sticking
with something quite generic but still potentially useful. The sample program
opens a new window in which it displays a pithy quote and the date and time (I
call this the *message*). The window stays on the screen until the user clicks OK.

Based on this description, you can list the elements that you must create to
complete the program:

- ✔ Obviously, the program has one window, so you need one form
  (UserForm).
- ✔ The form requires two controls: a label control for the message, and a
  button control for the OK button.
- ✔ You must also write code for two procedures: one that displays the message in the label control, and another to exit the program when the user
  clicks the OK button.

One thing that this program does *not* need is a separate module for its VBA code (a *module* is a unit of code containing one or more procedures — Chapter 7 offers much more detail on modules). You can write both procedures in the Code window associated with the form itself. After all, both procedures do their work in response to *events* that occur on the form.

Take the procedure that displays the message and date. You don't need it until the moment that the program window appears on the screen. In this program, of course, that happens faster than you can blink, but the point is still valid — the event of displaying the form should trigger this procedure.

The exit procedure is also triggered by a form-related event — namely, the fact that the user has clicked OK. You can write this procedure on the form's Code window, too.

Note that many VBA programs don't display their own windows or other dialog boxes. If you're creating such a program, you definitely need to create one or more modules to hold its code.

Step 2: Implementing the design

With a clear plan in mind, you can begin programming in earnest. Take a little visual form design as your base, season it with a pinch of carefully typed code, and you can look forward to a tasty little VBA morsel.

Adding a new UserForm

In the Visual Basic Editor, your first step is to create a new, blank form to serve as the sample program's window. From the Visual Basic Editor's menu system, choose Insert➪UserForm to place a new form on your screen.

See how easy that was? In the bad old days of Windows programming, you would have had to write out a long and very complex statement in code to add even something as simple as a blank window.

As you can see in Figure 3-10, a new UserForm is a featureless gray plane. Notice that you can control the form's size by dragging those little white squares along the right and bottom edges (they are the resize *handles*). The window for this program should be a little wider (to fit all the text in the message on one line) and much shorter (one line of text and a button take up very little room).

More interesting is the Toolbox, that palette of icons in its own little window that pops up when you work with a form. Use the Toolbox, shown in Figure 3-11, to place controls onto a form.

Figure 3-10:
A newly inserted UserForm, looking for a purpose in life.

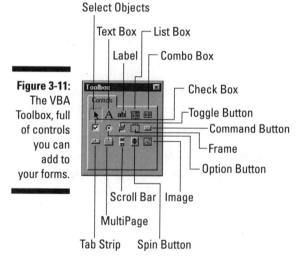

Figure 3-11:
The VBA Toolbox, full of controls you can add to your forms.

Select Objects
Text Box — List Box
Label — Combo Box
— Check Box
— Toggle Button
— Command Button
— Frame
— Option Button
Scroll Bar | Image
MultiPage
Tab Strip   Spin Button

Adding a label control to the UserForm

Now you're ready to liven things up a bit by adding controls to the form. Start with a *label control,* which simply displays text. This text is called the label's *caption.* When a program is running, a label control is a look-but-don't-touch affair — although users can read the caption text, they can't change it.

However, your program can. The sample program needs this capability because the date and time it displays are different each time it runs.

To place a label control on your new UserForm, follow these instructions:

1. Be sure the form window is active by clicking on it.

The Toolbox is only visible when a form window is active.

2. **Click the Toolbox icon that shows a bold letter A.**

3. **Move over to the form and, starting from the left side toward the top, drag a rectangle big enough to hold the message (see Figure 3-12 for guidance).**

Figure 3-12:
After plopping down a new label control, your form should look something like this.

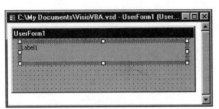

VBA gives every new label a caption automatically, so at this point you should see the magnificent text `Label1` within the label control's rectangular outline. Obviously, that won't do. To erase the automatic caption, you need the Properties window.

Using the Properties window to tweak controls

Each control on a form has a lengthy list of *properties*. These specify how the control looks and how it should act when the program runs. One of VBA's great strengths is that you can control these properties without having to write any code.

The control panel for properties is the Properties window. As Figure 3-13 shows, it contains a list of all the properties of the control that's currently selected. To change a property, you just find the property in the left column and change its setting in the right column.

For the label control in the sample program, you need to change just two properties: `Name` and `Caption`. Change the control's name from `Label1` to, say, `lblNow` (the first three letters identify the name as that of a label control). To do this, find the Name property at the top of the property list where (Name) appears — it's the only property shown in parentheses. Double-click in the right column of that row so that the existing name becomes selected, and then type in the new name. (You use a control's name to refer to the control when you're writing code, so try to select names that remind you of the control's purpose. Chapter 8 covers conventions you should use to identify the type of control in the names you create.)

Figure 3-13:
Use the
Properties
window to
change the
setting for
any of a
control's
properties.

Next, scroll down in the property list until you find the Caption property. Here, simply delete the current entry for the property. Why? Because your program will supply the text for the label caption when it runs.

Now, you do have to write code if you want your program to change a control's property while the program runs. But because most properties stay the same, you usually need very little code to take care of such changes.

As long as you're changing properties, you may as well re-title the form itself. Select the form by clicking the title bar of the UserForm window. In the Properties window, scroll to the Caption property and change it to **Did You See Where I Put My Keys?** or **VBA For Dummies First Sample Program**. The new caption appears in the form's title bar.

Adding a command button

Unlike a label control, a *command button* control (better known as a button) interacts with the user of your program. When someone clicks the button, it looks pushed in, and the program does something.

The sample program needs just one button: the one that stops the program when it gets clicked. To place this button on the form, do the following:

1. **Click on the form's window to activate it once more.**

   The Toolbox, which vanished when you went to the Properties window, should reappear.

2. **Click the little command button icon in the Toolbox (refer to Figure 3-11).**

3. **Starting just left of the midline and toward the bottom of the form, drag diagonally downward and to the right to create the button.**

At this point, the form should look like the example in Figure 3-14.

Figure 3-14:
The form for
the sample
program
after you
add a
command
button
control.

Now you can set the properties for the button. Using the Properties window, follow these steps:

1. **Change the button's** (Name) **property to** OKButton.

   Again, you refer to the button in your code by name, so this title helps remind you what it does (it okays and closes the window).

2. **Change the button's** Caption **property to** OK. **That's all the user of your program will see.**

You have completed the form for the sample program. Even without any further work, you already have a functioning VBA program — one that displays the hugely fascinating form you just designed. To run it, just press F5, or click the Run button on the Visual Basic Editor toolbar. It's the little blue arrow pointing toward the right, as shown in the margin.

When you run the half-baked program, the form appears on top of the document in your VBA application (not in the Visual Basic Editor). Check out Figure 3-15. The label control is blank and the OK button doesn't do anything — you haven't written any code yet, remember? To shut down the program, you have to click the Windows standard Close button, that X on the right end of the window's title bar.

Writing the code

Now comes the scariest, and the most exciting, part of VBA programming: writing the code that makes your program go. Recall that the sample program requires you to write two procedures, and that both are tied to events that occur while the program runs. The first procedure displays your message when the form appears on the screen, and the other terminates the program when someone clicks the OK button.

Figure 3-15:
Running the
custom
form as a
program
before you
add code.

Opening the form's Code window

To write code *behind* (associated with) a form or one of its controls, you need to display the form's Code window instead of the form itself. To do so, start by selecting the form or control. The procedure for the OK button is easier, so why not start there? Click the OK button so that the selection handles appear around its border. You can then use any of the following methods to display the Code window:

✔ Choose View➪Code.

✔ Press F7.

✔ Right-click the form and choose View Code from the shortcut menu.

When the Code window appears, it should already contain the skeleton of a procedure — see Figure 3-16. VBA automatically creates a procedure for the most common type of event, a simple mouse click on the button. Your program performs this procedure whenever someone clicks the OK button.

These two lines of code don't actually do anything; they simply provide the walls that tell VBA where the procedure begins and ends. The first line of code VBA generated for you is

```
Private Sub OKButton_Click()
```

Figure 3-16:
VBA creates
this
procedure
skeleton as
soon as you
switch to
the form's
Code
window
with the
OK button
selected.

Figure 3-16:
VBA creates this procedure skeleton as soon as you switch to the form's Code window with the OK button selected.

In all VBA procedures, the first line of code defines the type of procedure (in this case, a private Sub procedure) and the procedure's name. Private and Sub are VBA *keywords,* words or symbols that are part of the VBA language. Keywords have fixed, special meanings in VBA, and you can't use them as the names of items such as procedures. And by the way, Chapter 9 covers the various types of procedures available in VBA. In this case, VBA chooses the name of the procedure, OKButton_Click, for you. The name is a combination of the button's name and the event type.

The last line of automatically generated code is

```
End Sub
```

All Sub procedures must end with this line. It tells VBA to stop running the procedure.

Adding your own code

The insertion point should be blinking between the two lines of code that VBA created. By typing just one line of your own, you can enable the button to shut down your program. Here it is:

```
Unload Me
```

The Unload statement removes the named object from memory. Here, the named object is Me, a word with special meaning in VBA. In this case, it refers to the form and all its code.

Correcting errors as you write code

The VBA compiler watches over your shoulder, figuratively, as you write your code. If the compiler catches an obvious error, you see an immediate error message identifying the problem, at least in general terms. Suppose, for example, you type a stray character after the statement `Unload Me`. The compiler knows that `Unload Me` is a complete statement and nothing should follow it on the same line. When you move the insertion point to another line the compiler displays the entire statement in red and highlights the extraneous character. You see the message "Compile error. Expected: end of statement."

The compiler can only detect some types of errors as you write your code. It catches others when you try to run the program, as discussed in the section, "Running programs in the Visual Basic Editor" later in this chapter.

Creating a second procedure

The next procedure, the one that displays your message as the label control's caption, is only a bit more complicated. This procedure should activate when the form appears on the screen. With the form's Code window still active, proceed as follows:

1. **At the top of the Code window, click the arrow beside the text box at the left, which should still read** `OKButton`.

   This action drops down a list of the items that belong to the form (see Figure 3-17).

Figure 3-17: The Object drop-down list shows all the items belonging to the form that owns this Code Window.

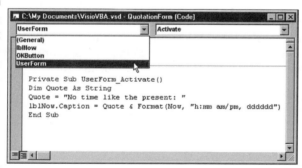

2. **In the drop-down list, choose the UserForm item.**

   VBA creates a new procedure for the click event. In other words, this procedure is triggered if someone using the program clicks over any part of the form that doesn't have a control. The sample program doesn't need this procedure, so leave it alone for the time being.

3. **Click the arrow at the top right of the Code window to drop down the Procedures list, which includes all the events that VBA can detect in connection with the UserForm.**

   The list is long, which gives you some idea of how responsive you can make your programs (see Figure 3-18).

4. Choose the very first item in the list, Activate. You have to scroll up the list to find it.

VBA dutifully creates a skeleton `UserForm1_Activate` procedure, which is triggered when the form gets loaded into memory.

5. Now you can delete the `UserForm1_Click` procedure if it bothers you by selecting all the procedure's text and pressing the Del key.

This step is optional — the code does no harm. But because it does nothing at all except distract you, you may as well end its lonely life.

Writing code for the new procedure

With the skeleton for the correct event procedure in place, you can now go to work and flesh it out. Between the lines VBA has entered for you, type three new lines of code. The final procedure should look like this:

```
Private UserForm_Activate()
Dim Quote As String
Quote = "No time like the present: "
lblNow.Caption = Quote & Format(Now, "h:mm am/pm, dddddd")
End Sub
```

The first line you type,

```
Dim Quote As String
```

creates a variable named `Quote` and defines it as a *string*, meaning a consecutive sequence of text characters.

The next line,

```
Quote = "No time like the present: "
```

stores the text "No time like the present:" in the `Quote` variable you just created. Just like in algebra class, you use the equal sign to assign a specific value to a variable. Notice also that a space occurs before the closing quotation mark to separate the proverbial statement from the next text.

The final line,

```
lblNow.Caption = Quote & Format(Now, "h:mm am/pm, dddddd")
```

has the code that actually displays the complete message on the form. This line begins by identifying the label control named lblNow as the object with which you're working. Then comes a period, showing that what comes next is a property belonging to lblNow — in this case, its caption. A property is like a variable because you can change its value while the program runs. Therefore, you use the equal sign to change a property setting in code.

The remainder of the line defines the message that should appear as the label's caption.

The first part of the message is the Quote variable. Then the plus sign tells VBA to add what follows to the text stored in Quote. Inside the parentheses, the Now *function* tells VBA to go fetch the current reading of the computer's clock, which keeps track of the date and time. The Format function then takes this raw information and converts it into a form you can read. Those letters inside the quotation marks define the particular format you see on the window, but I won't go into how they work in detail here — you can find more information in Chapter 9.

Step 3: Testing your program

This is only Step 3? Well, don't worry: The rest of the development cycle for the sample program doesn't take long.

Running programs in the Visual Basic Editor

You're ready to give the new program a trial run to see whether it works as planned. To run a VBA program from within the Visual Basic Editor:

1. **Click on either the UserForm window or the Code window for your program to to be sure it's active.**

   Remember, you can tell which window is active by looking at the title bar — the active window's title bar is a different color than the title bars of inactive windows (which by default are drab gray).

2. **Then use any one of the following methods:**

   • Choose Run⇨Run Sub/UserForm.

   • Click the Run button on the Visual Basic Editor Standard toolbar. (The Standard toolbar is the only one visible in the Visual Basic Editor unless you customize the screen as described in Chapter 5.)

   • Press F5.

After a brief pause, the program window appears over your VBA application (not the Visual Basic Editor). If all goes well, what you see should look pretty much like Figure 3-19.

Be sure to include Step 1 above whenever you try to run a VBA program! If you don't activate the UserForm or Code window for the program first, nothing happens when you try to run the program (or a different program runs).

Compiling

A VBA program must be compiled before it can actually run the first time (see Chapter 1 for the definition of compiling). As the compiling process prepares your program for life in the fast lane, the code is checked line by line to be sure that it matches the conventions of the VBA language. The compiler stops at the first deviation and gives you a chance to correct the error. Even the slightest spelling error brings the compiling process to a screeching halt.

The compiler shows you an error message in a little window if it finds any mistakes. Among the suggested choices, the Debug button is usually your best course. Clicking Debug takes you straight to the Code window, where the offending line is highlighted. The compiler keeps track of its work up to that point, so you can correct the error and continue compiling where you left off, using any of the techniques listed earlier for running your program (see "Running programs in the Visual Basic Editor").

You can try your luck with the Help button if you want, but don't be surprised if the information it provides is too general to be of much use. The End button halts the compiler and your program, returning you to the Visual Basic Editor.

Running clinical trials

The compiler may give your program a clean bill of health, but that doesn't mean the program works the way you want. Compiling a program without any errors is only a preliminary to real-life testing.

See, although the compiler never misses a VBA language error, it can't read your mind. It's perfectly content to pass lines that follow the VBA language conventions, even if they don't make sense in your program. Imagine a teacher who gives you an A for writing a poem such as

```
Roses are red.
Violets are blue.
I have a bicycle.
Do you like fish?
```

because each line is a complete sentence. The VBA compiler is that sort of grader.

After the compiler finishes its work, your program is running. You can now put it through its paces and see whether it works as you intended.

The sample program should be easy to test. If the window displays the intended message instead of `Inky Binky Bonky` and if clicking the OK button stops the program, congratulations. If not, you have bugs to eradicate.

Step 4: Debugging

As your programs get more complex, the likelihood for mistakes in the way they operate (*run-time errors*) grows exponentially. After you discover such an error, the task becomes identifying its cause and correcting the problem. In a word, that's debugging.

In smaller programs, this crude but reasonably effective debugging method sometimes works; simply read through your code line by line and see whether you can figure out what went wrong. After you understand the problem, it should be relatively easy to fix. (If something goes wrong with your sample program, all you have to do is compare your code against the printed version — if they don't match, change yours accordingly.)

Fortunately, VBA includes several debugging aids to complement the squint-and-scratch-your-head technique. Chapter 14 spells out the details.

Running a form from other VBA code

Be aware that the technique previously discussed — which works only inside the Visual Basic Editor — is the only way you can directly run a form-based program such as the example. To display the form from inside your VBA application, you must use the Visual Basic Editor to create a Sub procedure (macro) that runs the form, then run *this* macro from your application. Follow these steps:

1. **In the Visual Basic Editor, choose Insert⇨Module to create a module and open its Code window.**

2. **Type the following code:**

```
Sub ShowQuote()
    UserForm1.Show
End Sub
```

If your form is named something other than `UserForm1`, substitute that name in the second line of code above.

After you save your work you can run the `ShowQuote` macro with the techniques I describe in Chapter 4. Chapter 16 gives further details on running form-based programs.

Returning to Your VBA Application

For my money, the best way to access a document in your VBA application while you're working with the Visual Basic Editor is to use the standard Windows technique for switching between applications. Press Alt+Tab until the application's icon is selected in the pop-up window and then release the keys.

Any of these techniques also work:

- ✔ Choose View⇨AutoCAD (or whatever the application's name is).
- ✔ Click the View button at the far left of the Visual Basic Editor toolbar — it shows an icon representing the application's document.
- ✔ Press Alt+F11.
- ✔ Click the application's button in the Windows taskbar.

You can get back to the Visual Basic Editor with Alt+Tab, the taskbar, by again pressing Alt+F11, or by choosing Tools⇨Macro⇨Visual Basic Editor.

When you're ready to say goodnight to the Visual Basic Editor, either of the following options shuts down the Editor and takes you directly back to the VBA application you started from:

- ✔ Choose File⇨Close and Return to *<application>*.
- ✔ Press Alt+Q.

Chapter 4

Running VBA Programs

● ●

In This Chapter

▶ Running programs and macros from the Macros dialog box — reliable but not much fun

▶ Triggering macros from toolbar buttons and menu items

▶ Assigning macros to keyboard shortcuts

▶ Running programs automatically when something special happens

● ●

*N*o matter how much firepower a VBA program is packing, it doesn't do any blasting until you pull its trigger. For that matter, you have to *find* the trigger first. To put it more prosaically, until you find a way to run your VBA program, the program is worthless.

As you assemble a program in the Visual Basic Editor, you can always run it by pressing F5 or clicking the Run button on the Visual Basic Editor Standard toolbar. That's fine for testing purposes, but it doesn't help you in the real world. After the program is finished, you need to run it within your application.

This chapter covers the options you can use to start your VBA programs and macros from a VBA application. (Remember, a macro is just a VBA program that you happened to record.) The Macros dialog box is the easy way to start most of your programs, but it's cumbersome. VBA programs become really useful when you hook them up to a menu command, toolbar button, or keyboard shortcut instead — or when you get them to run automatically.

To try out these techniques, use them with macros you record following the directions in Chapter 2, or with procedures you create in the Visual Basic Editor according to the outline in Chapter 3 or the detailed instructions in Parts III and IV.

The Name Is Everything

You run VBA programs by name.

Sorry to hit you with the technicalities right at the outset, but I see no alternative. When you run a VBA program, you're running one specific VBA *procedure*. Your program may actually incorporate many different procedures, but only one of them contains the first line of code that you want the program to execute. This first procedure may run (*call*) other procedures, which in turn may call still others, and so on. Still, you have to run only the first procedure to get your program started — the rest of the procedures run automatically as the program goes about its business.

So what's the point? Here it is: To run a VBA program, you have to know the name of the procedure that kicks off the program. In programs that do contain more than one procedure, the launch-pad procedure is usually named `Main`.

Hungry for something more substantial on the subject of procedures? Skip to Chapter 7 for a satisfying luncheon.

Running from the Macro Dialog Box

The surefire method for starting a VBA program is via the Macro dialog box. If you haven't gotten around to assigning the program to a toolbar button or keyboard shortcuts, or if you just plain forgot where you assigned it, the Macro dialog box is always there.

Displaying the Macro dialog box

To display the Macro dialog box in Office programs or in Visio, do one of the following:

  ✔ Choose Tools⇨Macro⇨Macros.
  ✔ Press Alt+F8.

Other VBA applications may provide different methods for opening the Macro dialog box.

The Macro dialog box should look something like the dialog box shown in Figure 4-1. As usual, some of the details may vary, depending on the VBA application you're using.

Figure 4-1:
The Macro dialog box as it appears in PowerPoint.

Most of the dialog box is given over to a listing of the VBA programs currently available.

Technically speaking, all the procedures listed in the Macro dialog box are Sub procedures that take no arguments. (You may recall from Chapter 2 that this is the official definition of a macro.) After you run such a procedure, *it* can run other types of procedures, including Function procedures and Sub procedures that do take arguments.

Running a macro

Running a macro from the Macro dialog box is hardly a major challenge. The steps are

1. Select the macro in the list under Macro name.

2. Click the Run button.

Pretty tough, huh? Alternatively, you can just double-click the program name in the list.

The only complication you may face is finding the program you want to run in the Macro dialog box. See the next section if you have trouble locating your program.

Finding your macro in the Macro dialog box

In the Macro dialog box, the VBA programs (macros) in the Macro Name list can sometimes be confusing. Depending on where a program is stored, it may be listed with an identifying preface.

Take the example of Excel, in which you can run VBA programs stored in the active workbook (the one you're currently using) as well as those in any other open workbooks. In the Macros dialog box, a macro stored in the active workbook appears under its own name. However, a macro that comes from another open workbook is listed as the workbook name followed by an exclamation point and then the macro name. Figure 4-2 shows an example.

Figure 4-2: Excel's Macro dialog box lists VBA programs (macros) from non-active workbooks by workbook name.

In Word, each program in the Macros dialog box is listed by the name of that procedure — *except* when two or more procedures have the same name. In that case, the duplicate procedures are listed under their module names, followed by a dot (period) and then the procedure name. I submit Figure 4-3 as evidence.

If the program you want to run doesn't appear at all, you may need to tell the Macros dialog box to display a different selection. To do so, use the drop-down list labeled Macros in. If the dialog box shows only programs associated with the current document, try a choice such as All active templates and documents.

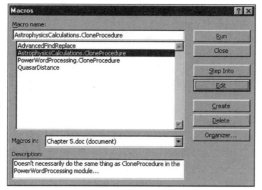

Figure 4-3:
The Macros
dialog box
in Word.

Launching Programs Quickly

The Macros dialog box may be foolproof, but it's ever so inefficient. When you want something done, you want it done *now*. Who wants to open up a dialog box, hunt through a long list of tiny names, and then click, click, oops, click, click, click.

There are better ways to fire up your VBA programs. Assign each one you use regularly to a toolbar button, menu item, or keyboard shortcut. Then one or two quick clicks or a single keystroke brings you immediate gratification.

As you may recall if you read Chapter 2, many VBA applications enable you to assign a macro to a toolbar button or keyboard shortcut at the time you record the macro. This capability is one good reason to start every new VBA program by recording a macro, which you can then edit with your own code. Refer to Chapter 2 if you need a refresher on how this process works.

After a macro is recorded, you should also be able to assign it to a button or keyboard shortcut, or even to a menu choice. The rest of this chapter discusses these options. Unfortunately, the techniques vary somewhat among different VBA applications. I discuss some of the wrinkles in the remainder of this (fairly lengthy) section.

Push button programs

Nothing is quite like the thrill of clicking a cute little button on your screen and getting an immediate response from your computer. True, more thrilling thrills exist, but button pushing definitely has its appeal. And you get a little extra tingle when that button you click triggers your very own VBA program.

Some VBA applications make setting up custom buttons for running VBA programs easy — even if you didn't create the program initially by recording a macro, as I discuss in Chapter 2. Office 2000 applications fall into this category, and with the exception of Outlook, so do those of Office 97. In other VBA apps, such as Visio, you may have to write VBA code to add custom buttons. Ouch! I thought VBA was supposed to be a visual interface designer.

Easy buttons in Office

In Microsoft Word, Excel, PowerPoint, or Access, as well as in Outlook 2000, assigning a VBA program to a new toolbar button is a simple matter of drag-and-drop with the mouse. After you have the button in place, you can dress it up with an appropriate picture.

Creating the button

Here's how to create a button that triggers a VBA program in any of the Office applications:

1. **Right-click any toolbar.**

   A shortcut menu pops up, as shown in Figure 4-4.

2. **Choose Customize at the bottom of the menu to display the Customize dialog box, which initially displays the Toolbars tab.**

   You can display the Customize dialog box directly, bypassing Step 1, by choosing Tools⇨Customize.

3. **Click the Commands tab of the Customize dialog box (as shown in Figure 4-5).**

4. **Scroll down the list under Categories until you see the Macros item. Click it to select it.**

   All the runnable VBA programs at your disposal then appear in the Commands list on the right. (If you look again closely at Figure 4-5, you can see that it shows the Customize dialog box set to display macros.)

5. **Finally, you're ready to create the new button. Locate the VBA program you want to assign to the button in the list. After you find it, drag it onto the toolbar of your choice.**

   When you release the mouse button, a new button labeled with the name of your program appears on the toolbar.

6. **Close the Customize dialog box to complete the job.**

Now, every time you click the new button, your VBA program runs. Miraculous!

Figure 4-4:
The
Customize
command is
at the
bottom of
this list of
toolbars that
appears
when you
right-click
any toolbar
in Office.

Figure 4-5:
The
Customize
dialog box
showing the
Commands
tab.

Putting on a pretty face

Of course, a super-wide button labeled something like

```
DummiesTemplate.GraphicsRoutines.MakeSalesGraph
```

is not only ugly as sin but also wastes lots of space on your toolbar. However, you can easily exchange that verbose text for a compact graphical image. Follow these steps:

1. **Open the Customize dialog box again, switching once more to the Commands tab (see Steps 1 through 3 in the previous section).**

2. **Right-click your new button on the toolbar.**

   A lengthy shortcut menu appears.

3. **About halfway down the menu, look for the Change Button Image choice. Select it to display a graphical menu of stock button faces.**

This procedure is illustrated in Figure 4-6.

Figure 4-6:
With the
Customize
dialog box
open, right-
clicking an
Office
toolbar
displays
this shortcut
menu.

4. **If you like one of the supplied images, click it to select it, and skip to Step 8. Otherwise, continue with Step 5.**

5. **Choose Edit Button Image on the shortcut menu.**

Figure 4-7 shows the Button Editor Window, a little art studio you get for painting the individual dots for your button.

6. **Pick a color from the palette, and then click the blow-up of the button image to daub it on.**

To get rid of color so that the toolbar background shows through, paint after clicking Erase. You can click the Move buttons to move the entire image in the direction of any edge that doesn't already have any colored dots.

Now that you have a graphical face for your button, you can turn off that text.

7. **Reopen the shortcut menu (see Step 2).**

8. **Select the Default Style choice.**

 After you're finished, a pretty little button should be parked securely on the toolbar, ready to spring into action whenever you click it. The button shown in the margin is the button face that I designed in Figure 4-7.

Removing buttons

In Office, you can delete a toolbar button you no longer need by simply drag-ging it off the toolbar. The trick is to hold down the Alt key as you drag the button to any part of the screen that doesn't have a toolbar. When you see a boxed X beside the mouse pointer, you can release the mouse button to delete the button.

Custom buttons via VBA code

I feel for you if your VBA application doesn't provide an easy drag-and-drop route to custom buttons. Early on in your experience with VBA, the code required to create buttons looks daunting. Actually, however, it's not *too* hard to create buttons this way. The trick is figuring out which objects your VBA application uses to represent toolbars and buttons, and which properties or methods are required to change them.

And they call VBA a standard . . .

In Visio, for example, the ToolbarItem object represents a single button. To work with a particular ToolbarItem object, however, you have to access the ToolbarItems collection to which it belongs. That ToolbarItems collection itself belongs to a Toolbars collection, which in turn is a member of a ToolbarSet collection, which in turn belongs to a particular UIObject (user interface object). I show you how all this works with some sample code later in this chapter.

In Office, on the other hand, buttons are called CommandBarButtons, and they belong to CommandBarControls collections. A given CommandBar (the toolbar that contains a CommandBarControls collection) resides in a CommandBars collection, which can belong to the Application object or a Document object.

If all that complication sounds terrifying, just remember that you probably don't have to write the code for the custom button from scratch. Hunt in the Help files for your VBA application on the subjects of customizing and toolbars, and you're likely to find an example that you can modify without much trouble.

A sample Visio procedure

The sample code printed here works in Visio to add a custom button to a toolbar. It begins by declaring variables for the types of objects involved in working with toolbars. It then defines those variables as the specific objects to be manipulated. First, it gets the Visio application's user interface object, and from that it extracts the set of toolbars visible when you are in the drawing mode. Next, it identifies the particular set of buttons (ToolbarItems) on a specific toolbar.

After the procedure has a specific ToolbarItems object to work with, it adds a new button to the set. After that, it modifies the AddOnName property to specify which VBA program to run when the button is clicked, along with other properties that determine how the button functions. Finally, it sets the whole thing in motion with a call to the SetCustomToolbars method for the ThisDocument object.

If you want to try the code here, change the item in quotes in the following line

```
objMyNewToolbarItem.AddOnName = "MyVBAProcedure"
```

to the name of one of your own VBA programs. Also, specify a different icon file in the line

```
objMyNewToolbarItem.IconFileName "rocket.ico"
```

Okay, here's the code:

```
Sub AddMyButton()
' Declare object variables
  Dim objMyUI As Visio.UIObject
  Dim objMyToolbarSet As Visio.ToolbarSet
  Dim objmyToolbarItems As Visio.ToolbarItems
  Dim objMyNewToolbarItem As Visio.ToolbarItem
'Define the declared variables
  Set objMyUI = Visio.Application.BuiltInToolbars _
    (visToolBarMSOffice)
  Set objMyToolbarSet = _
objMyUI.ToolbarSets.ItemAtID(visUIObjSetDrawing)
  Set objmyToolbarItems = _
    objMyToolbarSet.Toolbars(0).ToolbarItems
```

```
'This line adds a new button at the far left of the toolbar
' (position 0)
 Set objMyNewToolbarItem = objmyToolbarItems.AddAt(0)
'Select the button's VBA procedure and other properties
 objMyNewToolbarItem.AddOnName = "MyVBAProcedure"
 objMyNewToolbarItem.CntrlType = visCtrlTypeBUTTON
 objMyNewToolbarItem.Priority = 1
'Select the file containing the button image
 objMyNewToolbarItem.IconFileName "rocket.ico"
'This line makes Visio use the customized user interface
 ThisDocument.SetCustomToolbars objMyUI
End Sub
Sub MyVBAProcedure()
' Here's where your own code goes.
```

Custom menu items for your VBA programs

When you think about it, you can see that an item on a menu is basically no different from a toolbar button: It triggers some command when you pick it. A menu choice looks different from a button — for one thing, it usually displays text instead of a picture. And you use a different technique with the mouse to trigger it. But the result is the same.

Similarly, then, you use essentially the same technique to assign a VBA program to a custom menu choice as for a toolbar button. In Office, you can drag a VBA procedure from the list in the Customize dialog box (see Figure 4-8) up onto a menu. When the mouse pointer hits the menu name, the menu opens and you can drop your cargo where you like it.

In VBA applications that don't allow such easy customizing, you can use code to get your VBA programs onto a menu. In Visio, for example, you use essentially the same technique demonstrated in the preceding code. Just substitute menu-related objects for the toolbar-related ones. (Use a `MenuItems` collection instead of a `ToolbarItems` collection, for example.)

Keyboard shortcuts in Word, Excel, and Access

If you're any good at all as a typist, the commands that you use most often cry out for keyboard shortcuts. In most applications, even those that are heavily oriented toward graphics, pressing keys is quicker than moving the mouse around and clicking it. The only drawback to keyboard shortcuts is that you have to memorize them.

Figure 4-8:
Dragging a
macro (VBA
procedure)
to create a
custom
menu
choice in
PowerPoint.

At any rate, some VBA applications — including Word, Excel, and Access — give you direct access to the keyboard, allowing you to set up keyboard shortcuts for your VBA programs. If you're offered this kind of control, by all means take it.

Custom keyboard shortcuts in Word

When it comes to customizing the keyboard, Word is (hands down) the easiest and most versatile VBA application to manipulate. For example, if you want to assign a VBA program called `DoubleCurrentFontSize` to the keyboard shortcut Alt+> (that is, Alt+Shift+ the period key) in Word, follow these steps:

1. **Open the Customize dialog box by choosing Tools⇨Customize, or by right-clicking a toolbar and choosing Customize from the shortcut menu.**

   If you want another peek at this dialog box, refer to Figure 4-5.

2. **Click the Keyboard button at the bottom of the Options tab.**

   Up pops the Customize Keyboard dialog box, as shown in Figure 4-9.

3. **Select Macros in the Categories list.**

Figure 4-9:
Assign
your VBA
programs
to Word
keyboard
shortcuts
with this
dialog box.

4. Locate and select your program in the list that appears in the Macros list box.

If the program has already been assigned to a shortcut, that shortcut appears in the Current Keys list box.

Look really cool: Put your programs on shortcut menus

With just a little work, you can give your humble VBA program a high-fashion home on the shortcut (right-click) menu of your choice.

In Office, you can customize any shortcut menu in the Customize dialog box. The trick is to display first the Shortcut Menus toolbar. After choosing Tools⇨Customize to open the dialog box, display the Toolbars tab (if it isn't already visible) by clicking the corresponding tab at the top of the dialog box. Scroll down the list of toolbars until you see the Shortcut Menus item, and click in the little box beside it.

The Shortcut Menus toolbar should now be visible on your screen. You can navigate through this toolbar's menu system to the particular shortcut menu you want to customize. After you've opened it, use the technique discussed

at the beginning of this section to drag any macro from the Commands tab of the Customize dialog box.

Visio lets you place a macro on the shortcut menu for any shape. After selecting the shape, choose Window⇨Show ShapeSheet. In the ShapeSheet window, click in an Action cell. (If necessary, first insert an Actions section by choosing Insert⇨Section and checking Actions.)

Then choose Edit⇨Action. Now you can type in the text and other properties for the menu item and pick out which program you want it to run. After you're through, the shortcut menu that appears when you right-click the shape should include an item for your VBA program.

5. **Press the key combination for your shortcut.**

   If the shortcut you choose is already in use, the dialog box tells you which command it triggers so that you can decide whether to keep the existing shortcut or go ahead and replace it with the new one.

6. **Click <u>A</u>ssign, and then click Close to leave the dialog box.**

Your shortcut is now in effect.

Keyboard shortcuts in Excel

Excel lets you assign VBA programs to keyboard shortcuts, but it restricts you to key combinations based on Ctrl with the type-able keys (letters, numbers, and punctuation marks). To assign a program to a shortcut, proceed as follows:

1. **Open the Macro dialog box. (Why not use the Alt+F8 keyboard shortcut?)**

2. **Locate and select your program in the list.**

3. **Click Options.**

4. **In the resulting dialog box (see Figure 4-10), type the key you want to combine with Ctrl for the shortcut.**

   Excel distinguishes between upper- and lowercase letters. (In other words, an alphabet key typed with the Shift key is different from an alphabet key typed without pressing Shift.)

5. **Click OK to return to the Macro dialog box.**

Figure 4-10:
Assigning
a VBA
program to
a keyboard
shortcut in
Excel.

Keyboard shortcuts in Access

In custom Access database applications, you can easily create your own keyboard shortcuts. Access applications revolve around custom forms and their controls. All you have to do is create event procedures for these forms and controls, procedures that run when the user presses a key. Chapter 16 covers event procedures in lavish detail.

Things are different if you're working with an Access database directly, using the stock menu commands and toolbar buttons. In this case, you create custom keyboard shortcuts that run VBA programs by assigning them to special Access macros. (Access macros, you may remember, are *not* VBA procedures.) Access lacks a macro recorder, so you have to handcraft your macros as follows:

1. **In the Database window, select the Macros button (the Macros tab in Access 97) and then click the New button.**

   This action displays the Macro window (Figure 4-11).

2. **In the Action column, select the RunCode item, as shown in Figure 4-11.**

3. **Choose <u>V</u>iew⇨Macro Names to display in the window an extra column called Macro Name.**

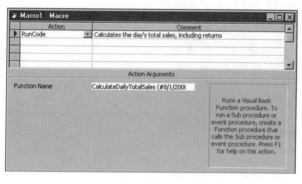

Figure 4-11:
Use this window to create Access macros.

4. **Enter the keyboard shortcut to which you want to assign your VBA program in the Macro Name column.**

   Use the ^ symbol to indicate the Ctrl key and the + symbol to indicate the Shift key. You can type ordinary letters and numbers, but you must stick braces around function keys. For example, you would type ^**k** to create a Ctrl+k shortcut, or +**{F8}** to create a Shift+F8 shortcut.

5. **Click the Function Name text box and type the name of the VBA procedure that the macro should run.**

   It has to be a Function procedure.

6. **Close the Macro window by clicking the x in the upper-right corner. When Access asks you to name the macro, type** AutoKeys.

Mouse macros in Visio

Visio provides yet another way to run VBA programs — by double-clicking a shape that you have associated with your code. Here's how to set up a double-click shape:

1. **Click the shape to select it.**

2. **Choose Format➪Double-Click.**

   The Double-Click dialog box materializes over the Visio workspace (as shown in Figure 4-12).

Figure 4-12: Use this dialog box to associate a Visio shape with a VBA procedure that runs when you double-click the shape.

3. **Select the VBA procedure of your dreams from the Run Macro list.**

4. **Click OK.**

Now, whenever you double-click that shape, your VBA program runs.

Running VBA Programs Automatically

Suppose that you come up with a VBA program you like so much that you want to see it in action first thing, every time you start your application. If you love your program that much, even the slight delay of clicking a button may be too much to bear.

Fortunately for you, many applications let you run VBA code automatically when the application starts up or shuts down, when a document opens or closes, and when other events take place. Tables 4-1 through 4-3 survey the techniques you can use in some popular VBA applications to run your VBA programs automatically.

Table 4-1 Automatically Running VBA Programs by Opening the Application's Shortcut

Application	Command to Type in the Target Box	Comments
Microsoft Word	/m*VBA*	Type the name of your VBA procedure in place of *VBA*.
Microsoft Access	/x *macro*	Runs the Access macro you list. To run a VBA procedure, the Access macro should contain a RunCode action (see "Keyboard shortcuts in Access," earlier in this chapter).

Table 4-2 Automatically Running VBA Programs in Word by Giving the VBA Program a Special Name

Name for the VBA Program	When It Runs Automatically
AutoExec	When Word starts up
AutoNew	When each new document is created
AutoOpen	When any existing document is opened
AutoClose	When a document is closed
AutoExit	When Word exits

Note: The AutoExec *macro must be stored in the Normal template (normal.dot).*

Table 4-3 Running VBA Programs by Writing Event Procedures in VBA Code (see Chapter 16 for details on event programming)

Application	When the Code Runs Automatically	Start with This Object	Write Code for This Event
Visio	When a new document is created	Document	DocumentOpened
Visio	When a document is saved using another name	Document	DocumentSavedAs

(continued)

Table 4-3 *(continued)*

Application	When the Code Runs Automatically	Start with This Object	Write Code for This Event
Microsoft Word	When a document opens	Document	`Open`
Microsoft Word	When a new document is created	Document	`New`
Microsoft Word	When a document is closed	Document	`Close`
Microsoft Excel	When any workbook opens	Application	`WorkbookOpen`
Microsoft Excel	When a specific workbook opens	Workbook	`Open`
Microsoft Excel	When a new worksheet is created	Workbook	`NewSheet`

Note: These are just a few of many available events pertaining to entire documents in Visio, Word, and Excel.

Working with Windows shortcuts

Some applications allow you to run VBA code by adding extra commands to the name of the application when you start it (see Table 4-1). Unless you want to type these commands at the DOS prompt, you need to modify or create a Windows *shortcut* to run the application.

In Windows, icons on the Start menu represent shortcuts. To modify one of these, right-click the Start button, choose Open from the little menu that pops up, and then open up the Programs folder and any appropriate subfolders until you see the shortcut for your application. Then right-click the shortcut and choose Properties from the shortcut menu to display the Properties dialog box.

Now select the Shortcut tab. In the Target text box, type the necessary command after the name of the application itself. For example, to have a VBA procedure run automatically when you start Word, the complete Target entry would look something like:

```
C:\Microsoft Office\WINWORD.EXE
    /mAutomaticNovel
```

To create a *new* shortcut, right-click in the Windows desktop, My Computer, or Explorer. From the shortcut menu, choose New⇨Shortcut and let Windows walk you through the remaining steps. You can then modify it as described earlier in this sidebar.

Part II
Mastering the VBA Development Environment

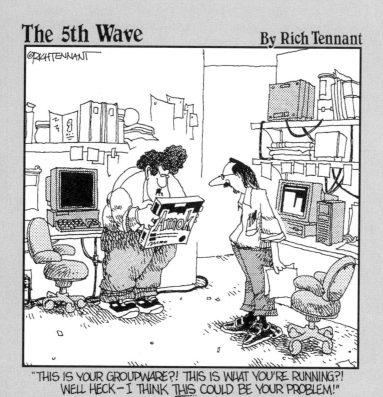

The 5th Wave   By Rich Tennant

"THIS IS YOUR GROUPWARE?! THIS IS WHAT YOU'RE RUNNING?!
WELL HECK – I THINK THIS COULD BE YOUR PROBLEM!"

In this part . . .

A carpenter has her workshop, a baker his kitchen, and you, well . . . now you have the Visual Basic Editor. The Visual Basic Editor is the official term for the VBA integrated development environment — the digital studio in which you sculpt your own software creations. Like any craftsperson, the VBA programmer must master the tools of the trade before producing great works reliably. In this part, you find out how to tame the resources of the Visual Basic Editor — I sometimes refer to it simply as the *Editor*. Chapter 5 orients you to the components of the Visual Basic Editor, including its toolbars, menus, and windows. In Chapter 6, you tour the individual windows and acquaint yourself with the unique contributions that each one can make on behalf of your programming projects.

Chapter 5

The Visual Basic Editor
at Your Command

. . . .

In This Chapter

▶ Finding commands in the Visual Basic Editor's menu system

▶ Displaying, moving, and customizing the Editor's toolbars

▶ Understanding how docking works in toolbars and windows

▶ Grappling with the multitudes of Editor windows

▶ Discovering keyboard shortcuts available in the Visual Basic Editor

. . . .

*R*emember that scene in *Fantasia* where Mickey Mouse plays the Sorcerer's Apprentice? A magic broom to help with the chores seems like a great idea, but pretty soon he has an out-of-control bucket brigade — and he just about drowns.

Your early experiments with the Visual Basic Editor may leave you feeling equally inundated. You can quickly open up so many unfamiliar windows that your mind starts sinking. But don't panic — those windows don't let any water into your basement, and each can perform an important job for you. Armed with a little experience and the tips you get in this chapter, you can put the Editor and its windows completely under your power.

Working with the Visual Basic Editor User Interface

The Visual Basic Editor user interface is standard Microsoft fare — the menus, toolbars, and keyboard shortcuts look and work much like those of Microsoft Office. You'll feel right at home if you're using VBA with an Office application.

On the other hand, you may notice a contrast between a non-Microsoft application's interface and that of the Visual Basic Editor. Remember, the other software publishers have licensed VBA from Microsoft and grafted it onto their own products, which in some cases took shape long before VBA arrived or the current Office interface emerged.

Out to lunch with Editor menus

I realize that you already know how to use menus. What you may be interested in, though, is where to find certain commands on the Visual Basic Editor menus.

For the most part, the Editor commands are organized logically. When you want to display a particular window, for example, you shouldn't have trouble locating the necessary command — it's on the View menu, of course. A few items aren't so obvious, however. The following little table clues you in to some of the Editor's hidden menu commands.

Task	Menu Command	Comments
Control the settings for an entire project	Tools⇨Project Properties	This is an odd location for a command pertaining to the VBA project you're working with — I expected to find it on the File menu.
Customize the Visual Basic Editor itself	View⇨Toolbars⇨ Customize and Tools⇨ Options	
Turn on Design Mode	Run⇨Design Mode	The Design Mode command sounds like it's intended for laying out forms, so why is it on the Run menu? Because it stops any running program. It isn't a very useful command, since you can design forms without it, and you don't need to leave Design Mode to run a program.

Tuning the toolbars

If you're familiar with Word, Excel, or PowerPoint, you're probably plenty comfortable with the way toolbars work in the Visual Basic Editor. If not, a few brief comments should suffice.

The Editor comes with four prefab toolbars:

- ✔ **Standard:** This is the only toolbar visible when you first run the Editor. It includes buttons for a broad range of functions, including saving your work, inserting new forms and modules, editing, and running your programs.

- ✔ **Edit:** The buttons on this toolbar are handy when you're editing code. They duplicate commands on the Edit menu.

- ✔ **Debug:** This toolbar contains buttons for commands that you're likely to need while tracking down errors in your programs.

- ✔ **UserForm:** Use this toolbar for forms design. Most of the buttons duplicate commands on the Format menu for aligning, ordering, and grouping controls on forms.

You can use the stock toolbars in any combination. Just two quick clicks display a toolbar (if it's not currently visible) or hide it (if it's already on the screen). Here's the procedure:

1. Start by right-clicking any toolbar.

A shortcut menu pops up (see Figure 5-1), listing the available toolbars. When a toolbar is visible, you see a check mark beside its name.

Figure 5-1:
Display or hide the toolbars using this shortcut menu.

2. On the menu, select the toolbar you want to display or remove.

As soon as you release the mouse button, the change occurs.

The Editor toolbars can exist in one of three states, as shown here:

Toolbar Status	*How the Toolbar Appears on the Screen*
Hidden	Not visible on the screen.
Docked	Stuck up against any of the four edges of the main work area.
Floating	In a separate window with its own title bar and Close button. Floating toolbars can be positioned outside the Editor.

Figure 5-2 shows the Visual Basic Editor configured with two docked and two floating toolbars. Most of the main windows in the Visual Basic Editor can exist in docked, floating, or hidden form.

To make a docked toolbar float, just drag it away from its edge of the work area toward the center of the screen. The most convenient place to "grab" a docked toolbar is in the area of those two little bars at the left or top — this region is called the *move handle*. Alternatively, you can just double-click the move handle to float the toolbar.

Vice being versa, you can convert a floating toolbar to a docked one by dragging its title bar toward any edge of the work area. As soon as it gets close enough, the window's gravitational field pulls the toolbar in tight. This effect is cool, but you can dock a floating toolbar more quickly by double-clicking the title bar (it returns to its last docked position).

Customizing your toolbars and menus

Suppose that you're not satisfied with the toolbars supplied with the Visual Basic Editor. Well, just make your own. You can add or remove buttons and menu items on the existing toolbars or menus, and if that's not radical enough for you, you can create your own toolbars from scratch (the process works just like it does in Office applications).

Moving and deleting toolbar buttons

If you only want to move or delete an existing button, all you have to do is hold down the Alt key while you drag the button to a new location. While holding down Alt, you can

✔ Drag a button to a new position on the same or a different toolbar. If you want to place a *copy* of the button at the new location, hold down both Alt and Ctrl as you drag.

✔ Add a separator line between a pair of buttons by dragging the button on the right just a little further to the right (go too far, and you move the button over one spot). To remove a separator line, drag the button on its right a bit to the left.

✔ Delete a button by dragging it to any location that isn't a toolbar. As soon as you see the X in the mouse pointer, you can let up on the mouse button — and that toolbar button is history.

Adding new toolbar buttons

For fancier modifications, you need to display the Customize dialog box. You use this dialog box to add new toolbar buttons, and it has to be open if you want to alter the menus.

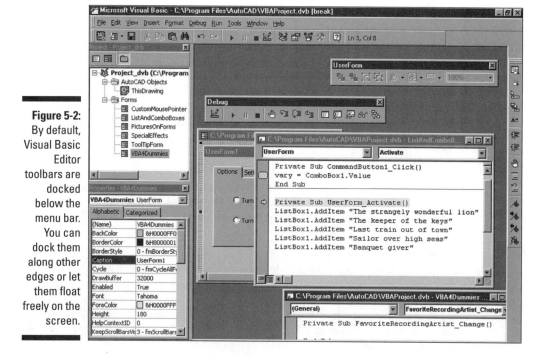

Figure 5-2:
By default,
Visual Basic
Editor
toolbars are
docked
below the
menu bar.
You can
dock them
along other
edges or let
them float
freely on the
screen.

Here are the steps for adding new toolbar buttons:

1. **Right-click any toolbar and then select Customize at the bottom of the shortcut menu.**

   This action brings up the Customize dialog box, shown in Figure 5-3.

Figure 5-3:
Using the
Customize
dialog box,
you can
make
sweeping
changes to
the Visual
Basic Editor
user
interface.

   2. **If the toolbar you want to customize isn't already visible, select the Toolbars tab of the Customize dialog box.**

      Check the box for the correct toolbar there. You can add a new toolbar by clicking the New button and typing in a name.

   3. **After you can see the toolbar you want to work with, switch to the Commands tab.**

      Now you can drag and drop items in the list to the toolbar or menu.

   4. **Close the Customize dialog box when the toolbar is the way you want it.**

Note that with the Customize dialog box open, you can move or delete existing toolbar buttons without holding down the Alt key. However, you still must hold down Ctrl if you want to copy rather than move an item.

Monkeying with the menus

To customize the Visual Basic Editor menus, you must first display the Customize dialog box (see Step 1 in the previous section). This accomplished, you can click a menu to open it and then drag individual menu items to other positions or to other menus. Dragging a menu choice into the work area deletes it. You can add or remove a separator line between two items by dragging the lower item just a tad down or up.

To add new choices to a menu, drag them from the Commands tab of the Customize dialog box, just as you would for new toolbar buttons. Figures 5-3 and 5-4 give you the idea.

As if customizing the main menu system isn't enough, the Visual Basic Editor enables you to modify the shortcut (right-click) menus as well. As shown in Figure 5-4, you start by opening the Customize dialog box, switching to the Toolbars tab, and checking the box for the Shortcut Menus item.

This action brings up a special little toolbar just for customizing purposes. Here, locate and click the specific shortcut menu you want to work with. You can then drag items from the Commands tab to the shortcut menu.

Keyboard shortcuts

Table 5-1 lists the keyboard shortcuts available in the VBA Editor. You can also use the standard Windows keyboard commands for cursor control and text editing. Remember also that pressing Shift+F10 pops up the shortcut menu for the window or other item that's currently active — just as if you had right-clicked the item.

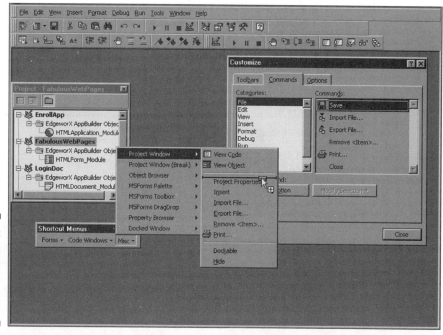

Figure 5-4:
Customizing
one of the
Visual Basic
Editor short-
cut menus.

Table 5-1   Keyboard Shortcuts in the Visual Basic Editor

Displaying Windows

To Do This	*Press*
Display the Code window for the selected form or control	F7
Display the form corresponding to the active Code window	Shift+F7
Move to the next Code or UserForm window	Ctrl+Tab
Activate the Object Browser window	F2
Activate the Properties window	F4
Activate the Immediate window	Ctrl+G
Activate the Call Stack window while a program is running	Ctrl+L

(continued)

Table 5-1 *(continued)*

Working with Code

To Do This	Press
Jump to the definition of the item at the insertion point	Shift+F2
Display the Find dialog box	Ctrl+F
Find Next (find the next occurrence of Find text)	F3
Find Previous	Shift+F3
Replace	Ctrl+H
Jump to the line previously edited	Ctrl+Shift+F2
Undo	Ctrl+Z
List properties/methods	Ctrl+J
List constants	Ctrl+Shift+J
Display Quick Info about the variable or object at the insertion point	Ctrl+I
Display parameter information for the function at the insertion point	Ctrl+Shift+I
Complete the word you're typing automatically	Ctrl+spacebar

Working with Properties

To Do This	Press
In the Property window, move to the next property in the list that begins with a particular letter	Ctrl+Shift+*<letter>*

Running Programs

To Do This	Press
Run the procedure or UserForm in the active window	F5
Pause code execution and enter Break mode	Ctrl+Break

Debugging (see Chapter 14 for information on how to use these commands)	
To Do This	*Press*
Execute code one line at a time *(step)*	F8
Execute statements one line at a time without stepping into procedure calls	Shift+F8
Run, stopping at the line containing the insertion point	Ctrl+F8
Specify *(set)* the next statement to be executed	Ctrl+F9
Run the error-handler code or return the error to the calling procedure	Alt+F5
Step into the error handler or return the error to the calling procedure	Alt+F8
Toggle the breakpoint in the code line with the insertion point	F9
Clear all breakpoints	Ctrl+Shift+F9
Add a watch for the item at the insertion point	Shift+F9

Managing the Windows

Unless you have a really gargantuan monitor, plan to spend lots of time moving windows around in the Visual Basic Editor. Those windows aren't there just for looks — each has something very valuable to contribute to your programming effort. The problem is that keeping them all open at once is not practical — you won't have enough space left for your VBA code and forms.

By the way, this chapter discusses only the mechanics of working with windows, not the functions of the windows themselves. Chapter 6 discusses each of the individual windows in some depth, and I also cover them in the relevant sections elsewhere in the book.

Some windows are loners; some run in crowds

Here's One Basic Fact to understand about Visual Basic Editor windows: You can have as many Code and UserForm windows as you need – but only one each of the other window types. This restriction may make perfect sense to you already, but it took me a while to figure out how the system works.

You need multiple Code and UserForm windows because you're likely to create more than one form and one VBA module. With a window for each, you can keep all your forms and modules in memory and available for quick access.

Some of the remaining windows — the Properties and Locals windows, to name names — change their contents automatically when you switch to a different Code or UserForm window. It's like getting multiple windows for the price of one. Others, such as the Object Browser, the Project Explorer, and the Immediate window, apply to everything you do in the Editor, so only one of each is necessary.

Viewing and hiding windows

Most Editor windows have their own keyboard shortcuts, which means that you can pop up a window that isn't currently visible without taking your fingers off the keyboard. Table 5-1 lists the shortcuts you need. If you can't remember the shortcut, you can display any window via the View menu.

Perhaps unfortunately, the keyboard shortcuts *aren't* toggle switches. If a window is already open, pressing its key combination doesn't hide it. To put a window back to bed, you have to click the window's little Close button (the one with the X in it at the far right side of the title bar).

To display a specific window that's open but buried, you can choose it by name from the Window menu. Only non-dockable windows are listed there.

As in many Windows applications, two keyboard shortcuts are available for switching from one window to the next: Ctrl+Tab and Ctrl+F6. In the Visual Basic Editor, however, only non-dockable windows become active in sequence as you press the shortcut keys repeatedly.

By now you may be asking, "So what is a non-dockable window?" You find the answer just ahead in the following section.

Docking windows, or not

Like the toolbars, most of the Editor windows are *dockable* — you can attach them along any of the four edges of the main workspace where they can't cover up other windows. Of course, docking a window makes the workspace smaller. Figure 5-5 shows the Editor with all visible windows docked.

Alternatively, you can let your windows float freely in the breeze. Floating windows leave you more room for writing code and designing forms, but they often cover up other windows. If you have a big monitor, you may prefer to display the Visual Basic Editor at less than maximum size and then move individual floating windows outside the Editor altogether.

No docking

Certain windows can't be docked. Docking is completely out for the Code and UserForm windows. In addition, you can make any other window *non-dockable*. To check or set docking status for all window types (except Code and UserForm windows, of course), choose Tools⇔Options and click the Docking tab. I'm sure that you don't need Figure 5-6 to get you there, but with the recent illustration drought, I thought you may appreciate something at least semi-graphical to inspect.

Figure 5-5: As you dock windows along the edges of the Visual Basic Editor window, the space available for editing code and designing forms grows smaller.

You can also make a dockable window non-dockable (if the window is currently docked) by right-clicking its title bar and choosing Dockable from the shortcut menu. Unfortunately, this trick doesn't work in the reverse direction.

Figure 5-6:
Set docking
status for
Visual Basic
Editor
windows
in this
dialog box.

Docking factoids

Points to ponder while you're trying to figure out how window docking works:

✔ A Code, UserForm, or any other non-dockable window can be maximized, minimized, or *restored* (Microsoft jargon for windows of user-determined size). Non-dockable windows have the full complement of standard Windows buttons at the right side of the title bar: Minimize, Maximize (or Restore, if the window is already maximized), and Close.

✔ You can tell whether a window is currently dockable by looking at the title bar. Dockable windows have only a Close button; non-dockable windows have the Minimize and Maximize (or Restore) buttons.

✔ When you maximize any non-dockable window, it fills whatever space is left by any other windows currently docked in the work area.

✔ To move a floating window to the edge of the work area without docking it, you must first make the window non-dockable.

✔ All open, non-dockable windows are accessible in sequence via the Ctrl+Tab keyboard shortcut. They're also listed on the Window menu.

Saving the screen layout

The Visual Basic Editor automatically preserves the layout that's in effect at the time you exit. The locations of your windows, menus, and toolbars don't change from one Visual Basic Editor session to the next.

Chapter 6

Getting Things Done in the Visual Basic Editor

In This Chapter
▶ A bird's eye view of your VBA projects with the Project Explorer
▶ Investigating project objects with the Object Browser
▶ Writing code — and having it written for you — in the Code window

*A*s you may have hoped — or feared — every window in the Visual Basic Editor has a genuinely meaningful — dare I say vital? — role to play in the process of VBA programming. This chapter introduces the individual windows and goes so far as to show you how to actually use some of them.

Specifically, I cover the Project Explorer, Object Browser, and Code windows in some detail — not just how they look and how their controls work, but how you put them to use during a programming session. Detailed coverage of the other windows — including the UserForm, Properties, and the four debugging windows — comes in Chapters 14 and 15, but you find basic information on them here.

Managing Your Projects with Project Explorer

In VBA, a *project* is all the code and forms that belong to one document, along with the document itself. In the Visual Basic Editor, you use the Project Explorer window for a bird's eye view of all projects currently open in your application — and more importantly, to navigate quickly to the Code or UserForm window you want to work with.

 To save the project you're currently working with — the one selected in the Project Explorer, as described later in this section — click the Save button on the Visual Basic Editor's Standard toolbar. You don't have to go back to your VBA application to save the document with its associated code.

Opening the Project Explorer window

The Project Explorer should already be visible when you first open the Visual Basic Editor. If it isn't, you can make it appear with any of the following techniques:

- ✔ Press Ctrl+R.
- ✔ Click the Project Explorer button on the Standard toolbar, shown in the margin.
- ✔ Select View➪Project Explorer.

Exploring the Explorer

If you've ever used the Windows Explorer to manage your disks and files (oops, *documents*), you are right at home in the Project Explorer. The Project Explorer gives you a branching hierarchical look at your open projects. Figure 6-1 shows an example.

Figure 6-1:
Here's the Project Explorer in Visio, showing several active projects open simultaneously.

At the top of the hierarchy are the individual projects themselves. They're listed farthest to the left in the Project Explorer window.

Each document that's open in your application automatically has a project, even if you haven't written any code or created any forms for its project so far. By default, a project takes on the name of its associated document, but you can change the name via the Project Properties dialog box or in the Properties window (see the "Renaming a project or module in the Properties window" section later in this chapter).

The next level in the hierarchy is formed by groups of related objects: forms, code modules, objects from the underlying application, and references to other object libraries (see Chapter 17 for instructions on adding such references to your project). Normally, the Project Explorer displays a folder for each of these groups. At the bottom of the hierarchy come the individual objects themselves.

Navigating the Project Explorer window

Fiddling around with the Project Explorer can be a way to avoid coding while still looking busy. Not only that, but it's also the fastest way to find and activate the modules, forms, and other objects you want to work with.

Just like the Windows Explorer, the Project Explorer displays a little box beside each item, or *node,* in its list. When only the project itself is visible and its contents are hidden, this box, the *expand indicator*, contains a plus sign. If the nodes at lower levels of the hierarchy are visible, the expand indicator displays a minus sign instead.

Here are the techniques you use to work with the Project Explorer:

✔ To expand a node, displaying items lower in the hierarchy, click the node's expand indicator when it contains a plus sign, or highlight the node and press the right arrow key.

✔ To collapse a node that is currently expanded, hiding its subsidiary items, click its expand indicator when it contains a minus sign, or highlight the node and press the left arrow key.

✔ To open the UserForm or Code window corresponding to a module, form, or class module item in the Project Explorer, double-click the item or highlight it in the list and press Enter.

✔ To activate a form's Code window, highlight the form in the list and press Shift+Enter.

✔ If you can't remember the difference between Enter and Shift+Enter, you can fall back on those buttons at the top of the Project Explorer window, just below its title bar. They work like this:

 ✔ At the left, the View Code button displays the Code window for the highlighted item.

✔ The middle button, View Object, shows you the highlighted item itself. If the item is a form, you see it in its UserForm window. If the item is a document, you're switched back to the underlying VBA application with that document active.

✔ At the right, the Toggle Folders button turns on or off the middle level of the project hierarchy. Normally, the Project Explorer separates the forms, code modules, and document objects into separate folders. If you click this button, those folders disappear, and you see all the individual objects in each project in one alphabetical list. Click the button again to turn the folders back on.

Using the Project Explorer shortcut menu

The Project Explorer shortcut menu, shown in Figure 6-2, gives you yet more ways to get up close and personal with the elements of your project. These commands are all available via the menus, but the shortcut menu provides faster access when you're already working with the Project Explorer.

Figure 6-2:
The Project
Explorer
shortcut
menu.

Setting project properties

The Project Properties dialog box lets you change the name of your project, add a brief description, attach a custom help file, and protect the project from unauthorized snooping or changes. Until you're a fairly advanced VBA developer, though, most of these options aren't terribly useful.

But, anyway, at least now you know that this dialog box exists. To display it, choose Tools➪*Project name* Properties, or right-click the Project Explorer window and select *Project name* Properties from the shortcut menu. Figure 6-3 shows the General tab of the Project Properties dialog box.

Renaming a project

The Project Explorer and the Object Browser list projects alphabetically by name; therefore you can move a project in either window by changing its name. (Of course, you may also want to change a project's name for purely artistic reasons.)

Figure 6-3:
The General
tab of the
Project
Properties
dialog box.

The easiest way to change the VBA-supplied generic project name is in the
Properties window. When you highlight the project in the Project Explorer,
the Properties window displays its name. You can edit the name to your
taste, right there in the Properties window. You can also change the project's
name on the General tab of the Project Properties dialog box, if you have it
open for other reasons.

Protecting your project

If there's any chance that someone else might get onto your computer and
mess around with your programs, consider protecting your VBA projects
with a password. To raise your security fence, display the Project Properties
dialog box and switch to the Protection tab, shown in Figure 6-4.

Here's how the settings on this tab work:

- **Lock project for viewing:** Checking this box completely locks out
anyone who doesn't have the password. They can't even view the project without the password. If you don't check this box, your password
prevents anyone else from opening the Project Properties dialog box —
and this prevents other users from locking *you* out of your own work.

- **Password:** Type the password you've chosen for your project.

- **Confirm Password:** Type it again to guarantee that you entered the
password correctly the first time.

Unless your memory is infallible, write down the password and put it somewhere you can find it. VBA encrypts the project quite stoutly. If you forget the
password, you will have to recreate the project from scratch.

Figure 6-4:
The
Protection
tab of the
Project
Properties
dialog box.

Using the Object Browser

Although it looks different and has more bells and whistles, the Object Browser has a lot in common with the Project Explorer. Like the Project Explorer, it lets you navigate quickly through the hierarchy of objects available to your VBA programs.

Cosmetics aside, though, a fundamental difference is that the Object Browser displays only one project at a time — but lets you access *all* objects available to that project, not just the ones that belong to the project itself. (Did I hear a "Hunh?") In other words, besides your project's code modules and forms, you can also view the objects provided by your application, by VBA itself, and in other object libraries you may have opened for use by the project (see Chapter 17 for instructions on adding references to other object libraries).

The Object Browser's other great advantage is that it can track down the procedures, methods, events, properties, and other such goodies from any of these object libraries.

Starting the Object Browser

The F2 key is your quick trigger command for displaying the Object Browser. Slower routes to the same destination include clicking the Object Browser button on the Standard toolbar (shown in the left margin here), or choosing View⇨Object Browser. Figure 6-5 shows the Object Browser window.

Figure 6-5:
The Object
Browser.

Browsing objects

Before you do any serious work with the Object Browser, be sure that you're browsing the right project. All you have to do is select the project you want to work with in the Project Explorer.

Clicking the Project/Library list box at the top-left displays the libraries available in the chosen project. (Your project should be there in the list — if it's not, go back to the Project Explorer and make sure that it's selected.) By choosing <All Libraries> in the Project/Library box, you can browse all the objects available to your project (that is, the objects of all libraries referenced in your project). To home in on a particular library, select it in the list.

Browsing panes

The Object Browser window is divided into several sections or panes (check out Figure 6-5 again). You can resize any of the panes by dragging the separator bars between them. The top pane contains the buttons with which you control the Object Browser. Below that comes the Search Results pane, discussed in the "Searching for members" section later in this chapter.

Below the Search Results pane are two side-by-side panes. On the left, the Classes list displays the objects, collections, modules, forms, and constants available in the selected library or project. Clicking any one of these items displays its members in the pane on the right, the Members Of list. The members may be procedures, methods, properties, events, or individual constants.

Want to know where your own VBA code lives? Just look for items displayed in bold in either the Classes list or the Members Of list.

The Details pane at the bottom of the Object Browser window displays information about the currently selected object, including the item's type and the object it belongs to (if you can't see all this information, drag the separator at the top of the pane upward or use the scroll bar at the right). Clicking the object that the item belongs to displays that object in the Object Browser.

Surfing the projects

The Object Browser works a lot like a Web browser. As in a Web browser, you can follow hyperlinks to related items — clicking the underlined object in the Details pane (at the bottom) displays it in the Object Browser.

And as in a Web browser, you can retrace your steps. To revisit objects you've previously examined, click the Go Back button at the top of the Object Browser window. Of course, you also have a Go Forward button, which reverses direction again, eventually returning you to the object you were looking at when you first clicked Go Back.

Instantly accessing your code

 If the item you've selected in the Object Browser is a module or procedure from your own code, just press Enter to bring up its Code window. Mouse lovers can click the Show Definition button (shown in the margin) for the same service.

Getting help in the Object Browser

 Pressing F1 or clicking the Help button at the top of the Object Browser window is supposed to bring up a Help topic on the object, method, property, or event you've selected in the Object Browser. In fact, it usually works this way. If your thinking style is more freeform than regimented, randomly nosing around with the Object Browser and displaying Help for any item that catches your eye is a great way to explore VBA painlessly.

Searching for members

Suppose you're not sure which of your code modules contains a particular procedure, or which object owns a particular method or event. Rather than comb through your modules in the Project Explorer or rummage through the Help system, you can get the Object Browser to locate the item for you. Here's how:

1. **Set the Library/Project drop-down list to <All Libraries> (if you need to search the entire project) or to a specific library.**

   If you select the wrong library, you may find something, but — since items in different libraries can have the same names — it won't be what you were looking for.

2. **Enter the text you want to search for in the Search box.**

   You can repeat any of your last four searches by reusing it from the Search box's drop-down list of items.

3. **Press Enter or click the Search button (the one with binoculars).**

   After the obligatory hard-drive rattle, matching items appear in a new Search Results pane above the list panes. You can resize any column that's too small for the item displayed.

4. **To close the Search Results pane, click the double up-arrow button next to the Search button.**

   Click the same button (which now displays a double down-arrow) to redisplay the Search Results pane.

Using browsed items in your code

The Object Browser does more than satisfy your curiosity about the objects in your project — it can be a modestly practical coding aid. After you locate an item that you actually want to use in your own code, you can press Ctrl+C or click the Copy to Clipboard button to place the term on the Clipboard. Then, after switching to the appropriate Code window, paste the Clipboard contents into your program. This technique ensures correct spelling — a little typo can make your code run amok (or it never gets running in the first place).

Coding Secrets

Code windows are the heart of the Visual Basic Editor. Here you construct the VBA statements that actually perform useful work. In this chapter, I don't say anything about the content of those VBA statements — well, not much, anyway. Instead, I focus on how to get the most out of the Code window when you're entering code. Three types of VBA items have associated Code windows: modules, class modules, and UserForms. Although each of these item types has a different function in VBA — covered in detail in later chapters — Code windows look and work the same for all three of them.

Opening Code windows

The VBA Editor gives you lots of different ways to open the Code window of an existing module, class module, or UserForm. First, you have to locate and select the item in the Project Explorer. After you have it in your sights, any of the following techniques brings up the corresponding Code window:

- ✔ Press F7.
- ✔ Click the View Code button at the top of the Project Explorer window.
- ✔ Right-click the object and select View Code from the shortcut menu.
- ✔ Choose View➪Code.
- ✔ For modules, double-click the item or just press Enter (this doesn't work for UserForms).

If you're currently viewing a UserForm window, pressing F7 or choosing View➪Code displays that form's Code window.

Creating new Code windows

Inserting a new module into your project automatically opens a new Code window for that module. Chapter 7 walks you through the process of starting new modules. When you create a new form, a Code window is automatically created for it (you don't see it until you use one of the techniques just listed).

Typing code

VBA Code windows are, in essence, simple text editors, but they include loads of special features designed for writing VBA code.

You type your VBA statements just as you would in a word processor, using the same cursor control and editing keys that are standard in Windows (you know, pressing Home takes you to the beginning of a line, while Ctrl+Home takes you to the top of the window — like *that*). You can select text with the mouse or by holding down the Shift key while you move the cursor.

Like every self-respecting text editor of the millennial era, the Code window supports drag-and-drop editing. After you select the text you want to work with, you can

✔ Move it, by dragging it into position and dropping it there.

✔ Copy it, by holding down the Ctrl key as you drag and drop.

You can drag text to another location in the same Code window, to a different Code window, or to the Immediate or Watch windows. If the destination is in a different Code window, you must arrange the two windows so that both the original text and the destination are visible before you start. (See the "A First Look at the Debugging Windows" section later in this chapter for quick descriptions of the Immediate and Watch windows.)

The Code window also lets you Undo previous changes you made to your code. Each time you press Ctrl+Z or choose Undo from the Edit menu, another change is reversed. The Edit menu does provide a Redo command as well — to undo the effects of the Undo command — but Redo has no keyboard shortcut in the Visual Basic Editor.

The ideal coach

Like that perfect servant you always wished for, the Visual Basic Editor is constantly (but unobtrusively) checking and correcting your work in these ways:

✔ If you indent one line of code, the following lines are automatically indented to match (you can shut off this feature in the Tools⇨Options dialog box by removing the check from the Auto Indent box).

✔ If the editor recognizes a VBA *keyword,* it automatically capitalizes it according to VBA conventions (if you type an `if...then...else` statement, the Editor changes it to `If...Then...Else`). In addition, keywords are automatically colored (blue, by default) so that they stand out from the other items you type.

✔ In Code windows, you create a new procedure by typing `Sub` or `Function` followed by parentheses and an argument list, if required. When you do, the Visual Basic Editor automatically supplies the required closing statement for you — `End Sub` or `End Function`. Notice that a separator line appears between procedures.

✔ Finally, and most importantly, typing a VBA statement that is obviously incomplete or otherwise at odds with proper coding syntax provokes a warning message from the Editor (see Figure 6-6). With this immediate notification, you can correct the problem while you still remember what you were trying to accomplish with the statement in question. Even if you dismiss the warning for now, the Editor displays the statement in red to remind you that something serious is wrong.

Figure 6-6:
You get a
warning
message
like this one
when a line
of VBA code
doesn't
follow
correct
syntax.

Navigating in a Code window

When you create a program of any complexity, a single Code window can contain pages and pages of code. Scrolling up and down randomly to find the section you're looking for would be much too primitive in such elegant surroundings. Instead, take advantage of those two drop-down list boxes at the top of the Code window. They zoom you directly to the procedure you want to see or edit, as follows:

✔ The list box on the left is the *Object box.* In a module window, the only item in this list is (General), and you don't need to worry about it. But when you're working with the Code window for a form, this box lets you pick out a specific control on the form (or the form itself). When you do, the Code window displays the default procedure for that object.

✔ The list box on the right is the *Procedures/Events box.* Here, selecting the Declarations section (for the entire window) or a specific procedure displays the code for the selected item. If you're working in a form's Code window, this box lists only the events available for the item you chose in the Object box. When you select an event, the Code window displays the corresponding procedure for that event.

Bookmarking your code

It's 3:00 a.m. Your eyelids are so heavy that they're falling on your typing fingers, but the deadline looms and you keep on knocking out line after line of fairly routine code. Suddenly, inspiration strikes — you've just realized how to solve a major programming problem that you were working on yesterday morning.

Before you jump to that other module to implement your brilliant idea, drop a *bookmark* where you're now working. That way, when it's time to get back to this module, you can make like Hansel and Gretel and find your way home in a flash.

To place a bookmark on a line of code (well actually, alongside the code — see Figure 6-7), click the Toggle Bookmark button. All the bookmark-related buttons appear on the Edit toolbar, so you have to display this toolbar if you want access to them. Alternatively, you can use the corresponding menu command (Edit⇨Bookmarks⇨Toggle Bookmark), but it's much slower. (Cruelly, Microsoft omitted keyboard shortcuts for the bookmark commands.) You can lay down as many bookmarks as you want.

  Of course, a bookmark does you no good by itself. Click the Next Bookmark or Previous Bookmark button to jump in sequence from one bookmark to the next until you arrive at your destination.

 To remove a single bookmark, place the insertion point on the line containing the mark and again click the Toggle Bookmark button. If you've accumulated so many bookmarks that the Next and Previous Bookmark commands work like scroll bar buttons, you can wipe them all out by clicking the Clear All Bookmarks button.

Splitting a Code window

You can split any Code window into two separate panes (see Figure 6-8). These allow you to see code in different parts of the same module at the same time. They also give you an easy way to cut and paste between sections of your code.

To split a Code window, use the split bar — it's that little gray bar just above the top-right scroll bar arrow. Drag the split bar downward until the panes are sized to suit you. To reunite them, remove the split bar by double-clicking it or by dragging it back to the top of the window.

Figure 6-7: Those light ovals along the left side of the Code window represent bookmarks. By default, they appear in light blue (cyan) on a color monitor.

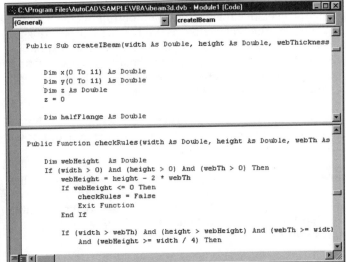

```
C:\Program Files\AutoCAD\SAMPLE\VBA\ibeam3d.dvb - Module1 (Code)          _ □ ×
(General)                              ▼   createIBeam                         ▼

    Public Sub createIBeam(width As Double, height As Double, webThickness


        Dim x(0 To 11) As Double
        Dim y(0 To 11) As Double
        Dim z As Double
        z = 0

        Dim halfFlange As Double

    Public Function checkRules(width As Double, height As Double, webTh As

        Dim webHeight  As Double
        If (width > 0) And (height > 0) And (webTh > 0) Then
            webHeight = height - 2 * webTh
            If webHeight <= 0 Then
                checkRules = False
                Exit Function
            End If

            If (width > webTh) And (height > webHeight) And (webTh >= widtl
                And (webHeight >= width / 4) Then
```

Figure 6-8:
I split this
Code
window.

More Code window creature comforts

Why write code when you can have someone else type it for you? The Visual
Basic Editor pampers you by automatically entering those wacky VBA terms
for you at just the right time. Not only does this minimize your typing, but it
also guarantees accurate spelling.

Several related Editor features, all found on the Edit menu, provide these
amenities. They are

- ✔ The List Properties and Methods feature.
- ✔ The List Constants feature.
- ✔ The Complete Word feature.

Using the List Properties and Methods feature

Of these, the List Properties and Methods feature sees the most use. Here's
how it works: To do anything useful with a VBA object, you change the setting of one of the object's properties or you activate one of its methods. To
identify the property or method you want to work with, you type the object's
name, a period (the *dot* operator), and then the property or method name,
like this:

```
ActiveWindow.Selection.Group
```

(See Chapter 10 for the full story on working in code with objects and their
properties and methods.)

With List Properties and Methods, all you have to type is the object name and the dot. As soon as you do, a little list of all the available properties and methods for that object pops up in the window. Figure 6-9 shows this list in action. To find the correct property or method, you can scroll the window (by using the arrow keys) or type the first letter or two of the item's name. After the correct item is highlighted, you can then press Tab to insert the item into your document.

Figure 6-9:
The List Properties and Methods feature gives you a power assist when entering — what else?— properties and methods in code.

The List Properties and Methods feature performs a similar service when you're declaring a variable (defining its type). When you start typing a statement such as

```
Dim Oatmeal As CerealObject
```

a list of the available data and object types pops up just when you finish typing the word *As*. Just as before, you pick from this list by scrolling or typing a letter or two and pressing Tab. By the way, Chapter 9 showers you with a gentle rain of information on declaring variables.

List Properties and Methods works not only with built-in VBA objects, but also with your own variables — *except for those of the variant type*. This gives you another good reason to explicitly define variables (see Chapter 9).

Oh, one other point. The Properties and Methods list pops up automatically only if the proper setting is turned on in the Options dialog box. If you don't get the list, choose Tools⇨Options and be sure that the box labeled Auto List Members is checked. You can pop up the list manually by using the appropriate command on the Edit menu or by using the keyboard shortcut Ctrl+J.

Listing constants automatically

The List Constants feature works just like the List Properties and Methods feature, except that it displays the names of the predefined constants for the property you're working with. This list pops up just after you type the = in a statement such as

```
Oatmeal.Texture = Gluey
```

It's beyond me why this is considered a separate command rather than just another part of the List Properties and Methods. But because it is, it requires a slightly different keyboard shortcut: Ctrl+Shift+J. If you want to know how named constants work, see "Working with Values Constantly" in Chapter 9.

Completing words automatically

The Visual Basic Editor's Complete Word feature enters just about any valid VBA term for you. To activate it, press Ctrl+spacebar. Doing so pops up a list that looks and works just like the one provided by the List Properties and Methods feature. The difference is that the Complete Word list includes just about everything you may want to type: objects, functions, procedures, constants, methods, properties, and your own variables. One exception is the keywords for built-in data types, such as Integer and Variant.

Typing a letter or two before you press Ctrl+spacebar limits the list to items starting with those characters. Better yet, if you've typed enough letters to match only one item, the Editor inserts it for you as soon as you press Ctrl+spacebar — the list itself never appears.

Getting into arguments

Many VBA procedures require you to specify one or more *arguments* when you execute the procedure. Such procedures base their calculations (or do whatever else they do) on the information supplied in these arguments. Many object methods require arguments just like procedures do.

Now, the Visual Basic Editor won't type the arguments for you — it can't, because it doesn't know which specific values you want the arguments to have. However, it does pop up a little bitty window containing a kind of cheat sheet — it tells you which arguments the function requires, which are optional, and the type of information each argument represents. You're looking at the Quick Info window, shown in action in Figure 6-10.

If the Auto Quick Info box is checked in the Tools⇨Options dialog box, the Quick Info window appears automatically as soon as you type the name of a function, method, or procedure that requires arguments. If you shut off this automatic response, you can still display the Quick Info window by pressing Ctrl+I.

Figure 6-10:
The Quick
Info window
in action.

Many functions and procedures require multiple arguments. To help you keep track of where you are in the list of arguments, the Quick Info window displays the argument you're currently typing in bold. As soon as you type the comma that indicates the end of one argument, the next argument turns bold in the Quick Info window.

Using the Properties Window

The Properties window lets you view and edit the properties of whatever object (project, module, form, or control) is currently active in the Visual Basic Editor. If you look at Figure 6-11, you can see that the title bar of the Properties window shows the name of the active object, which also appears highlighted in the Project Explorer (if the selected object is an individual control on a form, only the form itself is listed in the Project Explorer).

Quick Info versus Parameter Info

The Parameter Info feature complements Quick Info when you get into heavy VBA coding. Often, you want to use one function to determine the value of an argument required by another function, as in this simple example:

```
MsgBox(Str(AnIntegerVariable))
```

Here, the `Str` function converts the integer value stored in the variable `AnIntegerVariable` into a text string. This string is then used as the argument to the `MsgBox` function (it becomes the prompt you see when VBA displays the message box on your screen).

But because you can *nest* functions within functions within functions in this way, the Quick Info window isn't enough. It always shows you the argument list for the function containing the insertion point. An extra helper, the Parameter Info feature, displays the argument list for the *outermost* function, the one within which all the other functions are nested. The keyboard shortcut for the Parameter Info feature is Ctrl+Shift+I.

Properties - DefineBeam
DefineBeam UserForm
Alphabetic | Categorized
(Name)   DefineBeam
BackColor   &H8000000F&
BorderColor   &H80000012&
BorderStyle   0 - fmBorderStyleNone
Caption   Define Beam
Cycle   0 - fmCycleAllForms
DrawBuffer   32000
Enabled   True
Font   Tahoma
ForeColor   &H80000012&
Height   180.75
HelpContextID   0
KeepScrollBarsVisible 3 - fmScrollBarsBoth
Left   0
MouseIcon   (None)
MousePointer   0 - fmMousePointerDefault
Picture   (None)
PictureAlignment   2 - fmPictureAlignmentCente
PictureSizeMode   0 - fmPictureSizeModeClip

Figure 6-11:
The
Properties
window for
a form.

When a project or module is the selected object, the only property listed in the Properties window is the project name. With form and control objects, however, the Properties window gives you access to a myriad of properties governing the appearance and behavior of the selected object.

Because the Properties window is primarily useful for designing forms, I postpone a full discussion of how it works to Chapter 15. For now, I just show you how to display the window and use it to rename projects and modules.

Invoking the Properties window

You can do any of the following tricks to display the Properties window:

- ✔ Press F4.
- ✔ Click the Properties button on the Standard toolbar.
- ✔ Choose View➪Properties Window.

After the Properties window is visible, you can switch to a Code or UserForm window (or click an item in Project Explorer) to display that item's properties in the window.

Renaming a project or module in the Properties window

Projects and modules have only one property each: a name. Even so, you still use the Properties window if you want to change that one property.

To rename a project or module, follow these steps:

1. **Select the project or module in the Project Explorer.**

2. **Activate the Properties window. If you can't see it, display it by using any of the methods just listed in "Invoking the Properties window." If the Properties window is visible, be sure it's active — click it or press F4.**

3. **Type the new name.**

   Because this is the only property, you don't have to click the row for the (Name) property before you start typing.

A First Look at the Debugging Windows

Although Chapter 14 covers debugging in detail, this survey of the Visual Basic Editor's windows wouldn't be complete without a quick look at the debugging windows. You have four of them:

- ✔ **The Immediate window** lets you execute individual VBA statements on the fly. You can also have your programs display messages in this window for debugging purposes. Figure 6-12 shows the Immediate window in action.

- ✔ **The Locals window** displays details about the objects and variables used in the procedure currently running.

- ✔ **The Watch window** (or Watches window, take your pick) shows the current values of objects or variables you choose to display in the window. They can come from any part of your program, not just the currently running procedure.

- ✔ **The Call Stack window** lists the procedures that have been executed by your program up to the time you display the window.

Figure 6-12:
Executing a line of VBA code in the Immediate window.

```
Immediate
print 1001/2
 500.5
x = Now
print x
3/27/98 6:42:24 AM
x = IIf (x < #01/01/2000#, "Premillenium", "Now things get interesting")
print x
Premillenium
```

You can display three of the windows at any time — the exception being the Call Stack window, which you can see only when code is executing in *break mode.* However, you also have to be in break mode to see anything useful in the Locals and Watch windows.

With these caveats out of the way, I can safely mention the techniques you need for displaying the debugging windows. Of course, you can always open the View menu and select the appropriate menu choice there. For faster response, use these alternatives:

Window	*Button*	*Keyboard Shortcut*
Immediate	(Debug toolbar)	Ctrl+G
Locals	(Debug toolbar)	None
Watches	(Debug toolbar)	None
Call Stack	(Debug toolbar) or (at top right of the Locals window)	Ctrl+L

Part III
The Main Course in VBA Programming

IT'S FRICASSEE OF PYTHON WITH FRIED ANTS AND CRISPY GRASSHOPPERS.

YOU'RE GETTING RECIPES OFF THE INTERNET AGAIN, AREN'T YOU?

In this part . . .

*I*f you want to gorge yourself on VBA programming essentials, this part of the book is your meal ticket. While other parts cover important concepts and skills, this part offers satisfying staples of knowledge that fortify you for the day-to-day programming challenges you're bound to face. I foresee you returning to this part of the book for sustenance more often than any other.

Chapter 7 takes apart the structure of VBA programs, explaining every building block in detail. Chapter 8 lays out rules and conventions for naming things in VBA and suggests ways you can make your code prettier and easier to understand. In Chapter 9, you get an extensive tour of VBA variables and constants — named handles for the information you bandy about in your programs. In Chapter 11 comes a survey of the techniques you need for working with VBA objects.

I don't recommend reinventing the can opener, nor should you write a custom procedure when a one-line VBA function or statement can do the job for you. But you have to know what functions and statements VBA provides, and that's the task Chapter 11 sets for itself. Chapter 12 explores the techniques you can use to direct the sequence in which your program does things — techniques that are critical for giving your programs a modicum of intelligence.

In Chapter 13, I return to the subject of data management, covering advanced storage receptacles such as arrays, collections, and user-defined types. Finally, because nothing ever works the way you plan, Chapter 14 tells all about preventing, locating, and extinguishing errors in your programs.

Chapter 7

Anatomy of a Great VBA Program

. . . .

In This Chapter

▶ Details on the components of VBA programs and how they relate to each other

▶ When to create a new module, and where to put things in it

▶ How to write Sub and Function procedures

▶ Understanding all the types of VBA statements

. . . .

*I*n previous chapters, I refer to the various components of code in VBA programs whenever they need mentioning, in an offhand, rather casual fashion. Now it's time to get at least semi-formal in my definitions of these elements. First, I offer a brief tour of each item in the VBA coding hierarchy. The bulk of this chapter then covers these elements separately and in more detail, working from the top of the food chain down.

Program Building Blocks

A VBA program isn't just a random collection of instructions to the computer. *Au contraire,* it's a highly organized random collection of instructions. Lines of code are collected into procedures, which reside in modules, which in turn are housed within projects.

Programs defined

So what's a *program?* Conceptually, a program is a complete, functioning (or malfunctioning) software totality. A program consists of one or more statements that execute in the order defined by the programmer.

But a program isn't an official VBA entity. VBA recognizes by name procedures, modules, and projects, but not programs as such. A VBA program requires at least one procedure — because VBA executes only statements within procedures — but it can encompass two or more procedures, within one or more modules, spanning one or more projects.

In this book, I stick mostly to programs that confine themselves to single projects at most. Chapter 17 briefly touches on cross-project programming.

A sample program

To make the discussion of this hierarchy of VBA elements a little less abstract, you can refer to the following module of code. It contains all the elements I mention (except a project because modules go inside projects rather than the other way around). After the sample model come descriptions of each of these elements.

I guess you should know what the program does. It starts by creating a set (*array*) of six integers and filling them with random values between 1 and 1,000. After counting how many of those values exceed the cutoff value, 500, it displays the count in a little VBA message box.

```
Option Explicit
Const Maximum As Integer = 500
Const HowMany As Integer = 5
Dim ListOfNumbers() As Integer
Sub MAIN()
 Dim ItemsInList, n, x As Integer
 ReDim ListOfNumbers(HowMany)
 Randomize
 For x = 0 To 5
        ListOfNumbers(x) = Int((1000 * Rnd) + 1)
 Next x
 n = CountBigNumbers()
 MsgBox ("There were " & n & " values greater than " & _
        Maximum)
End Sub
Function CountBigNumbers()
 Dim Counter, y As Integer
 Counter = 0
 For y = 0 To 5
   If ListOfNumbers(y) > Maximum Then
    Counter = Counter + 1
   End If
 Next y
 CountBigNumbers = Counter
End Function
```

The entire block of sample code shown previously is a *module*. The module consists of a series of statements organized into three sections: the Declarations section, which starts with the Option Explicit statement, a Sub procedure, which starts with the Sub MAIN () statement, and the Function procedure, which starts with the Function CountBigNumbers () statement. Most of the module's statements occupy one line, but the statement that begins with MsgBox spills over onto a second line.

The VBA hierarchy

With the sample program in mind, you should be better able to understand the following definitions and descriptions of VBA code building blocks.

A *statement* is the smallest unit of VBA code that can accomplish anything. A statement may be used to declare or define a variable, set an option of the VBA compiler, or carry out an action in your program. A valid statement is a lot like a complete sentence — it has to include the proper "parts of speech" or it isn't really a statement at all.

A *procedure* is the smallest unit of code that you refer to by name. It's also the smallest unit of code that you can run independently. VBA recognizes two main types of procedures: Sub procedures and Function procedures. A procedure of either type consists of one or more statements, sandwiched inside two special statements: the procedure's declaration at the top, and the End Sub or End Function statement at the end.

A *module* is a named unit consisting of one or more procedures, plus declarations common to all procedures in the module. Although VBA allows you to place all your procedures in a single module, it makes sense to divide related procedures into separate modules to make it easier to keep track of them.

Two types of modules are available in VBA. By far the most common is the *standard module,* the kind you use for the code you want to run. The other type, the *class module,* is used to define custom objects and their properties and methods. I discuss class modules briefly in Chapter 17.

A *project* consists of all the modules, forms, and application-related objects associated with a particular document, plus the document itself.

Where Do Projects Come from, Mommy?

The stork brings them. Well, maybe not, but the point is that you never have to take special steps to create a project. Every document from a VBA application is a project automatically. Of course, a document's project doesn't contain any code or forms until you create them in the Visual Basic Editor or record macros in the application. (The section on the Project Explorer in Chapter 6 covers the techniques you need for working with projects.)

Totally Modular

The module comes just below the project in the hierarchy of VBA code elements. A module stores one or more VBA procedures, along with a Declarations section containing statements that apply to the entire module.

Planning your modules

Deciding how to organize your modules doesn't have to be a big deal. It does make sense to think about how many modules you should create and which procedures each one should contain. The basic points to remember are these:

- ✔ Your procedures can *call,* or run, procedures stored in other modules. One module can use variables declared in another module, too.

- ✔ However, using procedures and variables from other modules can introduce slight complications. For example, you can call a procedure in another module by entering the procedure's name alone. However, if the procedure you're calling has the same name as a procedure in the current module, you must enter the procedure name preceded by the module's name, as in `OtherModule.DoSomethingNow`. (I recommend using this *Module.Procedure* technique even when you don't have to, so you know which module contains the procedure you're calling.)

In general, you should place related procedures together in a single module. Typically, a module contains all the procedures for one complete VBA program — and no extraneous procedures. That setup simplifies your programming because you don't have to deal with the little complications involved in accessing procedures or variables in other modules.

However, if you create procedures that you plan to use in more than one program, you can organize them in modules according to type, as in `MyMathProcedures` or `TextHandlingRoutines`. You may also create modules called `BrandNewProcedures` or `OldProceduresIMightNeedSomeday`.

Adding a new module to a VBA project

To create a new module in the Visual Basic Editor, start by making sure that you're working with the correct project. In the Project Explorer, select the project itself or any of the objects it already contains (this can be a form, an application object, or an existing module — it doesn't matter). You can then use any of the following techniques to insert the new module:

✔ Click the Insert Module button, shown in the margin. This is a split (multi-function) button for inserting various items. If the module icon isn't visible, click the narrow bar with the arrow to the right of the main part of the button, and choose from the menu.

✔ Right-click the Project Explorer window — make sure that you do it over the correct project — and choose Insert Module from the shortcut menu.

✔ Choose Insert⇨Module.

The Visual Basic Editor automatically opens the new module's Code window. It also christens the module with a generic name. To change it, type a new name in the Properties window (see "Renaming a project or module in the Properties window" in Chapter 6).

What goes where in a new module

The Code window for a brand-new module has only one section, the Declarations section. You can tell which section you're in by looking at the list box at the top right of the Code window.

You can enter two types of statements in a module's Declarations section. These are:

✔ Declarations of variables, constants, and user-defined data types. These tell the compiler the name and type of each item (but not its value). Variables and constants declared in a module's Declarations section can be used in any procedure in that module.

✔ Compiler options that control the way VBA compiler operates.

What you can't place in the Declarations section are assignment or executable statements — statements that actually do something when the code runs. For example, you can't specify the *value* of a variable in the Declarations section. That requires an assignment statement, which must go inside a procedure elsewhere in the module. (I discuss the differences between executable statements, assignment statements, declarations, and compiler options in the section "Making Your Statements" later in this chapter.)

Statements in the Declarations section also go by a fancier name – *module-level code.*

Each procedure you add to the module is considered a separate section. After you add a procedure, its name appears in the list box at the top right of the Code window, enabling you to jump directly to that procedure by selecting its name in the list.

Standard modules and modules with class

The garden-variety VBA module is a *standard module.* Standard modules were known as *code modules* in older versions of VBA and Visual Basic. They contain statements that declare variables and constants, define custom (user-defined) data types, and set compiler options, as well as executable statements that actually get things done. You can make use of any existing objects you have access to in a standard module, but you can't create new object types in this type of module.

You use *class modules,* by contrast, to define your own custom objects. After creating a class module for the custom object, you fill it with the code for the object's properties and methods. Code in other modules can then access the custom object's properties and methods, just as if it were a built-in VBA object. Although I don't have room for more than this brief mention of class modules, creating your own objects is a very powerful programming technique.

Procedure types

The bulk of the VBA code you write lives within two types of procedures, Sub procedures and Function procedures. Event procedures, which VBA executes when an event such as a mouse click occurs, are specialized Sub procedures. VBA also has a third type of procedure, the Property procedure.

Here's a summary of the various procedure types:

- A *Sub procedure* is a general-purpose procedure for getting things done in VBA. Sub procedures are the only type you can run independently with the techniques covered in Chapter 4. However, one Sub procedure can also run, or *call,* another.

- A *Function procedure* can execute any VBA statements you like. However, it differs from a Sub procedure in that it calculates a value and then *returns* that value to the procedure that activated the Function in the first place.

- An *event procedure* is a special type of Sub procedure. I know, I already said so. What I didn't say is that Chapter 17 covers the particulars on event procedures.

- A Property procedure determines or assigns the value of a custom object's property. I don't cover Property procedures until Chapter 18, but I mention them here because you see them listed in the Add Procedure dialog box.

A VBA macro is, technically speaking, a Sub procedure that *takes* (requires) no arguments. Macros are the only kind of Sub procedures you can run directly, by name, in the Visual Basic Editor or your VBA application. To run a Sub procedure that does take arguments, you must call it from another procedure. Arguments are discussed in "Winning arguments" later in this chapter.

Writing Procedures

Procedures are critical functional units of your VBA code because code must be stored within a procedure or it won't run. There are two everyday types of VBA procedures: Sub procedures and Function procedures (see the "Procedure types" sidebar in this chapter).

Procedure skeletons

Here are two simple procedures, one of each type (Sub and Function):

```
Public Sub SubMarine()
 MsgBox "Up Periscope!"
End Sub
```

```
Public Function FunkShun (Birthdate As Date)
 FunkShun = DateDiff("yyyy", Birthdate, Date)
End Function
```

As you can see, each procedure comprises an opening declaration statement, one or more lines of code, and a terminating End statement. I go into these elements in the sections "Sub procedures in detail" and "Function procedures in detail" later in this chapter.

Creating a new procedure

Before you can start a new procedure, you have to first open the Code window for the module in which you're going to store the procedure. Create a new module with the steps laid out in the "Adding a new module to a VBA project" section earlier in this chapter, or open an existing module by double-clicking it in the Project Explorer.

After the module's Code window is open and active, you're ready to begin the new procedure. Your initial task is simply to insert into the module the procedure's declaration statement, and its complement, the End statement that signals the end of the procedure. You can accomplish this in two ways:

- ✔ By choosing Insert➪Procedure and completing the resulting dialog box
- ✔ By typing the statements yourself

Typing versus the dialog box

I recommend typing in the procedure's "shell" yourself, simply because the dialog box method doesn't save any time unless you're a *really* slow typist. The do-it-yourself approach also lets you control where in the module to place the procedure, which you can't accomplish with the dialog box. All you have to do is click where you want the procedure to go, type the procedure's declaration statement, and then press Enter. You don't have to type the closing End Sub or End Function statement — the Visual Basic Editor puts the correct one in for you.

 However, when you're getting started in VBA, you may feel more secure using the dialog box. To use the latter technique, click the Insert Procedure button (again, you probably have to click that little bar next to the Insert button and then pick Procedure from the shortcut menu). Alternatively, you can just choose Insert⇔Procedure.

The resulting Add Procedure dialog box appears. Here, type the procedure name in the Name text box. Then choose the Type of procedure and its Scope using the radio buttons, and check the box for static local variables, if that applies. I know, I haven't said anything about the terms *scope* and *static* so far, but all your questions are answered in the section "Scoping Out the Scope" later in this chapter.

After you click OK, the Visual Basic Editor inserts paired procedure declaration and End statements at the end of the module, regardless of where the insertion point was when you started.

Completing the procedure

Entering the declaration and End statements is definitely the easy part of creating a new procedure. Your real work consists of typing in the filling — a series of VBA statements — between those pieces of bread. This section isn't the place for details on what to type. Suffice it to say that the statements within a procedure are executed in the order in which they appear, except when your code instructs VBA to jump to another location.

Sub procedures in detail

The term *Sub procedure* still looks odd to me, but that's the proper usage in VBA. In some programming languages, "subprocedures" or "subroutines" are those that are called by main procedures. In VBA, while a Sub procedure can be called by another procedure, the main procedure of a program is itself *always* a Sub procedure. Weird.

Enough of my grousing — on to the facts. Here's a sample Sub procedure, with the declaration at the top, the terminating End statement at the bottom, and a few statements in between.

```
Public Sub ASweetProcedure()
  Dim ANiceMessage As String
  ANiceMessage = "Have a nice day!"
  Msgbox ANiceMessage
  (more statements)
...
End Sub
```

The first line, the Sub procedure declaration, performs two vital duties. First, it tells where the procedure starts, so that VBA knows where to start executing code when you run the procedure. Second, it declares the procedure's characteristics, as discussed in the next section.

Every Sub procedure must be terminated with an End Sub statement. This line lets VBA know that it's time to stop executing code.

Items in a Sub procedure declaration

In the procedure's declaration statement, the first term, Public, specifies the procedure's scope. This can be Public or Private. Public is the default, so you don't need to include this keyword. However, doing so makes the scope obvious so you don't have to wonder. Again, I leave a full discussion of scope to the section "Scoping Out the Scope."

Next comes the Sub keyword, which simply indicates that you're declaring a Sub procedure. After that comes the procedure's name, which can be anything you like, as long as it conforms to the naming rules described in Chapter 8.

Forgoing arguments

Closing out the declaration is a pair of parentheses. Why are they there when nothing is inside them? Those parentheses would hold *arguments,* if the procedure had any. Arguments are elements of data that the procedure expects to receive when it is launched. In this case, the procedure has no arguments, so not only is it quite friendly, it has nothing inside the parentheses. Arguments are further discussed in "Winning arguments," later in this chapter.

To repeat a point I make elsewhere, a VBA macro is by definition a Sub procedure that requires no arguments. To run a Sub procedure that does take arguments, you must call it from another procedure.

Calling Sub procedures

You can run, or *call,* any Sub procedure — whether or not it takes arguments — from another procedure. To call a Sub procedure, just include a
statement consisting of the name of the Sub procedure you want to call, as
in the following code fragment. The line that reads WashMyOldCar calls the
Sub procedure.

```
. . .
MyOldCar = "Valiant"
WashMyOldCar
NumberOfCarwashTrips = NumberOfCarwashTrips + 1
. . .
```

Function procedures in detail

A Function procedure can conduct general business just like a Sub procedure, but its main *raison d'être* is to calculate a value. When the Function
completes its work, it returns that value to the calling procedure, which can
use the value in further computations.

Here's a sample Function procedure:

```
Public Function DeFunction (x As Integer, y As Integer)
   Dim z As Integer
   z = x + y
   DeFunction = x ^ z
End Function
```

Obviously, the basic form of a Function procedure is much like that of a Sub
procedure. The declaration begins with an optional keyword defining the procedure's scope (in this case, Public). Next comes the Function keyword,
specifying the type of procedure, then the procedure's name, and finally its
arguments. I explain arguments in "Winning arguments," but you can see how
they work by reading the code. Like a Sub procedure, a Function procedure
ends with a terminating statement, End Function.

I must pause here to point out that VBA comes with numerous built-in functions. Like a Function procedure, a VBA function returns a value to a calling
procedure. Also, you use the same technique to call both functions and
Function procedures. The only difference between Function procedures
and functions (besides the name) is that you don't have to write code for
functions! Chapter 9 offers an overview of the functions available in VBA.

The difference between Function and Sub procedures

There is one critical difference between Sub and Function procedures: Somewhere in the Function procedure, at least one statement specifies the value of the function itself. It does so by using the name of the procedure as if it was a variable. In the above example, this occurs in the line DeFunction = x ^ z. After this line executes, DeFunction holds the value that will be returned to the calling procedure and used there.

Calling Function procedures

You can only run Function procedures by calling them from within other procedures. Typically, you do so by setting a variable equal to the name of the function. In the following example, the variable called ZPower receives the value returned by the DeFunction procedure:

```
. . .
ZPower = DeFunction(3, 4)
. . .
```

After this statement runs, the ZPower variable would contain the value calculated by DeFunction, a Function procedure; the value equals 3^7. Note that this statement passes the arguments required by the DeFunction procedure in parentheses following the procedure name.

Winning arguments

Arguments represent values that VBA is to transfer, or *pass*, from one procedure to another. The procedure on the receiving end is said to *take* the arguments. You build arguments into a procedure when you want the procedure to modify its behavior based on values you supply at the time you call the procedure. Both Sub and Function procedures can take arguments.

Here again is the Function procedure DeFunction:

```
Public Function DeFunction (x As Integer, y As Integer)
   Dim z As Integer
   z = x + y
   DeFunction = x ^ z
End Function
```

The procedure takes two arguments, x and y. As the code illustrates, a procedure's arguments are declared as part of the declaration of the procedure itself. They always appear in parentheses following the name of the procedure. In this *argument list,* you declare individual arguments by listing each argument's name and its data type (see "Writing procedures that take arguments" later in this chapter for further details).

A procedure that takes arguments requires those arguments to do its job. Within the procedure in detail, arguments serve exactly the same role as variables that you declare in the usual way.

Look carefully at the code for the `DeFunction` procedure. After declaring a variable z, the procedure calculates z's value as the sum of the two arguments, x and y. Then, to calculate the procedure's own return value, the next line of code raises the x argument to the power of z. As you can see, x, y, and z all have similar roles. If you wanted, you could have raised z to the power of x instead of the other way around.

Productive arguments

So if arguments are so much like variables, why use arguments at all? Actually, you don't have to — you can use ordinary variables to accomplish everything you can do with arguments. But arguments make your procedures easier to use and your code easier to read.

It's time for a couple of comparative examples. This first pair of procedures uses the arguments `Model` and `Year` to communicate values:

```
Public Sub CallingProcedure()
    ProceedsFromOldCar = SellOldCar ("Rambler Classic",1962)
End Sub

Public Function SellOldCar(Model As String, _
    Year As Integer)
Dim AgeFactor As Integer
Dim PriceFactor As Single
 AgeFactor = Year - 1900
 If Model = "Rambler Classic" Then
    PriceFactor = .001
 Else If Model = "Dodge Dart" Then
    PriceFactor = .005
 Else If ...
    (more statements)
 End If
 SellOldCar = AgeFactor * PriceFactor * 1000
End Function
```

To summarize what's going on here in English, the procedure named `CallingProcedure` uses `SellOldCar`, a `Function` procedure, to calculate a result called `ProceedsFromOldCar`. Because the `Function` procedure takes arguments, you can tell right away which car you're selling and how old it is.

Now, here are two comparable procedures that conduct the same sort of business without arguments. Note that you must declare two variables at the module level, outside either procedure, so that both procedures have access to the variables.

```
Dim Model As String
Dim Year As Integer
Public Sub CallingProcedure2()
 Model = "Dodge Dart"
 Year = 1963
 ProceedsFromOldCar = SellOldCar2()
End Sub
Public Function SellOldCar2()
Dim AgeFactor As Integer
Dim PriceFactor As Single
 AgeFactor = Year - 1900
If Model = "Rambler Classic" Then
   PriceFactor = .001
 Else If Model = "Dodge Dart" Then
   PriceFactor = .005
 Else If ...
   (more statements)
 End If
 SellOldCar2 = AgeFactor * PriceFactor * 1000
End Function
```

So why argue?

With the preceding examples fresh in your mind, I can list the advantages of using arguments when sharing information between two procedures. Here you go:

- ✔ Again, when you're reading through a procedure's code, arguments make clear which values the procedure requires from elsewhere in the program to do its job.

- ✔ When you're writing code, arguments help you minimize the number of variables you need to create (in the Declarations section of the module, outside any procedures). One obvious problem with such module-level variables is that you can't see their declarations when you're writing code for a procedure that uses them.

- ✔ When you call a procedure that takes arguments, VBA *forces* you to state values for those arguments. This requirement helps ensure that the procedure gets the correct values it needs.

Writing procedures that take arguments

To write a procedure that takes arguments, enclose the arguments in parentheses immediately after the name of the procedure in the procedure's declaration. Here's an example:

```
Sub Novelizer(Title As String, Pages As Integer, Deadline As
      Date)
```

As the example illustrates, you designate the data type for each argument by following the argument name with `As type`, where `type` can be any VBA data type or object class. If you list only the argument name, omitting `As type`, VBA assigns the argument the `Variant` data type. (I know, I know, I haven't discussed data types and object classes in this chapter, but you can find out all about them in Chapters 9 and 10, respectively.)

Calling procedures that take arguments

To call a procedure that takes arguments from your code, you simply list each argument's value following the name of the procedure you're calling. You must list the values in the same order the corresponding arguments appear in the procedure declaration.

The only complication you face is knowing whether or not to place the arguments in parentheses. The rules are as follows:

```
ProceedsFromOldCar = SellOldCar ("Rambler Classic",1962)
```

When you use a `Function` procedure to return a value, you surround the arguments in parentheses, as shown in the above line of code.

Omit the parentheses when calling a `Function` procedure without using its return value in the calling code.

When you call a `Sub` procedure that takes arguments or when you call a `Function` procedure but you don't want to use its return value, omit the parentheses, as in these examples:

Organizing your procedures

An entire VBA program, no matter how large, can fit in a single procedure. Then why go to the trouble of writing separate procedures? The main reason is to keep track of your work more easily.

As a program grows in size, the likelihood that you'll get lost in all that code grows even more quickly. By dividing the program into a series of procedures, each named for what it does, you can jump to the part of your program you want to concentrate on. Remember, you can use the list box at the top right of the Code window to select the procedure from an alphabetical list and get beamed directly to that procedure, wherever it happens to be in the module.

Another good reason to place a block of code into a separate procedure is to eliminate redundant code. If your program repeatedly uses the same sequence of code statements in various places, you can minimize its size and complexity by placing those statements into a procedure. You can then call that procedure from anywhere in the program.

As a bonus, creating a separate procedure for the repeated statements minimizes drudgery and the mistakes that you otherwise may make (*will* make, truth be told) if you have to revise a bunch of identical series of statements. When you consolidate the repeated statements into a single procedure, you need to change only that one procedure.

Scoping Out the Scope

Each VBA procedure has a defined *scope*. The scope determines the parts of your program from which you can call that procedure. If you have a visual imagination, think of it this way: A procedure's scope decides which parts of your program can "see" the procedure.

Procedures can have three different scopes:

✔ By default, VBA procedures (except event procedures) are *public* in scope. That means that you can call them from any part of your program — from the same module, from another module, or even (if your program includes multiple projects as discussed in Chapter 17) from a different project.

✔ When it suits your programming needs, you can create procedures that are *private* in scope. Private procedures are visible, if you will, only within the same module. In other words, you can call a private procedure from another procedure in the same module, but not from procedures in any other modules.

✔ In a VBA program that includes more than one project, you can create procedures that are accessible to all the modules within a given project but off-limits to other projects.

Variables have scope, too, and scope works in a similar way for them. See the section on "Specifying a variable's scope" in Chapter 9.

Specifying a procedure's scope

To specify the scope of a procedure, all you have to do is place the `Public` or `Private` keyword at the beginning of the procedure's declaration. Look at these examples:

```
Public Sub IKneadYou()
... (procedure statements)
End Sub

Private Function IKneedYou()
... (procedure statements)
End Function
```

Because procedures are public by default, you don't have to include the `Public` keyword to give a procedure public scope. If a program contains any private procedures, however, I recommend that you explicitly declare the public procedures so you can tell at a glance which is which.

To restrict the scope of a public procedure to its project only, so that it is inaccessible to other projects, place the statement `Option Private Module` in the Declarations section of the module in which you declare the procedure. See the "Declarations" and "Compiler options" sections later in this chapter for details on working with such statements.

Using private procedures

Making a procedure private helps prevent errors. Because you can only call the procedure from within the same module, you can more easily control the conditions in effect at the time the procedure gets called (conditions such as the values of variables that the procedure uses).

Making a procedure private in scope is easy enough, but why bother? After all, VBA doesn't *demand* that you call a procedure from another module, just because that procedure is public.

Well, the reason is self-protection. You may forget that you designed a procedure so that it should only be called from within the same module. If the procedure is private, VBA won't let you call it from another module even if you try to. As a bonus, in programs of substantial size and complexity, limiting the number of access points to a given procedure helps you better keep track of the program's organization.

Making Statements

Procedures are made up of statements, the smallest viable units of code. Most statements occupy only one line of code, and a line of code usually has only one statement — but not always, as I discuss later in this section. VBA distinguishes four different statement types: *declarations, assignment statements, executable statements,* and *compiler options*.

Declarations

A declaration is a statement that announces to the VBA compiler your intention to use a named item — a variable, constant, user-defined data type, or procedure — in your program. The declaration goes further, specifying which type of item it is and providing any additional information the compiler needs to make use of the item. Once you've declared an item you can use it elsewhere in your program.

The first example declares a *variable*. Variables are named values that can change as a program runs (see Chapter 9 for full details). The following statement declares the variable named MyLittleNumber and specifies that it always contains an integer:

```
Dim MyLittleNumber As Integer
```

Also discussed in Chapter 9, *constants* are named values that never change. This statement creates a *string* (text) constant named UnchangingText and consisting of the characters Eternity:

```
Constant UnchangingText = "Eternity"
```

You can place a declaration for a variable or constant in the Declarations section of a module or within an individual procedure. Your choice of location determines where the item will be accessible — I refer you to the section "Specifying a variable's scope" in Chapter 9 for details. Anyway, here are some examples of declaration statements.

The next sample statement declares a user-defined data type called MadeThisUpMyself, defining it as a structure that includes a string variable called Name and a date variable called Birthday. In this case, the declaration spans several lines:

```
Type MadeThisUpMyself
 Name As String
 Birthday As Date
End Type
```

The following declaration creates a Sub procedure named HiddenProcedure, specifying that the procedure is Private in scope. The End Sub statement that closes the procedure is considered part of the declaration. You must go on to write the other statements that form the body of the procedure:

```
Private Sub HiddenProcedure()
(the procedure's other statements go here)
End Sub
```

You can find more examples of procedure declarations in the section "Writing Procedures" earlier in this chapter.

Assignment statements

Assignment statements set a variable or a property of an object to some specific value. These statements always have three parts: the name of the variable or property, an equal sign, and an *expression* specifying the new value.

I define the term *expression* in a moment. First, though, some examples of executable statements are in order. This statement sets the value of the My-LittleNumber variable to the sum of the SomeOtherNumber variable plus 12:

```
MyLittleNumber = SomeOtherNumber + 12
```

The following statement sets the Color property of the AGraphicShape object to Blue (presumably, Blue is a named constant representing a numeric color value):

```
AGraphicShape.Color = Blue
```

To assign a value to the SquareRoot variable, this statement calls the Sqr function — a built-in VBA function for calculating square roots — with the current value of the MyLittleNumber variable:

```
SquareRoot = Sqr(MyLittleNumber)
```

Just before the examples I used the term *expression*. In VBA, an expression is any snippet of code that specifies a particular numeric value, string of text, or object. It can contain any combination of actual numbers or characters, defined constants, variables, object properties, built-in functions, and Function procedures, all combined with any of the *operators* (such as + or *) that act on these items. The following are examples of expressions.

Expression	Value
3.14	3.14
AGraphicShape.Sides	5 (assuming the AGraphicShape object represents a pentagon)
(12 - Sqr(x))/5	2 (assuming the x variable = 4)
"Roses are red," & " violets are blue"	Roses are red, violets are blue

Executable statements

Executable statements do the program's work. You use statements of this type to do the following:

- ✔ Call another procedure in your own code.
- ✔ Activate a method belonging to an object.
- ✔ Control the order in which other statements get executed, by defining loops or by choosing which section of code (of several alternatives) to execute.
- ✔ Execute one of VBA's built-in statements or functions.

Gaze upon the following examples. The following statement executes the Rotate method of the AGraphicShape object:

```
AGraphicShape.Rotate(90)
```

This small block of code contains two executable statements: The If...Then statement checks to see if the current value of the AudibleThreshold variable is greater than 3. If so, it directs the program to execute the next executable statement, the one that calls the PlayLoudSound procedure:

```
If AudibleThreshold> 3 Then
  PlayLoudSound
End If
```

Compiler options

Instructions that control the VBA compiler's behavior constitute the last class of statements. The following compiler option statements are available:

Statement	What It Does
Option Base number	This statement sets the default numbering system for array variables to begin with 0 or 1 — see Chapter 11 for details.
Option Compare method	This statement determines the method VBA uses for comparing string (text) variables. The method term can be Binary, for comparisons based on each character's numeric code; Text, in which upper- and lowercase characters are considered equivalent; or Database, which is available only in Access and which uses the database's sort order.

(continued)

Statement	What It Does
Option Private Module	When you include this statement in a module's Declarations section, other *projects* can't access the module's procedures, variables, or constants, even if those items are declared as public in scope. See "Scoping Out the Scope" in this chapter for more on the topic of scope.
Option Explicit	The Option Explicit statement is one compiler option you need to know and use. When you place it in a module, VBA doesn't allow you to use variables without declaring them first. See Chapter 9 for details.

Multiple-line statements and multiple-statement lines

Although most statements fit on a single line of code, VBA doesn't limit you to one-liners. If a statement is too long to fit on one line, break it up over two or more lines by adding an underscore (the _ character) at the end of each line in the statement except the last. Chapter 8 shows examples of this practice.

Conversely, you can place more than one statement on a single line of code. I don't recommend this because it makes your code harder to read. For the curious, the technique required is simple: Just place a colon after each statement on the line, except the last one. Here's an example:

```
Dim A As Integer, B As Integer: A = 3: B = 5: A = A + B
```

The line above is equivalent to the following four lines:

```
Dim A As Integer, B As Integer
A = 3
B = 5
A = A + B
```

Chapter 8

Manners, Please! VBA Etiquette

In This Chapter

▶ Following VBA rules when naming variables, forms, modules, and the other elements of your programs

▶ Choosing names to make your code more understandable

▶ Indenting to clarify complex code

▶ Splitting statements over multiple lines of code

▶ Adding comments to explain your code to your future self

*T*his chapter devotes itself to the service of readable, understandable, working code. Here you discover rules and conventions for naming variables, procedures, and other items. You also get tips on formatting your code for legibility, and on adding explanatory comments that keep you from forgetting why you wrote the dang procedure that way, anyway.

I'm sure you're eager to get started writing useful code, and if the urge is overwhelming, you're welcome to skip over this chapter for now. But you know what they say — it's harder to unlearn a bad habit than to learn to do things right from the beginning.

Naming Your Babies

Within limits, you're free to choose your own names for your variables, procedures, and what have you. The following rules apply to all the named elements in a VBA program, including variables, constants, data types, procedures, modules, forms, controls, and projects:

✔ Names must begin with a letter, not a numeral. After the first character, however, you can use numerals and the underscore character, as in

```
Hidden_Variable3
```

✔ Aside from the underscore character, punctuation marks are off limits altogether in VBA names. *Verboten* characters include these:

```
! @ & ' $ # ? , * . (period) { } ( ) [ ] = + - ^ % /
~ < > : ;
```

✔ Names can't include spaces.

✔ You're limited to a maximum of 255 characters (40 characters, for forms and controls).

✔ A name can't duplicate a VBA keyword, function, or statement.

✔ You can't use the same name more than once in the same scope. For example, all procedures in the same module must have different names. For that matter, a procedure and a module-level variable — one declared in the Declarations section of a module — can't share the same name. However, you can use duplicate names for variables declared inside procedures. (I clarify the muddy issue of scope in Chapters 7 and 9.)

If you enter a name that violates any of these rules, the Visual Basic Editor warns you as soon as you move the insertion point off that line of code. The line appears in red characters, and the Editor displays a quasi-explanatory error message (see Figure 8-1). The exception: You won't be notified of duplicate procedure names until you run the program.

Figure 8-1: The Visual Basic Editor lets you know when you enter an invalid name.

Here are some examples of law-abiding and illegal VBA names:

Valid	Unacceptable
a	AReallyLongNameOfMoreThan255CharactersThatWon'tAllFit . . .
Go4It	4ScoreAnd7
You_Did_It	WhoDunIt?
IrishEyes	Spanish Eyes

How VBA handles capitalization

VBA ignores the capitalization of names, but preserves the capitalizations you use as a courtesy. Suppose that you declare a variable in all uppercase letters, like this:

```
Dim LOUDVARIABLE As String
```

You can turn around and type the variable in your code in any case you like. Typing any of the following statements manipulates that same variable:

```
loudvariable = "Bright red"
lOuDvArIaBlE = UCase(lOUDvARIABLE)
MsgBox (LoudVariable)
```

Of course, you don't see the alternative versions of the name for very long. The Visual Basic Editor remembers the capitalization pattern you used when you declared the name. If you then type the variable any which way, the Editor automatically corrects any mismatched capitalization as soon as you move the insertion point to another line.

VBA naming conventions

As long as you live by the rules listed earlier in this section, you can give any name you like to any item in your program. Nevertheless, you can make your programming life a lot easier by sticking to a logical naming scheme. As your programs get longer, remembering the purpose and type of your variables gets harder — much harder. So drop yourself hints by designing names that make some sense.

Ideally, adopt and stick to a systematic naming practice. One method that many people use is to start each name with a short prefix that indicates the type of item, and follow that with a capitalized brief descriptive name. For an obvious example, say that you're writing a program that tracks inventory. If the program needs an integer variable to store part numbers, you may call it intPartNo.

Table 8-1 lists suggested prefixes for the most commonly used VBA items. You can make up your own, or use them as suffixes, if you prefer. The important thing is to use them consistently.

I don't use this convention in this book in Chapters 1 through 7 because the convention requires an explanation first. But in this chapter and in the later chapters in this book, I try to practice what I preach.

Table 8-1	Suggested Prefixes for Naming VBA Items	
Use This Prefix	*To Name This Type of Item*	*Example*
Variables		
byte	Byte	byteDaysInMonth
bool	Boolean	boolClearedStatus
int	Integer	intWeeksOnChart
lng	Long integer	lngPopulation
sng	Single	sngRadius
dbl	Double	dblParsecs
cur	Currency	curUnitPrice
str	String	strLastName
date	Date/Time	dateBirthdate
var	Variant	varSerialNumber
obj	Object	objStampCollection
Controls		
txt	Text box	txtEnterName
lbl	Label	lblAnswerMessage
cmd	Command button	cmdCalculateInterestRate
mnu	Menu	mnuTools
cmb	Combo box	cmbToyCategory
fra	Frame	fraHabitat
opt	Option button	optGasolineGrade
chk	Check box	chkCaseSensitive
Other Items		
bas	Module	basTextFormatFunctions
frm	UserForm	frmOptionsDialog

Making Your Code Pretty

Okay, your code doesn't really need to be good-looking — just easy to read. This section offers a few simple suggestions for writing code that you can decipher when you come back to it tomorrow, next week, or next year.

Judicious indenting helps organize your code

The Eleventh Commandment: Develop and practice a consistent indenting style. The VBA compiler ignores blank space at the beginning of a line, so you're free to use indentation to set off related lines of code. Compare these two sample code fragments and tell me which one is easier to understand:

```
If intA = 27 Then
If txtChooseColor.Text = "Beige" Then
intA = 33
intB = 0
End If
For Each objCbar in CommandBars
If objCbar.Name = "Big Toolbar" Then
If objCbar.Visible = False Then
objCbar.Visible = True
End If
End If
Next objCbar
End If


If intA = 27 Then
  If txtChooseColor.Text = "Beige" Then
    intA = 33
    intB = 0
  End If
  For Each objCbar in CommandBars
    If objCbar.Name = "Big Toolbar" Then
      If objCbar.Visible = False Then
        objCbar.Visible = True
      End If
    End If
  Next objCbar
End If
```

Although both fragments produce identical results, the indenting in the second one makes it (reasonably) easy to tell which `End If` statement belongs to which `If...Then` statement above it. As a result, you can readily trace the flow of program execution, depending on the conditions in effect when you run it.

Indenting customs

So which lines of code should you indent, and by how much? Your goal is to indent related statements by the same amount, so that the relationship between them is visually obvious. More specifically, statements that are executed only when some condition is in effect should all be indented together.

For example, VBA executes the statements within an If...Then...Else construction or inside Do...Loop and For...Next loops as a group; so they should have the same indentation. Here's another example:

```
Do While intC <> 20
  intA = intA + 1
  If intA = intB Then
    intA = 5
    intB = 10
  Else
    intA = intB
    intC = 20
End If
```

VBA executes the statement intA = intA + 1 and the If...Then...Else structure with every pass of the Do...Loop structure. For this reason, I used the same indentation for the intA = intA + 1 statement and the three statements that define the If...Then...Else structure (If intA = intB Then, Else, and End If). The two statements immediately following the If ... Then statement are only executed if intA equals intB, so they receive additional indenting, as do the two statements following Else.

Note that *control structures* like Do...Loop and If...Then...Else always consist of at least two statements — one that starts the structure, the other that terminates it. For Do...Loop, the terminating statement is Loop; for If...Then...Else, it's End If. Statements that are part of a given control structure itself should all be indented by the same amount. This format allows you to see clearly the outline of the structure, and which other statements fall inside it. Control structures are one of the major topics covered in Chapter 9.

How to indent

To indent a line of code, you can simply press the spacebar or the Tab key to move the insertion point over. You can control how far the Tab key moves each time you press it by choosing Tools⇨Options. The Editor tab of the Options dialog box has a box labeled Tab Width where you type the number of spaces you want. Because space in the Visual Basic Editor is so dear, I decreased my Tab Width setting to 3, but you can enter any value from 1 to 32.

  If pressing Tab or the spacebar is beneath you, you can always use VBA's Indent and Outdent buttons to move the beginning of your lines of code to the right or left, respectively. These buttons work on selections, not just single lines, so you can indent or outdent an entire block with one click. Note that they ignore the location of the insertion point — they always indent or outdent the entire line, no matter where the insertion point rests.

Automatic indenting

To cut your workload to a minimum, the Visual Basic Editor automatically indents each new line of code to match the previous one. When you get to a line that requires a smaller indentation, just press the Backspace key to back up. If you don't like the assistance, you can shut off automatic indenting in the Editor tab of the Tools⇨Options dialog box.

Space-iousness is good

Placing a blank line between groups of related statements clues you in to meaningful units of code. Besides, it makes your program a little less dense and easier on your visual cortex. To see this practice, peek up ahead at Figure 8-2.

Don't scroll if you don't have to!

As Chapter 7 makes plain, extending a single statement over multiple lines is perfectly acceptable in the Visual Basic Editor. A single line of the Code window can hold over 300 characters (would you believe that 308 is the maximum?), so you can certainly write some very long one-line statements if you like. Obviously, however, each line will be much easier to read if it all fits into the visible portion of the Code window so you don't have to scroll sideways.

Using the line-continuation character

To continue a statement onto another line, place an underscore (_) at the end of the line. For example, the following three lines together constitute one statement:

```
sngWackyNumber = Cos(12 * 57.5 / Sqr(intMyTinyNumber + _
   intMyBigNumber) + CustomDataMassage(sngrawinfo, 12) + _
   (bytFirstTuesdayInAugust * curLastPayCheck) + 1)
```

Be sure that you remember to type a space before the underscore (also called the *line-continuation character*) on every line where you use it. Otherwise, VBA gives you an "invalid character" error message.

One more caution about breaking up statements over multiple lines: Don't place the underscore within a pair of quotation marks that enclose a string of text — not unless you want to include the underscore character as part of the string. Chapter 10 tells all about using strings in your code, including how to split them across two or more lines.

Not using multiple-line statements

Although multiple-line statements are better than long single-line statements that trail off the edge of the Code window, they're not at all ideal. VBA may have no trouble interpreting statements that continue over two or more lines, but most human beings find them confusing.

Unless you've made the Code window very skinny, you can usually break up a long statement into several separate statements that get the same job done. You may need to create additional variables for temporary storage of some intermediate calculations, but this is a fair price to pay for improved clarity in your code.

```
For instance, you may rewrite the above sample code as
        follows:sngTemp1 = Sqr(intMyTinyNumber +
        intMyBigNumber)
sngTemp2 = 12 * 57.5 / sngTemp1
sngTemp3 = CustomDataMassage(sngrawinfo, 12)
sngTemp4 = bytFirstTuesdayInAugust * curLastPayCheck
sngWackyNumber = Cos(sngTemp2 + sngTemp3 + sngTemp4 + 1)
```

This code is longer and it does involve extra variables, but it makes the calculation you're performing easier to follow. Also, if you get the wrong final results, you can follow each part of the computation individually as the program runs to see whether you can catch the error — this *stepping* isn't possible when one long statement performs the entire calculation (Chapter 14 covers the process of stepping through your code).

Remarks About Comments

Like all serious programming languages, VBA lets you add explanations to your code. *Comments* allow you to translate the code into understandable English and to record the purpose of each statement or group of statements. For that matter, you can use them to embed phone numbers, recipes, and positive affirmations in your code.

The comments you type are totally ignored by the VBA compiler. They live only in the text file representing the contents of the Code window, not in the compiled program. They don't make the compiled program any longer, nor do they slow it down in any way. Comments cost you nothing except a minuscule amount of disk space, so use them freely.

How to make comments

A comment begins when you type an apostrophe. Everything you type to the right of the apostrophe on that line of code is part of the comment. You can place comments on lines all by themselves, or add comments after a line of active code. Figure 8-2 shows a Code window with lots of comments interspersed among the active code statements.

```
Sample code for chapter 9.xls - TeachingMachine [Code]
(General)                                              DisplayQuestion

' This procedure displays a question that meets current selection criteria
Public Sub DisplayQuestion()

SelectNextQuestion ' Call procedure to select a prospective question
' If we're screening questions by their weighting factors,
' compare the prospective question's weight against the random cutoff value
If boolWeightingFlag = WTurnedOn Then ' If
ReEnterQuestionLoop:
    Do While Questions(intQNumberCurrent).intQWeight < intRandomWeight
        SelectNextQuestion ' Repeat selection process if prospective ? fails the test
    Loop
End If

' A question that passes the first criterion has been found. Now be sure it
' wasn't the last question displayed.
If intQNumberCurrent = intQNumberLast Then
    SelectNextQuestion
    GoTo ReEnterQuestionLoop
End If

' We have a valid question for display. Take care of housekeeping before displaying it.
intQNumberLast = intQNumberCurrent ' store the selected question number for the next pass
QAsked(intQAskedPointer) = intQNumberCurrent ' also store the number in the list of previo
```

Figure 8-2:
Comments,
please?

One place you can't put a comment is on a line that ends with the line-continuation character, the underscore. In other words, you get an error message if you enter code like this:

```
a = b _ ' This is the first line of a multi-line statement
+ c
```

To comment a multiple-line statement, you must place the comment on a line of its own before the statement starts, or on the last line of the statement, like this:

```
' Here is a properly commented multi-line statement
z = x - _
y ' The last line CAN take a comment.
```

When to use comments

Be lavish with comments. Train yourself to add at least a brief clarification to every line of code, and to record in detail the function of each group of statements. When you declare a variable, add a comment about what it's for and where it will be used. When you declare a procedure, write down what it does, which arguments and variables it uses and why, and which other procedures it calls. Train yourself to type comments whenever you experience a lull in your creative coding process.

Excuse my preachiness, but this point is really important! When you're actively working on a particular project, the logic behind your coding choices may seem transparently obvious. However, that lovely sense of clarity soon fades. If you turn your attention elsewhere, even for a few days, only your comments save you from laboriously translating the work you've already done back into terms your mind can understand. Comments are critical when you are working on a project with other people — they let you explain your program's goals and choice of programming techniques in context.

Commenting is a good way to take real code statements off of active duty without deleting them for good. This can come in handy when you want to try two alternative approaches to the same coding problem, or to shut off code that you know contains an error while you test another part of the same module. By the way, the same goes for blank lines, which I also recommend highly (see the "Space-iousness is good" section in this chapter).

Long-winded comments

To include a long comment spanning two or more lines in your code, you still have to place an apostrophe at the beginning of each line. But fortunately, VBA provides a one-button command for commenting blocks of lines in bulk.

To insert a multiple-line comment in your code, type the comment as you would in a word processor, dismissing any error messages you get when you press Enter to start each new line. After you're through, select the entire block that you intend for comment-hood, and click the Comment Block button. The Visual Basic Editor adds the required apostrophe at the beginning of every line in the selected block.

You can also "uncomment" a block of lines that currently begin with apostrophes. Select the block and click the Uncomment Block button.

Using the Comment Block and Uncomment Block buttons, you can quickly deactivate and reactivate any code block. *Commenting out* a block of code that isn't working properly at the moment can be a boon when you want to test some other part of the program.

One little note about the way these buttons work is in order. If a line already starts with an apostrophe, the Comment Block button adds a second apostrophe to it, and so on. Likewise, each time you click the Uncomment Block button, only one apostrophe is removed. This means that when you comment and then uncomment a block of active code, you don't lose any real comments that it contained.

Rem sleep for your comments

A holdover from the original versions of BASIC, the keyword Rem performs the same function as the apostrophe in VBA: It indicates the start of a comment. (*Rem* stands for *remark,* not rapid eye movement.) If you like letters better than punctuation marks, you can use Rem anywhere you can an apostrophe, and you can mix and match the two comment indicators at whim.

One difference exists between them, however: If you use the Rem keyword on a line that contains active code, you must type a colon (:) after the code, before Rem.

```
Rem This is a comment marked by the Rem keyword
```

a = b + c: Rem See the colon after the active code?

Chapter 9

Storing and Modifying Information

In This Chapter

▶ Using variables as named storage bins for whatever data you want to store

▶ Declaring variables in your code for fast, error-free programs

▶ Lightening your programming workload by defining named constants

▶ Expressing your values in VBA code as expressions

▶ Calculating and computing with VBA operators

▶ Understanding practical details on the different data types for variables and constants

o tap the full potential of VBA, programs require *variables* to store information that can change. Variables are the key to writing programs that alter their own behavior based on up-to-date information or other changes in prevailing conditions. This chapter surveys the topic in some depth, explaining how variables work and how to use them in your programs. The various types of data that you can store in variables receive special attention, as do related topics such as *constants,* which represent unchanging values, and *operators,* the symbols and keywords you use to calculate a new value from two or more existing ones.

Although fairly hefty, the material here isn't the last word in this book on variables. Chapter 13 discusses variables in relation to arrays and user-defined data types, and Chapter 10 shows you how to use variables to work with objects.

The forms in this chapter are available on the CD in its fullest form.

Working with Variables

In essence, a variable is an ID tag for a chunk of information stored by your program.

It's like when you go to the theater and leave your hat at the hatcheck. The attendant puts your hat away somewhere in a back room — you couldn't care less where, as long as it's safe. In return, you get a slip with a number on it.

When you leave, you give the attendant the number and you get your hat back. At the next performance, the staff uses that same number for somebody else's hat.

What, you say you don't have a hat? Well, until now, you haven't had any variables, either.

A variable lets you access a whole chunk of information all at once via the variable's name, instead of working with each individual digit, character, or what have you. What's more, you don't need to know the details of where your program stores the data, or in what form — all you need is the variable's name. Finally, you can change the information represented by the variable any time you like.

This last characteristic is the key to creating programs that can respond automatically to changing conditions. Whenever appropriate, your program can examine the information the variable stands for, comparing it to criteria that you specify. If the information matches the criteria, the program can execute one set of statements; if not, it executes a different set.

Technically, a difference exists between the variable (which is a named information container) and the information it contains. However, people don't go around saying things like "the information represented by variable *x*" very often. You can refer to the information itself by the variable name, as long as you keep in mind that the information can vary.

Declaring variables: The overview

Chapter 7 introduces the concept of *declarations,* VBA statements that notify the compiler that you plan to use a named item and that describe exactly the type of item it is. One of the most common uses of declaration statements is to declare variables. Variable declarations look like this:

```
Dim varAnyOldVariable
Private intIntegerVariable As Integer
Static strNewYearsResolution As String
```

Most variable declarations are `Dim` statements. The `Dim` keyword is short for *dimension,* used as a verb. The idea is that the `Dim` statement gives VBA the dimensions for the storage area that the variable refers to. You can also use the `Private`, `Public`, and `Static` keywords to declare variables and at the same time specify their *scope.* (See the "Specifying a variable's scope" section later in this chapter or see Chapter 7.)

After you declare a variable, you can then use it in other statements in your program. Typically, the first time a variable sees action is when you place specific information in it using an assignment statement (see "Giving variables their values," later in this chapter). You can then go on to use that information (via the variable's name) anywhere else you like in your code.

Where to declare variables

You can declare a variable in either of two places in your program:

- ✔ The Declarations section of the module (at the module level)
- ✔ Anywhere within a procedure (at the procedure level)

The choice of this location helps determine which procedures can access the variable —, that is, they determine the variable's scope. In general, if you declare the variable at the module level, any procedure in the module can use the variable. If you declare it in a particular procedure, it can be used only in that procedure. You can also use the Public, Private, and Static keywords to specify a variable's scope. (I introduce *scope* in Chapter 7 and offer further detail in the "Specifying a variable's scope" section in this chapter.)

Although VBA won't object if you interleave variable declarations with executable statements within a procedure, your code will be clearer if you declare all the procedure's variables at the very beginning. Note how the following procedure follows this practice:

```
Public Sub VariableProcedures ()
  Dim strChildsName As String
  Dim intToyCount As Integer
  Dim curAllowance As Currency

  strChildsName = InputBox ("Enter the child's name:")
' in the next two lines, CountToys and NewAllowance
' represent Function procedures that are presumably
' defined elsewhere in your code
  intToyCount = CountToys(strChildsName)
  curAllowance = NewAllowance(strChildsName, intToyCount) .
End Sub
```

When to declare variables

All the experts agree that declaring variables ahead of time, before you use them in your program, is the best practice. One simple reason for doing so is to make your code easier to understand. Other advantages come into play when you use the `Option Explicit` compiler directive, covered in "Pros and cons of explicit declarations" later in this chapter.

By default, however, VBA permits you to use variables without declaring them first. If you type `A = 7` anywhere in your code, VBA dutifully creates a variable named `A` and stores the value 7 in that variable. Variables you create without declaring them are automatically defined as *variant variables*, which are discussed in the next section.

Choosing and using data types

When you write a variable declaration, you can simply name the variable. The following statement tells VBA to set aside storage space for a variable named `varIable` but does not say what sort of information that variable should hold:

```
Dim varIable
```

Alternatively, you can declare the variable's *data type* explicitly. The statement

```
Dim sngMyOldSocks As Single
```

declares the variable `sngMyOldSocks` as of the *single* data type, meaning that it holds a relatively small floating-point number (the kind written in scientific notation — you know, with a decimal point and an exponent, as in 6.02×10^{23}.

VBA recognizes a variety of other distinct data types for your variables, including helpful types like `Date` and `Currency`. Familiarize yourself with the available types because collectively they are an important key to writing code that works right. Table 9-1 summarizes key facts about the data types. The "Details on Data Types" section of this chapter offers tips on working with many of the specific types.

Table 9-1	VBA Data Types	
Data Type	*Explanation*	*Range of Permitted Values*
Boolean	Logical True or False	True (-1) or False (0)
Byte	Small whole number	0 to 255
Integer	Smallish whole number	-32,768 to 32,767
Long	Large whole number	-2,147,483,648 to 2,147,483,647
Single	Single-precision floating-point value	-3.402823E38 to -1.401298E-45 for negative values; 1.401298E-45 to 3.402823E38 for positive values
Double	Double-precision floating-point value	-1.79769313486232E308 to -4.94065645841247E-324 for negative values; 4.94065645841247E-324 to 1.79769313486232E308 for positive values
Currency	Large, precise number; 19 significant digits	-922,337,203,685,477.5808 to 922,337,203,685,477.5807 including four fixed decimal places
Decimal	Even larger, more precise numbers with 29 significant digits and up to 28 decimal places	+/-79,228,162,514,264,337,593, 543,950,335 with no decimal point; +/-7.9228162514264337593 543950335 with 28 places to the right of the decimal
Date	Dates and times	January 1, 100 to December 31, 9999
Object	VBA object	Any object reference
String	Sequence of text characters of variable length	0 to approximately 2 billion (variable length)
String	Sequence of specified number of text characters	1 to approximately 65,400 (fixed length)
Variant	Anything goes	Any numeric value up to the range of a Double; same range as for variable-length String
User-defined (requires	Group of variables used together as a unit	The range of each variable the Type statement) in the group corresponds to its data type, as shown in this table

Pros and cons of using specific data types versus variants

Depending on whom you talk to, declaring a variable as a specific data type — that is, as a type other than `Variant` — is either a great idea or a bad one. The practice helps prevent some errors, but fosters others. It definitely makes for smaller and faster programs — but in most real-world scenarios, these improvements probably aren't significant.

Here's some background on error prevention: When you specify a particular data type when declaring a variable, VBA bars you from placing other types of data in that variable. Suppose you declare a variable as in this example:

```
Dim dateAnniversary As Date
```

VBA displays an error message if you try to assign text to the variable with a statement such as

```
dateAnniversary = "Trip to Fiji" ' Error
```

An error message may be a nuisance, but it's better than allowing your program to keep running with erroneous information.

You wouldn't get that error message if you had declared `dateAnniversary` as a variant, a catch-all type that can hold any kind of data. You can declare variants just as you would variables of other types, as in this example:

```
Dim varTootSuite As Variant
```

However, since `Variant` is the default data type, you automatically get a variant variable if you omit the data type. Just listing the variable name in your declaration will do, as shown here:

```
Dim TootSuite
```

Now, how about the performance question? Declaring a variable with a specific data type lets you select the type that requires the least storage space to hold the information you plan to keep there. Variants consume more memory than variables of other types, and accessing their information slows down your program. However, these effects are trivial unless you work with very large numbers of variables. And by declaring all variables as variants, you can reduce errors and make your code easier to write, more flexible, and less complicated to modify. I don't have room to explore this issue in detail, but you should be aware that some very good programmers recommend coding exclusively with variants.

Decide on one of these strategies — declaring the specific data type of every variable, or using variants for all your variables — and resolve to stick to it, at least within a given program.

Explicit declarations are good

Whether or not you decide a particular data type for each variable, it's always a good idea to declare each variable before you use it. As a Serious Programmer, you can set VBA so that it forces you to do so. When you place the statement

```
Option Explicit
```

in the Declarations section of a module, VBA displays an error message every time you try to use a variable that you haven't declared. Duly reminded, you can go back and add the necessary declaration.

Requiring explicit declarations in this way produces an even more important benefit: It prevents spelling errors or typos from introducing major problems into your code.

Imagine this scenario: You decide to wing it without the `Option Explicit` statement in your module. Somewhere in the body of a procedure, however, a random finger spasm strikes while you're typing one of your variables' names. When the VBA compiler encounters the line with this misspelling, it thinks that you've just designated a new variable and cheerfully creates it for you. Your program may still run, but don't be surprised if it turns all your text purple or tells you that the world's population just hit 12.

By now, maybe you're convinced that the `Option Explicit` statement should be a part of every module you create. If that's the case, why should you have to type it each time? You don't have to, of course. Go to the Options dialog box by choosing Tools⇨Options. On the Editor tab, check the Require Variable Declaration check box. From now on, the Visual Basic Editor automatically inserts an `Option Explicit` statement in every *new* module. You still have to type the statement yourself in *old* modules that don't have it.

Specifying a variable's scope

A variable's *scope* — that is, where in your program the variable is accessible — depends on two interacting factors:

- ✔ The location where you declare the variable (either inside a procedure or in the Declarations section of a module — see "Where to declare variables" earlier in this chapter)

- ✔ The keyword you use to declare the variable (`Dim`, `Public`, `Private`, or `Static`)

If you declare a variable inside a procedure using Dim, you can only use that variable inside that procedure. Elsewhere in your program, VBA won't recognize the variable. Variables declared with Dim in the module's Declarations section are accessible throughout the module — but not from other modules.

Private variables — the default

The Private keyword works exactly like Dim. The two declaration statements shown here function identically:

```
Private strLouie As String
```

```
Dim strLouie As String
```

Because Private and Dim work the same way, you can forget about Private if you like. You may want to use Private instead of Dim, however, to remind yourself when you read the code that the variable is accessible only in the current module or procedure.

Public knowledge

Declaring a variable with Public makes the variable accessible throughout your entire project. Here's an example:

```
Public intUnclassified As Integer
```

However, Public has its special power only if you declare the variable in the Declarations section of a module. Although VBA accepts Public declarations within procedures, the variables so declared are still inaccessible outside the procedure where you declare them.

The Static advantage

Use Static to declare a variable within a procedure when you want the variable to remain in memory — and even more importantly, to retain its value — even when the procedure isn't running. In the following example, the variable intLastingVariable acts as a counter, recording the number of times the procedure runs:

```
Sub TransientProcedure()
  Dim strTransientVariable As String
  Static intLastingVariable As Integer
  strTransientVariable = Format(Now(), "Medium Time")
  intLastingVariable = intLastingVariable + 1
  MsgBox "The time is " & strTransientVariable & ". " & _
    "You have executed this procedure " & _
    intLastingVariable & " times."
End Sub
```

In the above example, the statement `intLastingVariable = intLastingVariable + 1` adds 1 to the value of the variable each time the procedure runs. If you declare `intLastingVariable` with `Dim` instead of `Static`, the variable always starts with the same value (zero) with every pass through the procedure, which makes the procedure essentially worthless.

You can only declare `Static` variables within a procedure. If you want *all* the variables in a procedure to remain intact — even when the procedure isn't running — declare the whole procedure as `Static`. In the procedure declaration, place the keyword `Static` immediately before the `Sub` or `Function` keyword that defines the type of procedure you're declaring. Here are a couple of examples of this technique:

```
Private Static Sub DoItAll ()
```

```
Static Function DontDoVeryMuch(intTimeToWaste as Integer)
```

Note that `Static` comes after `Private` or `Public` in the procedure declaration, if you include either of these optional scope-related keywords.

Declaring multiple variables on the same line

To conserve space, you're free to declare more than one variable on the same line of code. You have to type the `Dim` keyword only once per line. A comma should separate each variable.

Just remember to specify the data type for *each* variable that you declare — even if all the variables on the line are of the same type. Here's an example of the right way to do it:

```
Dim intA As Integer, intD As Integer, intL As Integer
```

Mixing data types on the same line works, too:

```
Dim curNetWorth As Currency, datSecondTuesday as Date
```

Declaring multiple variables on the same line increases the likelihood that you'll accidentally fail to specify a data type. Any variables on the line for which you don't supply a data type are automatically registered as variants. If your declaration reads

```
Dim strX, strY, strZ As String
```

`strX` and `strY` are treated as variants, not string variables.

Giving variables their values

After you've declared a variable, the next thing you do with it, usually, is fill it with information (putting known information into a variable for the first time is called *initializing* the variable). To place information in a variable, you *assign* the value of the information to the variable. Whenever it suits your purposes, you can store different data in the variable by assigning a different value to it.

Giving assignments

To assign a value to a variable, all it takes is one little equal sign. For example, to store the number 3 in a variable named intC, just type

```
intC = 3
```

In VBA, an *assignment statement* consists of an equal sign between a variable on the left and an *expression* specifying the variable's value on the right. In the example, the expression is simply the number value, 3. Values you specify directly like this are called *literal* values. (Expressions are discussed in the "Expression-ism" section later in this chapter.)

Take a look at another assignment statement:

```
strQuote = "Ask not what your country can do for you, " & _
  "ask what you can do for your country."
```

In this case, the statement assigns all the text to the right of the equal sign to the variable strQuote. As before, the information in this statement's expression consists entirely of literal values — the actual text you want to place in the variable. However, the statement is broken up over two lines, so the text expression has to be divided into two separate strings. That & (ampersand) sign tells VBA to join them together.

The point I'm trying to illustrate here is that expressions very often have two or more components. No matter how many parts an expression has, VBA computes its overall value and *then* assigns that value to the variable.

Understand that until an assignment statement actually executes, it isn't a statement of fact. In math, when you write an equation such as $2 + 2 = 4$, you're proclaiming that the values on either side of the equal sign *are* actually equal. By contrast, a VBA assignment statement *compels* the variable to become equal to the expression's value. Another assignment statement can change the variable's value at any time.

Using variables in assignment statements

You can base a variable's assigned value on other variables, as well as on literal values. The statement

```
curSalePrice = curCost * sngMargin
```

multiplies the `curCost` and `sngMargin` variables together and assigns that result to the `curSalePrice` variable. Note that in this statement, the expression consists of other variables, not literal values. VBA makes the necessary calculation based on the current values stored in those variables. (By the way, following the naming convention recommended in Chapter 8, `curSalePrice` and `curCost` are variables of the `Currency` data type.)

Using functions in assignment statements

Functions and `Function` procedures can also be used in assignment statements, as in this example:

```
strFavorite = InputBox("What's your favorite flavor?")
```

VBA functions and the `Function` procedures you write can be used in an assignment statement because each returns a value. The `InputBox` function used in the above code displays a little dialog box with the specified message and provides space for the user of your program to type a response. That response is the value returned by the function, in the form of a string (more on the `InputBox` function in Chapter 11).

Expression-ism

An *expression* is a portion of a VBA statement that can be evaluated to give a value, such as a number, a text string, or a reference to an object. It can consist of one or more of the following, in any combination:

- ✔ Variables, such as `bytMonth` or `boolWinter`
- ✔ Literal values, such as `1234` or `This is only a test`
- ✔ Constants, which stand in for literal values and are covered in the section "Working with Values Constant-ly" later in this chapter
- ✔ VBA functions, such as `InputBox()` or `Sqr()`
- ✔ Function procedures in your code

If the expression has more than one of these elements, they are joined with *operators* such as the + sign, or in some cases, by nesting functions and `Function` procedures inside other functions and `Function` procedures.

Note that if an expression has more than one component, each component is itself an expression — it has a value.

Working with Values Constant-ly

When your program uses a value that *doesn't* change, you don't need a variable to represent that value. Although you can always place literal values in the meat of your procedures, declaring *constants* to represent these values is usually better.

Declaring constants

Use a `Const` statement to declare constants:

```
Const cstrPetsName As String = "Foo-foo"
Const cdateTargetDate As Date = #5/26/2000#
Const cboolUp As Boolean = True
```

What's in a variable before you assign it a value?

When VBA runs a procedure, it creates storage space for each variable and assigns an initial "nothing in here" value to the variable. Most of the time you assign your own information to a variable before using it in any other statements. But it's quite possible, and sometimes useful, to access a variable before you know for sure whether it contains any of your own data.

Suppose that your program has a procedure that runs only under certain conditions. Suppose also that this procedure assigns a value to one of the program's variables. In this situation, another procedure may check to see whether the variable contains a value as a way to see if the first procedure has already been executed.

Here are the values that your variables contain before you assign any values to them yourself:

Data Type	Initial Value
All numeric data types	0
String (variable-length)	A string of zero length ("")
String (fixed-length)	A string of the specified length consisting of ASCII character code 0 — which isn't a visible character
Variant	Empty (a special value indicating a variant with no contents)
Object	Nothing (a special value indicating that no object reference has been assigned to the variable)

Note that this technique is quite similar to the way you declare variables. The difference is that you specify the value of the constant when you declare it. You can declare constants as any of the same data types you use for variables, except object, user-defined, and, for now, decimal (refer to Table 9-1).

Notice also that I declared the name of each constant with an initial lowercase *c* (which stands for "constant"). This method is the simplest way to indicate that a declared name is a constant rather than a variable. However, you can choose another meaningful prefix if you prefer.

You may follow the example of VBA and Visual Basic and choose a prefix based on your name or on the name of your VBA project. VBA and Visual Basic identify constants with the prefix vb, as in vbBlue (representing the code number for the color blue, 16711680) or vbKeyTab (representing the code for the Tab key, 9). VBA applications often name the constants they define using an application-specific prefix, as in xlBarStacked (representing the code for an Excel stacked bar chart, 58).

By the way, you're free to use the constants defined by VBA or your VBA application in your own programs. You can use the Help system or the Object Browser to locate information on these predefined constants (see Chapter 6 for a discussion of the Object Browser).

Reaping the benefits of a constant approach

After you declare a constant, you can use it by name in your program wherever you would have entered the corresponding literal values. For instance, let's say that you write a program that determines an employee's salary based on his shoe size. One way to code a part of the program would be:

```
If bytShoeSize > 12 Then
    CurJoesSalary = 75000
End If
```

One problem with this approach is that it "hard-codes" the exact salary amount in your program. If a rising cost of living increases salaries across the board, you have to dig through your code to find the amount that needs to be changed. And if you use the same value more than once in the program, you have to change each occurrence — and you run a bigger risk that typing errors will creep in and gum up the works.

Here's the same code written with a constant:

```
Const ccurTopSalaryStep As Currency = 75000
...
If bytShoeSize > 12 Then
    CurJoesSalary = ccurTopSalaryStep
End If
```

With this solution, you can easily locate the constant declaration at the top of the module or procedure. Change the constant's value there, and you instantly alter your code to match at every place the constant appears. As a bonus, the code is much easier to understand. Instead of asking, "What does this number 75,000 represent?" you know at a glance that Joe is due the top step of the salary scale if he wears size 12 shoes.

You *could* use a variable to gain the advantages of a constant. However, variables take up more space in memory, and more importantly, you run the risk of accidentally changing the variable's constant value in your program.

Using constants to represent attributes

Constants are handy for working with a group of named elements or characteristics such as days of the week (Monday, Tuesday, and so on) or tastes (sweet, salty, sour, and bitter). Instead of manipulating the names of these items as text strings in your program, an easier approach is to pick a number to represent each item and then declare a constant equal to that number based on the item's name. From then on, you can refer to the items by name rather than number. Here's a little bit o' code that uses this technique:

```
Const cbytSweet = 1, cbytSalty = 2
Const cbytSour = 3, cbytBitter = 4
Do While intTaste = cbytSour
  AddSweetener
  intTaste = CheckTaste()
Loop
```

Hello, Operators

In VBA, an *operator* is a special symbol or keyword in an expression that combines two values (sub-expressions, if you will) to give a new result. The two values are listed on either side of the operator.

In the following expression, the + (addition) operator adds 3 to the value of the intA variable.

```
intA + 3
```

The result of this addition is the expression's value. (Remember, an expression is only a part of a VBA statement and you can't run it by itself — you must include it in a complete statement such as `intB = intA + 3`. For information on expressions, see "Expression-ism," earlier in this chapter.)

VBA includes operators in three main categories — arithmetic, comparison, and logical — plus a few miscellaneous operators such as the ones for string *concatenation.* I review each category separately later in this section.

When used with text strings, the + operator performs concatenation, not addition — it joins the two strings together. But it's better to use the "real" concatenation operator, the & symbol. VBA interprets the expression:

```
"My name is " & "Ellie."
```

as "My name is Ellie."

By the way, you can use the + operator to add numbers to text, if the text consists only of numerals. After running the statement

```
intC = 123 + "456"
```

you get 579 as the value of variable `intC`.

Here's a comparison operator at work:

```
Tan(sngAngleA) <> 1.4
```

The <> symbol is the "not equal to" operator. It tests to see whether the two values in the expression are unequal, returning a result of `True` or `False`. If the tangent of `sngAngleA` is *not* equal to 1.4, the result of this expression is `True`. Otherwise, the result is `False`.

Taking precedence

In fancier expressions that include more than one operator, VBA has to figure out which operation to perform first, second, and third. The expression

```
intA + intB * intC
```

contains two operators: + (the addition operator) and * (the multiplication operator). In English, you would read the entire thing as "`intA` plus `intB` times `intC`."

Although the * symbol is the second operator in the expression, it has *precedence* over the addition operator. VBA multiplies `intB` times `intC` first, and then adds this result to `intA`. As this example illustrates, VBA follows a fixed sequence in evaluating the parts of an expression when it contains more than one operator.

You can use parentheses to override the predetermined precedence order by which operators are processed. If you type

```
(intA + intB) * intC
```

VBA adds the first two variables first, and then multiplies `intC`'s value by that number.

Without parentheses to guide it, what are the rules VBA follows when deciding which operator to process first? If the expression includes two or more categories of operators, VBA evaluates all the operators in each category in the following order:

1. Arithmetic and concatenation operators come first.

2. Comparison operators follow.

3. Logical operators are processed last.

Within a category, VBA applies preset rules to determine which operator comes first. Arithmetic, comparison, and logical operators are processed according to the order shown in Table 9-2. VBA takes comparison operators as they come, working from left to right. If two or more operators at the same level of precedence appear in an expression, VBA processes them from left to right as well.

Table 9-2	Precedence Order for VBA Operators (Within Each Category, Operators Are Processed in the Order Listed)
Operator	*Operation Performed*
Arithmetic	
^	Exponentiation
–	Negation
* or /	Multiplication or division
\	Integer division
Mod	Modulus arithmetic
+ or –	Addition or subtraction

Operator	Operation Performed
Concatenation	
&	String concatenation
Comparison	
=	Equality
<>	Inequality (not equal to)
<	Less than
>	Greater than
<=	Less than or equal to
>=	Greater than or equal to
Like	String comparison to pattern
Is	Test whether two items refer to the same object
Logical	
Not	Logical not
And	Logical and
Or	Logical or
Xor	Logical exclusive or
Eqv	Logical equivalence
Imp	Logical implication

Performing calculations with arithmetic operators

VBA has seven arithmetic operators (refer to Table 9-2). You can tell what four of these do — that would be the +, -, *, and / operators — just by looking at the symbols. For example, the expression 6/2 gives 3 as the result, of course.

The other three arithmetic operators are less self-evident, however. Here's how they work:

  ✔ The ^ operator raises the first value in the expression to the power of the second value. The expression

```
2 ^ 3
```

calculates out to 8 (2³).

✔ The \ operator performs integer division, giving an integer result. VBA simply discards any fractional part of the answer rather than rounding it up or down. (**Note:** This operator is the backslash character, whereas the operator for ordinary division is an ordinary forward slash.) Try this example:

```
244 \ 7
```

The answer, 34, tells you how many full weeks occur in 244 days.

✔ The Mod operator divides the first value by the second but returns only the *remainder* as the result. Continuing with the last example, if you want to know how many days were left over after all 34 complete weeks have been accounted for, the expression you need is

```
244 Mod 7
```

which gives 6 as the result. Note that the result given by the Mod operator is always a whole number. If for some reason you want to know the fractional part of a division result expressed in decimal form, use an expression like this:

```
(244 Mod 7)/7
```

This is the same as 6/7, which works out to .857 or so.

Comparing values

VBA has six all-around comparison operators for comparing numeric and string values, plus two special-purpose comparison operators, Like (for strings) and Is (for objects). The comparison operators are summarized in Table 9-2.

Note that VBA uses the equals sign, =, in two different ways. In declarations, it serves to assign values to variables, as discussed in "Giving variables their values," earlier in this chapter. In addition, the equals sign functions as a comparison operator to determine whether two values are the same.

The result of an expression based on any of these operators is always either True or False. For example, here's an expression based on the <= (less than or equal to) operator:

```
intX <= 11
```

If the value of `intX` is 12, the result of the expression is False because 12 is not less than 11. Most often, you use comparison operators in *conditional statements* such as `If...Then` statements. I discuss conditional statements in detail in Chapter 12, but a simple sample is in order here:

```
If intX = 2000 Then
  MakeWhoopee
End If
```

The = operator tests to see whether the values on either side of it are the same. The expression's result is `True` if they are the same and `False` otherwise. The English translation of this code would be, "If `intX`'s value equals 2000, run the `MakeWhoopee` Sub procedure."

Comparing strings

You can use the comparison operators to compare strings of text as well as numbers. The expression

```
"Sweetpea" = "Daffodil"
```

gives `False` as a result — obviously, these two strings are not equal.

But in other cases, the results of a string comparison aren't so easy to predict. To get the results you want when comparing strings, you have to understand the rules VBA uses to decide whether one string is "greater than" another one.

Unless you specify otherwise, VBA uses a *binary* comparison method. The two strings are compared on the basis of the numeric codes in which the characters are actually stored in your program. In this coding system, common punctuation marks have the lowest numbers, followed by numerals, uppercase letters, lowercase letters, and then accented characters. Because the code numbers for lowercase letters are larger than those for uppercase letters, the expressions `"a" > "A"` and `"a" > "Z"` both give `True` results.

To use a different, more intuitive method for comparing strings, include the statement `Option Compare Text` in your module's Declarations section. With `Option Compare Text` in force, the strings are compared alphabetically, ignoring case (accented letters are still treated as higher in value than the corresponding unaccented versions). Under these conditions, the following are all `True` expressions:

```
"a" = "A"
"a" < "Z"
"Aunt Hill" < "Äunt Hill"
```

When comparing two strings, VBA starts by comparing the first characters in each string. If these characters differ, the greater string is the one with the greater character. If the first characters in each string are the same, VBA then compares the next, and so on.

Comparing strings of unequal length

What happens when you compare strings that aren't the same length? If the strings are identical except that one is shorter than the other, the longer string is greater than the shorter one. For example,

```
"In a canyon, in a cavern" > "In a canyon"
```

is a True expression.

However, if the two strings differ in content as well as length, the usual comparison criteria apply. The expression

```
"I'll take two" > "I'll take three"
```

is True because the w in *two* is greater than the h in *three* — even though the first part of the expression is shorter than the second.

What's not to Like?

The Like operator compares a string to a wildcard pattern rather than to a specific set of characters. Use it to see whether a string falls within, or outside, a given range. I don't have room to explain the many details involved in using this operator, but you should know that it exists — it's a powerful tool for handling text.

Using comparison operators in code

The results of a comparison operation can be stored in a variable, typically one of the Boolean data type, using a standard assignment statement:

```
boolTheAnswerIs = 5 > 4
```

Because 5 *is* greater than 4, the result of the greater than operation is True, and in turn VBA assigns True as the value of the boolTheAnswerIs variable.

The True and False keywords are actually built-in VBA numeric constants, representing the values –1 and 0, respectively. You can assign the result of a comparison to any numeric variable.

Comparison operators are frequently used in conditional statements to decide whether to execute a particular branch of code:

```
If intP <= intQ Then
  SomethingWentWrong 'call error-handling procedure
End If
```

Stringing text together

The *concatenation operator,* & (ampersand), joins strings together. You can use it with literal strings, string variables, or any function that returns a string value. You can use it repeatedly to construct a long string from multiple string values, as in this example:

```
strA = "You answered " & InputBox("Type an answer:") & _
    " . The correct answer was " & strAnswer & "."
```

After this statement executes, strA might contain "You answered Portugal. The correct answer was Spain." Or some similar string.

When assembling large strings from smaller ones, don't forget to build in the spaces and punctuation marks the final string needs.

Details on Data Types

This section offers tips on when and how to use the various VBA data types, with an exception or two. The object data type is crucial but quite complex, so it rates special treatment in Chapter 10. User-defined data types are mentioned, albeit briefly, in Chapter 13.

Converting between data types

Data types are a convenience for human beings — VBA actually stores all information in numeric form. That being the case, conversions between different data types aren't a big challenge for VBA.

VBA comes with many functions for converting one data type to another under your control. These are reviewed in Chapter 11. Realize, however, that whenever possible, VBA automatically converts between different types of data as the context suggests. For example, the + operator adds the number in a string to a numeric value, as long as the string contains only numerals. Similarly, if you assign a decimal value to an Integer variable, VBA automatically rounds off the value for you.

Sometimes these automatic conversions are just what you want. But the real point is that even if you take pains to declare your variables precisely, errors are still possible because of VBA's efforts to anticipate your needs.

Understanding variants

The Variant data type provides a one-size-fits-all container for your data storage needs. Variants can hold any kind of data you can use in VBA, including numeric values, strings, dates and times, and objects. What's more, the same variable can store different types of data at different times within a single program. The following code is perfectly acceptable, though hardly very productive:

```
Dim varAnythingGoes as Variant
varAnythingGoes = 3
varAnythingGoes = "I suppose."
varAnythingGoes = #12/31/99 11:59:59 PM#
```

Not only does VBA permit such statements, but it also figures out and keeps track of the type of data you're placing in the variant. After that last statement in the series above, for example, varAnythingGoes is cataloged as a Variant/Date variable. You can find out which type of data VBA is currently storing in a variant, using the TypeName function. Suppose the code fragment above continues with the following statement:

```
strVariantType = TypeName(varAnythingGoes)
```

After this statement executes, the value of strVariantType is Date — because that's the data type it currently stores.

Because they're so flexible, Variant variables are very convenient. Instead of worrying about which data types to use, all your variables can be variants, and you can stash any type of data in them as the need arises. But there are potential drawbacks to this approach, as discussed in the "Pros and cons of using specific data types versus variants" section earlier in this chapter.

Even if you declare most variables using specific data types, variants can still have a role as temporary scratch variables for simple computations in short procedures. Also, in VBA 5 and 6, you must use variants for variables of the Decimal type, used to maximize the precision of calculations (see the bulleted points in the next section).

Choosing a numeric data type

If you declare variables as specific data types rather than variants and choose the smallest possible data type, your programs will be faster, smaller, and more likely to work properly. Of course, the variable should have enough storage capacity to accommodate the range of values that it may contain — any extra room is just wasted space.

For example, suppose that your program requires one variable for the day of the week (possible values 1 – 7) and one for the month (1 – 31). You can get away with using the `Byte` data type, which holds values between 0 and 255. To work with the 365 days of the year, you would need an `Integer` variable.

Table 9-1 summarizes the value ranges for each type of numeric data type.Here are some tips on specific data types:

- ✔ Use the `Boolean`, `Byte`, `Integer`, or `Long` data types to hold whole numbers (the kind without decimals).

- ✔ Use the `Single` and `Double` data types to store floating-point numbers of up to 15 significant digits and their exponents. Though the range of values is huge, be aware that rounding may introduce errors — and these may be significant in operations on values of very different sizes. To assign a floating-point value such as $4.72 \times 10\text{-}22$ to a `Single` or `Double` variable, use the following format (VBA assumes the exponent is positive if you leave out a + or - sign after the letter E):

```
sngFloating = 4.72E-22
```

- ✔ If you need more precise calculations, the `Currency` data type gives you up to 19 significant digits, and with the `Decimal` type you can have as many as 29 (neither type provides exponents). In the current version of VBA, however, `Decimal` isn't a standalone data type — in other words, you can't declare a `Decimal` variable. Instead, `Decimal` is available only as a subtype of the `Variant` data type. To ensure that a number is stored as a `Decimal` variant rather than one of the floating-point types, use the `CDec` function in the assignment statement.

Here's an example of how to do this (notice that within the `CDec` function you must enter long numbers as strings):

```
Dim decvarPi As Variant
decvarPi=CDec("3.141592653589793238462643383")
```

If your program does calculations with the numbers in a variable, you may need to choose a data type large enough to hold the *result* of those calculations, even if you don't assign the calculation results to the variable itself. Peruse this example:

```
Dim bytByte1 As Byte
Dim bytByte2 As Byte
Dim intInteger As Integer
bytByte1 = 255 ' maximum permitted byte value
bytByte2 = 1
intInteger = bytByte1 + bytByte2 ' error!
```

Here, even though `intVariable` has enough storage capacity to hold the results of the calculation, VBA gives an overflow error on the last line. To make the calculation work, you must change at least one of those byte variables to integers.

When to use Boolean variables

Variables of the Boolean data type can hold only one of two values: `True` (stored as -1) or `False` (0). Declare a Boolean variable whenever you need to know which of two alternative conditions currently prevails. For example, you may have a variable called `boolIsOn`, whose value would be `True` if whatever it is, is on, and `False` if it's off.

Another way to use Boolean variables is to define other constants with the same values as `True` and `False`. Your variable names can then be neutral, while the constants explicitly refer to the two alternative conditions. This technique is definitely easier to show than to explain, so look here:

```
Dim boolBellyButtonStyle as Boolean
Const Innie As Boolean = True
Const Outie As Boolean = False
If boolBellyButtonStyle = Outie Then
   TickleLightly
End If
```

This is a great tip! To toggle the value of a Boolean variable or object property to its opposite, use the `Not` operator. In Word, for example, you can turn on the document map if it's off, or turn it off if it's on, with this line of code:

```
ActiveWindow.DocumentMap = Not ActiveWindow.DocumentMap
```

Working with currency values

The main reason to use the Currency data type is to ensure accurate results. True, the floating-point data types Single and Double can store numbers with decimal points — which is basically what currency values are. However, calculations involving floating-point values often produce small errors, and these drive the bean counters crazy.

Adapting to local money formats

One of VBA's many strengths is its capability to adapt automatically to the local customs regarding formatting of items such as dates and currency values. If you write your program properly, you don't need to build currency symbols such as $, ¥, or £ into your code — VBA adds the right one for you, based on the language and country selections in the Regional Settings applet of the Windows Control Panel.

For example, consider the following code:

```
Const ccurMoneyTalks As Currency = 5463.72
MsgBox Format(ccurMoneyTalks, "Currency")
```

In the U.S., the message box displays $5,463.72. When exactly the same program runs in France, you see 5463,72F in the message box. Chapter 11 discusses the Format function in some depth.

But you don't need to declare a variable as Currency to display it as a properly formatted money amount. Used with the "Currency" named format, the Format function dresses up any numeric value as dollars, francs, or whatever is appropriate locally.

Other uses for the Currency data type

Regardless of whether you're working with money, however, you can use variables of the Currency type any time:

✔ you need to store larger numbers than will fit in a Long integer variable

✔ you need to make calculations on large numbers with more precision than you could get from the floating-point data types.

Currency values can have up to 19 significant digits, 15 to the left of the decimal point and 4 to the right (the decimal point is fixed).

Working with dates

Use the Date data type to work conveniently with dates, times, or both. Behind the scenes, VBA encodes a date or time as a number such as 35692.9201273148 — apparently meaningless to mere mortals. But you can ignore this detail and work with dates and times in your programming as you would on paper or in a word processor.

The one trick you have to remember is that you must always type date and time values — date literals — between paired number sign characters. For example, the following statements declare two Date variables and assign them values:

```
Dim dateWeddingDay As Date, dateTimeOfCeremony As Date
dateWeddingDay = #4/20/99#
dateTimeOfCeremony = #3:15:00 PM#
```

As with currency, VBA automatically outputs dates according to local formatting customs. The expression Format (#10/24/89#, "Long date") gives the string "Tuesday, October 24, 1989" in the U.S., but "Terça-feira, 24 de Outubro de 1989" in Brazil.

Entering date values

You can type date literals in just about any format that appeals to you. The following are all acceptable:

```
#09/1/1998#
#Sep 25, 93#
#Janua 9 1905#
```

If the Visual Basic Editor recognizes your entry as a valid date, it converts it into the "short form" date format specified in the Windows Control Panel. If you omit the year, VBA adds the current year for you. The conversion happens as soon as you move the insertion point off the line of code, before you run your program.

Time has value

Enter time literals in the format #*hours:minutes:seconds symbol*#, where *symbol* is AM or PM. Examples include:

```
#10:45:00 PM#
#2:3:30 AM#
```

You don't have to type in leading zeros, as in #01:02:03 PM#, but VBA adds them for you when you move the cursor to another line of code. Similarly, you can omit portions of the time value you don't need, but VBA fills in the blanks. For example, you can enter seconds alone by typing something like #0:0:23#, but VBA changes such an entry into a complete time value — in this case — #12:00:23 AM#.

Date and time math

Adding or subtracting dates with the standard VBA arithmetic operators is *possible*, but unfortunately it doesn't work the way you would expect. For example, #3/19/2005# - #3/19/2004# does not equal "1 year," but #12/30/1900#. The explanation has to do with the way VBA stores date data, which I won't trouble you with here. All you really need to know is that VBA has two functions, DateAdd() and DateDiff(), that handle your needs for date math. Chapter 11 reviews their use.

In contrast, you *can* do time calculations fairly easily with the standard arithmetic operators. Take a gander at the expressions in the following code:

```
Dim dateThen As Date
dateThen = #07:15 AM# + #12:00# ' = #07:15:00 PM#
dateThen = #07:15:00 AM# - #0:15 AM# ' = #07:00:00 AM#
dateThen = #07:15:15 AM# + #0:0:30 AM# ' = #07:15:45 AM#
```

The examples show the minimum entries you can type. As always, VBA converts your entries into complete time literals — `#0:0:30 AM#` becomes `#12:00:30 AM#`, for example. One other point: As shown in the sample code, you must explicitly declare variables using the Date data type to get the expected results when you subtract times.

Stringing you along

Because VBA so freely converts between different data types, you may need string variables less often than you think. If all you need to do is display a non-string value in a form that humans can read, you don't need to convert it into a string first. Instead, you can use a number or date — or a variable containing one — as the argument to a function or as the value of an object property that by rights should be a string.

This example is based on the ever-popular `MsgBox` function, used for displaying string data in little dialog boxes (see Chapter 11 for more on this function). The statements

```
Dim dateThisIsADateNotAString As Date
dateThisIsADateNotAString = #17:23:16#
MsgBox dateThisIsADateNotAString
```

produce the message you see in Figure 9-1.

Or how about this heresy:

```
Dim intSmall As Integer, sngTall As Single
Dim varYouAll As Variant
intSmall = 3
sngTall = 9.99E+33
varYouAll = intSmall & sngTall
```

Following this sequence, `varYouAll` contains "39.99E+33". The presence of &, the concatenation operator, causes VBA to convert both numeric variables into strings so it can concatenate, by golly.

Figure 9-1:
The text
shown
in this
message
box was
never
explicitly
converted
into a string.

What you *really* need string variables for is to work with non-numeric characters, that is, letters and punctuation marks. You can't get these out of number values, not no way, not no how.

Careful programming practice dictates that you explicitly convert numeric values into strings before manipulating them as such. If you follow this advice, you're likely to make fewer errors and produce code that's more understandable. Still, it's nice to know that you can output variables with so little work.

Quotes in string declarations

Along the same lines, you don't really have to use those quote marks when you assign numeric, date, or currency values to a string variable (one that you've declared using the string data type). Ever the pampering parent, VBA makes its best effort to convert such values into strings, with never a mutter of complaint. If your program executes this code:

```
Dim strGString As String
strGString = #July 22, 1904#
```

the `strGString` variable contains the string "7/22/1904" until some other statement changes it. But humor me — use the quotation marks to make sure that the variable contains exactly what you intend.

Use VBA's `Chr` and `Asc` functions to convert a numeric value representing an ANSI character code to the corresponding text character and vice versa. `Chr` lets you place characters you can't type, like quotation marks, in your strings. `Asc` returns the numeric code of the *first* character in a string.

Fixing your strings

VBA lets you declare string variables in two ways. The standard string declaration, such as `Dim strMessage As String`, sets up a variable that can hold a string of any length. You can change the size of the variable at will, too, simply by assigning it a string of different length.

In some circumstances, presetting the size of a string variable is handy. This is primarily of value when you read and write records in a *random-access* file, a technique not covered in this book but discussed on the companion Web site (`www.seldenhouse.com/vba`). For now, showing you how to declare a fixed-length string is enough. Here's an example:

```
Dim strFixed As String * 5
```

Declared this way, the variable always contains exactly 5 characters. If you assign a shorter string to it, VBA adds spaces in after the characters. If you assign it a longer string, VBA stuffs the first 5 characters of the string into the variable, summarily discarding the remainder:

```
strFixed = "abc" ' strFixed now contains "abc  "
strFixed = "Fourscore and seven years" ' now, "Fours"
```

Chapter 10

Objectivity

● ●

In This Chapter

▶ Conceptualizing objects

▶ Grasping properties, methods, and events — important components of VBA objects

▶ Working with object models

▶ Using forms as objects

▶ Getting and setting object properties

▶ Calling methods

▶ Using object references to identify the object you want to work with

▶ Assigning object references to variables

▶ Creating your own objects with class modules

▶ Using objects efficiently with `For Each...Next` and `With` statements

● ●

A core aspect of VBA's identity is its status as an object-oriented software development tool. An understanding of objects is fundamental to VBA programming, especially when you want to create custom dialog boxes or put the features of the host application under your control. This chapter starts by charting the object territory conceptually, and moves on to cover the nuts-and-bolts of programming with objects.

Objects are vital features of the VBA landscape. Through them, you have access to the functionality of the underlying VBA application you're working in. Eventually, you can expand your prowess to the point where you can access objects from other compatible applications and even build your own objects.

So What's an Object?

Although it's possible to come up with a formal definition of a VBA object, it's a lot easier to understand objects by way of examples and in terms of their functions.

Objects as components of VBA applications

The easiest way to start thinking about objects is to see them as parts of your VBA application and its documents. A shape in a Visio drawing is an object, as is each *connect* that joins two shapes (see Figure 10-1). So is each layer to which shapes can be assigned, and so is each page where the layers reside. And so is the document itself, to which all the pages, layers, shapes, and connects belong.

Similarly, Excel objects include the cells in which you enter data or formulas, named ranges of cells, the charts that grace many worksheets, individual worksheets, and complete workbooks. And in all Microsoft Office applications — as well as many other VBA applications — the toolbars and menus, and the buttons and menu choices they contain, are objects as well.

VBA objects exist in a hierarchy in which one type of object contains objects of other types. These object hierarchies are the topic of "What's an Object Model?" the next major section in this chapter. For the time being, though, I concentrate on understanding individual objects.

Objects conceptualized

You may not be able to touch a drawing shape, a worksheet cell, or a toolbar button, but you can fairly easily think of them as *things*. In your imagination, at least, you can cut out a circle shape and paste it on another piece of paper. You can write numbers into that worksheet cell, or you can push that button.

In addition to fairly concrete items like these, however, VBA applications offer up all kinds of more abstract objects. Here are some examples:

- Microsoft Excel has a `CustomView` object, representing a workbook custom view (in Excel, a custom view defines the look of the workbook and its print settings).

- The Microsoft Word FileSearch object "represents the functionality of the Open dialog box," to quote the relevant Help topic. Note that this object doesn't represent the dialog box itself, but rather its functionality.

- Visio has a `Style` object, which represents a combination of line, fill, and text attributes for shapes.

- VBA itself has a few objects that are available in all VBA applications. A `Collection` object, for example, represents a grab-bag set of variables or other objects that you want to work with as a unit, regardless of their type.

Figure 10-1:
Examples
of VBA
objects.

A practical definition of objects

As you can tell, it's often difficult to imagine a VBA object as a material thing.
But that's okay — the more you can let go of such mental models, the more
freely you can work with the whole range of available objects. The programmer's pragmatic definition of an object is simple, really. An object is a named
item that has

   ✔ **Properties:** settings you can check and change

   ✔ **Methods:** actions the object can perform when your program asks it to

   ✔ **Events:** things that happen to the object, to which it can respond by
     automatically taking a predetermined action

If you have any poetic sensibility, the term *objects* may not seem fitting for
such richly endowed creatures. Indeed, objects are more like animals than
inert lumps. A tiger or a whale has characteristic features such as eyes,
limbs, and a tail; an object has properties. A horse or a dog can do tricks on
command or run away from danger; an object has methods and events.

Do you still want a technical definition? Try this one: An object is a named unit within a program that possesses both data and the code that acts on that data. An object is said to *encapsulate* the data as well as the related code.

Object classes versus specific objects

Here's yet another technicality to keep in mind: A distinction exists between a given specific object and the pattern on which the object is based. A particular object represents one specific document, shape, worksheet cell, or what have you. A document object, for example, includes the text of that one document.

An *object class,* on the other hand, can be compared to a set of building plans. You can build many houses from one set of plans, but nobody can live in the plans themselves. In the same way, a class lays down the types of data that can be stored in an object and defines the object's methods, properties, and events. Based on this description, you construct an *instance* of the class — an object — in which you actually store data. You can create, or *instantiate*, as many objects of a class as you like, each with a separate existence, and each containing different data.

Collection objects

A *collection* is a special type of VBA object. As the name suggests, its role is to simplify working with a set of objects as a group. In a typical collection, all the objects it contains are of the same type. A Shapes collection in Visio, for example, contains multiple Shape objects, and a Pages collection contains multiple Page objects.

Some collections, however, are less discriminating about which objects they allow in. VBA proper comes with a generic Collection object, which you can use to store objects of any type in any combination. If you're into jumbled hodgepodges, a VBA collection is just the ticket.

The section "Working with Collection objects" later in this chapter describes how to access the individual objects in a collection. In Chapter 13, I show you how to use a collection's properties and methods (a collection is itself an object, remember), and how to create collections of your own based on VBA's generic Collection object.

What's an Object Model?

As you see earlier in this chapter, VBA objects exist in a hierarchical relationship to one another. In addition to having properties, methods, and events of its own, an object at the top of the hierarchy serves as a *container* for one or more other types. These objects in turn each contain other objects, and so on.

For a given VBA application, the specifics of these hierarchical relationships are referred to as the application's *object model*. Often presented graphically, the object model specifies which object contains which other objects. Figure 10-2 shows one such representation of an object model.

As Figure 10-2 makes plain, the *Application object* is at the top of a VBA application's object model. It is the container for all the other objects from the application that you can manipulate. Your own VBA programming *project* is also a container object. It contains all the code *modules* (units of code) you write and the forms you design, as well as the project's document. (Chapter 7 defines and discusses VBA projects and their components in more detail.)

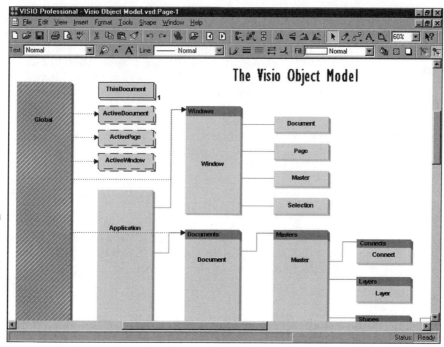

Figure 10-2: The Visio object model, taken from the Visio 5 CD-ROM.

Understanding why the object model is important

Because you need to tell VBA which specific object you're working with, a good grasp on the object model of your VBA application is critical to efficient work. Following a chart of the object model such as the one shown in Figure 10-2, you can quickly locate the branch that contains the object you're after. In this example, for instance, you can see that a `Connect` object is a member of the Connects collection, which belongs to the `Master` object, which in turn. . . .

Extending the object model

In the programs you write with VBA, you aren't limited to using the objects in only one VBA application. In fact, you're not even limited to VBA applications per se. Other applications and specialized "components" are fair game, as long as they adhere to Microsoft's *Component Object Model* (COM) standard.

COM is the technical specification detailing how objects are defined within applications and other software elements and how those objects are *exposed* so they can be used by other applications. The jargon word *Automation* refers specifically to the capability of a COM-based application to be controlled by another program. And by the way, COM isn't specific to VBA or even Visual Basic. Many software development tools such as C++ compilers understand COM and can access objects.

Anyway, COM opens up fantastic possibilities for powerful, customized VBA applications. You can readily (I didn't say "easily") build an application that processes information from Visio diagrams, Word documents, Excel worksheets, and so on. Your custom application can show all this information in windows that you have designed but that also use the display capabilities of the individual component applications.

Custom application development on this scale is decidedly an advanced VBA topic and one that I only briefly touch on in this book (in Chapter 17). Still, I want to stress that VBA is capable of a great deal.

VBA Forms Are Objects, Too

As I say in Chapter 1 — and don't be surprised if you hear this elsewhere in the book — a *form* is any custom window you build with VBA. If your program has its own user interface, the program's main window is a form and so are any dialog boxes the program may display (see Figure 10-3).

A key understanding to seal into your brain is that VBA forms are themselves objects. That is, they constitute entities that contain information — representing the layout of the form — and a set of tools for doing things with that information. The official term for a form is *UserForm object*.

As self-respecting VBA objects, forms fit comfortably into the object model paradigm. Each UserForm object belongs simultaneously to two collection objects — the VBA project in which the form is stored and the UserForms collection, which holds all the forms currently loaded by your program. For its part, a UserForm object is a container for a Controls collection object, which in turn contains the individual controls you have added to the form.

Likewise, a form's controls — each button, check box, and other doodad you can see and play with on the form — are also objects. VBA offers a different object type corresponding to each type of control.

Figure 10-3:
Examples of
VBA forms.

The techniques you use in your code to access a particular form or one of its controls, and to use the properties, methods, and events of these objects, are exactly the same as those you use for other objects, as detailed in this chapter. Part IV of this book delves into the application of these techniques to forms and controls. Also, see the bonus Web chapter at www.dummies.com/bonus/vba.

Using Objects in Code: An Introduction

Since the theoretical groundwork has been laid earlier in this chapter, practical directions for programming with VBA objects are now in order. I start by exploring the use of object properties, methods, and events in detail. After that, I move on to more fundamental techniques — those for identifying the specific object you want to work with in your code.

The basic rule about object programming

Although the object concept itself can be tough to wrap your mind around, *using* objects is easy. Because objects have names, you always know with which one you're working. In your code, all you need to do to identify one of the object's properties or methods is type the object name, a period, and then the property or method name.

For example, `MyShape.LineStyle` identifies the `LineStyle` property of a Visio object called `MyShape`. Similarly, `MyWorksheet.Calculate` identifies the `Calculate` method of an Excel worksheet object called `MyWorksheet`.

At this point, though, you may be asking yourself, "But how do I know what the object's name is in the first place?" An excellent question, indeed. The answer takes some explaining, however, so I put it off until the section "Identifying the Object You Want to Work With," which comes after the discussion of properties, methods, and events. For now, just assume that you can call an object by name.

What's your object?

As the earlier section "What's an Object Model?" makes evident, each VBA application has a different *object model* (hierarchical set of objects), and each of its objects has its own set of properties, methods, and events. You need a working familiarity with the details of the application's object model to put these objects to work in your programs.

In many applications, the VBA Help file has a topic devoted to a map of the application's object model (see Figure 10-4). If you don't see the object model map when you first open the Help system, look for it in the Contents tab where it should be listed as something like, say, Microsoft Excel Objects. With the object model map as your guide, you can view information on the individual objects by clicking them on the map or by looking them up in the Help index. Typically, the topic for each object has jumps to other topics detailing the object's properties, methods, and events. (I'm talking here about your particular application's VBA Help files, not the general Help system for the application or for VBA. See Chapter 4 for details about working with the VBA Help system.)

The Visual Basic Editor's Object Browser is another vital tool for viewing the relationships between the different objects of the application and exploring their properties, methods, and events. Chapter 6 describes the Object Browser in full.

Figure 10-4:
The Excel object model.

Getting and Changing Object Properties

Properties are probably the easiest object-related concept to grasp. A *property* stores information about some aspect of the object's appearance, behavior, contents, or pedigree, if you will.

A `Document` object may have a `Pages` property that tells how many pages are in the document. A `Shape` object may have a `Fill` property that specifies the shape's color. `CommandButton` objects (representing buttons on dialog boxes) have a `Caption` property that contains the text on the button.

A VBA program can retrieve the current settings stored in most properties. This capability allows the program to decide whether to take some action or whether to simply display the current setting in a window. Conversely, a program can change a property's setting to alter an object's appearance or behavior — but only if the property permits change (many properties can be retrieved but not modified).

The properties for appearance are the easiest to understand. A `Shape` object in Visio, for example, has the following appearance-related properties, among others.

Property	Description
AreaIU	The area of the shape in internal units
FillStyle	The Visio style describing the shape's color and other fill characteristics
Text	The text displayed on the shape

These properties correspond to the way the object looks in a document.

Behavior-related properties define the way the object reacts to various stimuli. Controls on UserForms are objects, and they have properties such as Enabled, which specifies whether the control responds to events such as mouse clicks.

Some properties, like the AreaIU for a Visio Shape, can take on an infinite range of different values. Others are limited to a list of predefined choices, such as Mauve, Teal, and Chartreuse. Many properties can take only two possible settings, such as True or False, Hot or Cold, or Wet or Dry.

In any case, you can use simple VBA statements to retrieve the current setting of a given property and to change the setting to one you prefer.

What you can't do with some properties

Just knowing *how* to access a property's value doesn't mean that you *can* access them. By design, some properties allow you to retrieve their values but not to change them. These are *read-only* properties. Less commonly, a property is *write-only* — you can set its value but cannot retrieve the current setting. However, most properties are the *read-write* kind — you can both retrieve and change their values.

Property settings are data

Although a property functions metaphorically to describe some characteristic of the object, you should realize that the setting it contains consists of data — no different in kind from the data you stuff into VBA variables. As such, you can think of a property simply as a more-or-less permanent variable that you don't have to declare.

After you understand properties this way, it makes sense that each property stores a particular data type exactly as variables do. A property that can take only two alternative settings (such as `True` or `False`, `Happy` or `Sad`, or `Left` or `Right`) is of the Boolean type. Some properties are strings, some are integers, some are floating-point or decimal numbers, and so on. Properties can even be objects. (See Chapter 9 for information on the available VBA data types.)

Retrieving a property's current setting

To find out, or *get,* the current setting of a given property, use the property as if it were a function or Function procedure. That is, assign the property to a variable in your code. The variable should be of the same or a compatible data type as the property.

In the sample shown here, the object in question represents, say, a question on a computerized test for graduate school admission. The property you're interested in checking is the one that describes how hard the question is on a scale of one to ten.

```
Dim intHowTough As Integer
intHowTough = objTestQuestion.DifficultyLevel
```

The first statement declares a variable to hold the property's current value, while the second statement assigns the property to that variable.

So why bother retrieving a property's current value? Often, you use it in a conditional statement to decide whether to take some other action, based on the value. (In this case, something like "If the question's `DifficultyLevel` is above 8, and if the answer is correct, award double credit" may be in order.) You may also store a property value in a variable so that you can assign the value to the same property of other similar objects.

If you're going to use the property's value only once, you don't need to assign it to a variable — you can access it directly in an expression. The example illustrates this practice:

```
If objTestQuestion.DifficultyLevel > 8 Then
  intTestScore = intTestScore + (intPoints * 2)
End If
```

This practice is convenient, but remember that your program slows down if you repeatedly retrieve a property's value. If you need the value more than once or twice, storing it in a variable is better — VBA can access the value of an ordinary variable more quickly than it can retrieve a property's value.

Changing a property's setting

Remember, properties are just glorified variables. Therefore, you can assign values to them just as you would any other variable — by placing the property name on the left side of an equals sign and the new value on the right. The statement

```
objMetalTune.GrungeFactor = 999
```

sets the `objMetalTune`'s `GrungeFactor` property — presumably, a measure of distortion, feedback, and extraneous noise — to 999.

```
objMetalTune.Ballad = False
objMetalTune.Title = "I have fleas. Bad."
```

Default properties

Many objects have a default property. You can retrieve or set its value using the object only, without mentioning the property itself by name. Sticking with the last example, suppose that the default property for the `objMetalTune` object is `Title`. In that case, you can simplify the last statement to read

```
objMetalTune = "I have fleas. Bad."
```

Default properties are convenient, as long as you're sure that you know which property is the default. If you have any doubt, or if you think that you may forget later, you had better go ahead and type out the property name.

Objects as properties

As I mention in "Property settings are data," a property of one object can identify another object. This arrangement lets your code access the subsidiary objects that belong to a given *container* object, just as you would the container's other properties. For example, in the expression

```
Toolbar.ToolbarItems
```

`ToolbarItems` is a property of the `Toolbar` object, but its value is a `ToolbarItems` object.

In fact, using object properties in this way is the critical technique for identifying the specific objects you want to work with. See "Identifying the Object You Want to Work With" later in this chapter for details.

Climbing the family tree

Just as an object's properties can identify other objects that belong to it, they can also tell you to which container objects it belongs. In Visio, if you have a `Pages` object stored in a variable and you want to know which document it belongs to, the expression

```
Pages.Parent
```

returns a reference to the correct document. If you need to know which *application* an object belongs to, you can often skip up to the top of the object hierarchy by getting an object's `Application` property:

```
Pages.Application
```

Method Acting

Methods are the named actions an object can perform at your command. Because the code for each method is part and parcel of the object, the object itself knows what to do when you trigger the method.

A graphical shape object, for example, may have a `Resize` method that changes its size and a `Rotate` method that rotates it on the document page. A worksheet cell object may have a `Calculate` method that recalculates the cell value and a `Clear` method that removes its contents. An object representing an entire document probably has `Print` and `Save` methods.

Methods are actually nothing more than procedures that are tied directly to specific objects. To call a method, you type the object's name, a period, and then the method name. Leaving behind metal madness, let's say that an object named `objJazzTune` represents a digital jazz recording in a multimedia program. Most likely, the object has a method called `Play`. Here's how to call the method:

```
objJazzTune.Play
```

In more detail, the techniques for calling methods are consistent with the ones you use to call procedures and VBA functions, as described in Chapter 7. To summarize:

✔ To call a method that takes arguments, type the argument after the method name. Here, the `Play` method takes an argument specifying how many times to repeat the tune:

```
objJazzTune.Play 3
```

✔ If the method takes two or more arguments, separate them with commas (in this example, pretend that Soft is a named constant specifying a quiet playback volume, and intSpeed is a variable representing play-back speed):

```
objJazzTune.Play 2, Soft, intSpeed
```

✔ To call a method that returns a value, assign the method to a variable or use it in an expression as you would a Function procedure. In this situation, any arguments must be enclosed within parentheses:

```
datePlayTime = objJazzTune.Play (2, Soft, intSpeed)
```

As with properties, many different object classes may have methods with the same names. Objects that contain groups of items or other objects typically have an Add method, for instance.

Just so it doesn't surprise you, I should mention that a method can change the value of one or more properties. For example, the objJazzTune object may have a read-only property called TimesPlayed that can be altered only by the Play method, but that you can retrieve via a property statement such as intPlaybacks = objJazzTune.TimesPlayed. Some objects even have special methods whose sole purpose in life is to set property values.

Events

An *event* is something that happens to an object and to which it can respond to an event with a predetermined action. Events include:

✔ **Physical actions the user of your program does,** such as clicking, just moving the mouse, pressing a key, or jumping up and down and scream-ing. (Okay, so VBA can't recognize "jumping up and down and screaming" events.)

✔ **Things that happen to the object as the application conducts its busi-ness.** If you're talking about a document object, events may include the opening or closing of the document or the addition or removal of a page. In Word, the Application and Document objects recognize such events. In Visio, Page objects can respond to nine different events, such as BeforeShapeDelete and TextChanged. See Chapter 4 for more exam-ples of such non-form events.

Your VBA application specifies which events, if any, a given object can recog-nize. *Your* job is to write the code that determines what the object does when the event occurs. One point may bear clarification: You don't call an event from your own code. Instead, the object automatically takes whatever action you've programmed it to do when the event occurs.

Event programming for forms is the subject of Chapter 16. The same basic techniques are applicable to non-form events, but details vary from application to application and sometimes even within the same application. Your application's documentation or Help files should provide the specifics.

Identifying the Object You Want to Work With

To do anything useful with an object, you have to tell VBA which object you want to work with. You use an *object expression* for this purpose. This is a special kind of VBA expression that uniquely identifies the specific object that interests you. Behind the scenes, the value that VBA calculates based on an object expression is an *object reference,* a value that you can think of as a street address for the object.

Figuring out the correct object expression you need is most of the battle. After you've done that, you can make your life much easier by creating a named variable for the object, using the expression to assign the corresponding object reference to the variable. From then on, you can refer to the object by the variable's name in your code.

Understanding object expressions

An object expression is a *code fragment* — an expression — that "points" at a particular object. Using a valid object expression, you can set the object's properties, activate its methods, or assign the object to a variable.

The ideas covered here are critical to daily work with VBA, yet they're not easy to grasp at first. Because your program can work with many different objects of the same type, a complete object expression must specify all the objects that contain the one you have in mind. It's something like this: Suppose that you were told to go get "the boy." You'd immediately ask, "Well, which boy?" If you were told instead to get the oldest boy who lives in the third house on Mayflower Street, Arhoolie, Nebraska, United States of America, you wouldn't need to ask that question. (Of course, you might ask "Why?") Of course, if you're already in the third house on Mayflower Street, and if only one boy lives there, a command such as "feed the boy" is quite adequate. In the same way, if the context is clear, VBA doesn't need the entire list of objects.

Working with properties that are objects

A property of one object can be another object. Objects exist in a hierarchy, with one object, such as a document, serving as a *container* for other subsidiary objects, such as pages, worksheets, or what have you.

The connection between these ideas is probably obvious: If an object contains subsidiary objects, you can identify a subsidiary object via a property of the first object. The expression you use to specify this property *is* the object expression.

For example, consider the following expression, which identifies a specific object in a Word document:

```
ThisDocument.Sections(2).Range
```

Notice that this object expression contains two periods, not just one. See, Range is a property of the Section object, which is in turn a property of the ThisDocument object. This idea may make sense to you right away, but if not, the next section, "Getting objects," explains it in detail.

Getting objects

The Application object occupies the very top of the object hierarchy in most VBA object models. However, you usually don't need to include it in object expressions — VBA is smart enough to assume you're working with objects from the current application, unless you specify otherwise.

The Application object contains a Documents object, which is a collection representing all the open documents. If you want to work with a specific document, you identify it as a member of this Documents collection object. For example, Documents (5) represents Document object #5 in the Documents collection.

The example expression above, however, starts with the special keyword: ThisDocument. In many VBA applications, ThisDocument stands for the Document object associated with your project.

In Word, each Document object has a Sections property. This in turn refers to a Sections collection, an object that represents the set of all the pages in the document. So the first part of the above expression — ThisDocument. Sections — identifies the particular Sections collection that belongs to the ThisDocument object. Once you've identified the Sections object, you can select a single member of its collection. Thus Sections(2) refers to the second section in the document.

Now for the final part of the expression. The tricky part here is that, although .Range specifies a *property* of the Section object, the value of that property is a Range *object*. The entire expression, then, supplies an object reference to that Range object. Using an expression that threads its way through the object hierarchy like this to a specific object is called "getting an object" in VBA lingo.

Working with Collection objects

In the example object expression we've been working with:

```
ThisDocument.Sections(2).Range
```

the Sections object is a *collection*. A VBA collection is a special type of object that may contain any number of other objects.

Collection objects defined in VBA applications usually store just one type of object. Word's Sections collections contains only Section objects. In the case of the Pages collection in Visio, only Page objects can belong to it. (VBA offers a generic Collection object in which you can store objects of any type. Chapter 12 describes how to create and manage your own collections.)

What you need to know about Collection objects is how to access the individual objects they contain. You have two options:

- ✔ Refer to the object by its slot or *index number* in the collection. That's the method used in the example expression — (2) refers to the second Section object in the Sections collection.

- ✔ Refer to the object by name. Many objects have names. If you know the name of the object you want to get, you can use it in the object expression instead of a number. Because Page objects in Visio can have names, the following example works:

```
ThisDocument.Pages ("My special page.")
```

Creating object variables

Nobody likes to type a long, complex object expression, even a relatively straightforward one such as ThisDocument.Sections(2).Range. If your program uses the same object more than once, create a named variable to hold a reference to that object. Then, wherever you would have typed the complete object expression, you can enter the variable name instead.

Besides being shorter, easier to remember, and easier to type than the original object expression, an *object variable* has two other plusses. First, it makes your code run faster. VBA can locate the object directly, rather than having to look up a series of properties in a series of objects. Second, you can use the same object variable to store references to different objects. That way, you can write flexible code that decides which specific object to store in the variable when the program runs.

In outline, the technique for creating an object variable requires two steps:

1. **Declare a variable you will use to refer to the object.**

2. **Assign the object you want to work with to that variable.**

The next two sections cover the details on each of these steps.

Declaring an object variable

You declare object variables just as you do variables of other data types. The standard method is with a Dim statement (just as with other types of variables, though, you can also use the Public, Private, or Static keyword instead of Dim to declare object variables). Here are two examples of object declarations:

```
Dim objGreatBigObject As Object 'A generic object
Dim objShapeObject As Shape 'A Shape object
```

The difference between these two declarations is important. The first statement declares an object variable but doesn't specify the type of object it will contain. You can use this variable to hold different types of objects as the need arises. The second statement declares the particular type, or *class,* of object that you want the variable to store. VBA doesn't allow you to place other object classes in the variable.

These two types of object declarations are referred to as *late binding,* in which no specific class is specified, and *early binding,* in which you do declare the variable as a definite object class.

Whenever possible, you should use early binding, declaring the object variable as a specific class. The benefits of early binding include:

- ✔ **Fewer mistakes.** As I mentioned, VBA doesn't let you assign incorrect objects to the variable. Just as important, by knowing which class of object you're working with, the compiler can check the rest of your code to make sure that you use properties and methods that are valid for that class. If you use late binding, the compiler can't perform this check. An error occurs while your program is trying to run if it attempts to use invalid properties or methods.

- ✔ **Faster performance.** Because the compiler can determine whether the object has the methods and properties you use in your program, the program doesn't need to pause to check this when it runs.

- ✔ **More understandable code.** You can tell by looking at the declaration what class of object the variable is supposed to contain.

In spite of these advantages, using late binding is better in two situations:

✔ You may *intend* to use the same variable for different classes of objects. This can be a good idea when the different classes share methods or properties that you need to access in your code. With a variable, you don't need to rewrite code that does the same things using different objects.

✔ Some objects can't be declared via early binding when they are accessed from another application. Using objects from other applications is an advanced VBA technique (it's introduced in Chapter 17), but you should know about this potential limitation.

As you know, a variable of the variant type can hold any type of information, and this includes object references. If you declare a variable without explicitly stating that it's an object, you can fill it with an object reference via late binding.

Assigning an object reference to a variable

After you've declared an object variable, you must fill it with a reference to a specific object before you can use the variable. To do so, assign an object expression to the variable using the Set keyword, as in this example:

```
Set objShapeObject = ThisDocument.Pages(1).Shapes(4)
```

Note that this syntax differs a bit from the way you assign other types of data to variables (see Chapter 9). As with other data types, you place an equal sign between the variable name and the object to be assigned. The only difference is that you must start the statement with the Set keyword.

Emptying an object variable

When you no longer need to access an object, good form requires breaking the tie between the object and the variable with which it's associated. This way, your program can use the memory occupied by the object for other purposes, and you can be sure that your code won't mistakenly make changes to the object.

The technique is simple. Using a Set statement, just assign the Nothing keyword to the variable, as in this example:

```
Set objPriceIsNoObject = Nothing
```

Creating new objects

If the object you want to work with doesn't yet exist, you have to create it. In simple VBA programs, you use the Add method for this purpose. The Add method should work if you're trying to create one of the built-in objects available in your VBA application, that is, the application with which your project is associated. (In some applications, you may need to use a method named something like `AddShape` or `AddDocument` — check with the application's VBA Help files to be sure.)

Using the Add method

The trick is knowing which object's `Add` method you should use. What you're looking for is the *container* object in which the object you want to create resides. The container is usually, but not always, a collection object.

For example, say that you want to create a new `Layer` object in Visio. A `Layer` object corresponds to a Visio drawing layer, which is a group of shapes that you can manipulate together. Each `Layer` object is contained in a `Layers` object, which represents a collection of (one or more) drawing layers. With this fact in mind, you choose the `Layers.Add` method to create a new individual layer.

Of course, you have to identify the specific `Layers` object in which VBA should create the new `Layer` object. A `Layers` collection object belongs to a particular `Page` object in a given `Document` object. With this in mind, the complete statement required to add a new `Layer` looks something like this:

```
ThisDocument.Pages(2).Layers.Add("NewLayer")
```

The `Layer` object has an `Add` method but, you can't use it to create a new layer. The `Add` method of the `Layer` object adds a `Layer` object to an existing layer rather than creating a new `Layer`.

Similarly, if you want to add a new slide to a PowerPoint presentation, a statement like the following would be in order:

```
ActivePresentation.Slides.Add 1, ppLayoutTextAndClipart
```

Again, the new slide is added to the appropriate container object, a `Slides` collection.

Creating a variable for an object you create

Because you've gone to the trouble to type out a long object reference — that's what an `Add` statement amounts to — you may as well create a variable for the new object at the same time. That way, you can use the variable instead of another lengthy object reference whenever you want to access the object in your code. These two statements illustrate this technique:

```
Dim objMyBaby As Slide
Set objMyBaby = ActivePresentation.Slides.Add 1, _
    ppLayoutTextAndClipart
```

Creating objects with New and CreateObject

Other situations require different techniques for creating new objects. These alternatives apply when you're creating:

- New copies of an existing form in your own project
- Objects from a *different* application or ActiveX (COM) component
- Specific objects based on classes you write in class modules

Depending on the details of the situation, you may use the New keyword in variable declaration or Set statements, or the CreateObject function to create these objects. I bring up this possibility not to tell you how to do these things here — they're advanced techniques covered in Chapter 17. Instead, I just want to steer you clear of the New keyword and the CreateObject function when you're trying to create ordinary objects.

What the definition of Is is, really

If you use variables to store object references, a time may come when you want to know whether the object a variable refers to is the same object referred to by another variable, or by an object expression.

Use the Is operator in an expression to check whether two object references refer to the same object. The expression's value is True if they do, or False if they refer to different objects. Here's some sample code to illustrate how Is works:

```
Dim objObject1 As Object, objObject2 As Object
...
If objObject1 Is objObject2 Then
  MsgBox "It's the same object!"
Else
  MsgBox "They're different objects."
End If
```

Of course, you can also compare an object variable against an object expression with the Is operator, as in the expression used in this line:

```
If objObject3 Is ThisDocument.Pages(2).Shapes(3) Then
```

Note that you can't use Is (or any other operator) to compare the *contents* of two different objects.

Efficient Object Coding

VBA includes two multiple-line code structures designed to make your work with objects easier. These are the `With` and `For Each...Next` statements.

Using With statements

Whether you refer to an object with a short, mnemonic variable or with a lengthy, inscrutable object expression, typing it over and over again gets old in a hurry. But you may not have to.

If your program uses the same object in two or more consecutive statements, the `With` statement allows you to name the object only once. Not only is this easier than retyping the object in each statement, it also makes your code easier to understand, and faster, too. Here's an example:

```
With objIHaveNoObjection
    .Name = "The Last Straw" ' Set the Name property
    .DisplayName ' Call the DisplayName method
    sngArea = .Area ' Get the Area property's value
    intStretchFactor = .Rotate (60) ' Call the Rotate
    ' method, assigning its return value to a variable
End With
```

As you can see, within the `With...End With` structure, you can mix statements that get and set properties with statements that call methods. Note also that the `With` structure is not a loop — the statements it contains are executed only once.

`With` structures can be nested, that is, placed one inside another. This is perfect when you must perform multiple actions on both an object and one of the objects it contains. The following example illustrates how this works. It performs a series of sundry actions on an AutoCAD `Block` object. A nested `With` structure further manipulates one of the drawing objects contained in the `Block`. The comments in the example should give you a feel for what's going on.

```
With Blocks.Item("Gizmo")
' With the Block named "Gizmo" perform the following:
 ' Rename the Block object via the Name property
 .Name = "Doohickey"
 ' Use Count property to see how many objects it has
 intNumberOfObjects = .Count
 ' Call AddCircle method with centerpoint = 0,
 ' radius = 5
 .AddCircle (0#, 5#)
 With .Item (1)
 ' This nested With refers to the first
 ' drawing object in the Block object
  ' Use Move method to move the drawing object
  .Move (15, 20)
  ' Change Color property of the drawing object
  .Color = 221
 End With
End With
```

One thing that this example doesn't illustrate is the fact that you can also use values returned by the object's properties or methods in conditions and other expressions. The following statements would be perfectly at home in the outer With statement of the preceding example:

```
intNewColor = InputBox ("Enter a new color value for " _
 & "the first object in the " & .Name & "block.")
If .Count > 12000
 MsgBox "This is a big Block!"
End If
```

Using For Each...Next structures

Although Chapter 11 is devoted to VBA *control structures* (groups of statements designed to direct program flow) I mention one of these structures here since it applies exclusively to objects. A variation on the For...Next loop idea, VBA's For Each...Next structure performs a set of statements for each object stored in a collection. Although the two statements look much alike, they have some real differences — one of which is that For Each...Next is easier to use. Here's the syntax:

```
For Each element In group
 (statements to be executed during each pass of the loop)
Next element
```

One key difference between a For Each...Next and the standard For...Next structure is that you don't have to specify the number of times that the loop should execute — VBA figures that out for you. The For Each statement requires an element variable that corresponds to the type of object stored in the collection. You must also indicate which collection you want to work with in the For Each statement by including a group argument.

For Each...Next in action

The following simple example of a For Each...Next statement works in AutoCAD, where the Blocks collection is, of course, a collection of Block objects and where each Block can hold an unlimited number of individual drawing objects, such as Cone and 3DFace objects. All that this code does is display the name of each Block in the Blocks collection:

```
Dim objB As Block
For Each objB In Blocks
  Debug.Print objB.Name
Next objB
```

The example may be less than earthshaking, but you should appreciate the potential power. A For Each...Next loop can efficiently perform any combination of actions that are available via the methods or properties of each object in a collection.

Hasty escapes from For Each...Next

When you're searching for that particular needle in a box of them, the other needles in the box don't interest you. To perform some action on a specific object in a collection, place a nested If...Then statement inside the For Each...Next loop. When the If...Then condition locates the object of your desire, you have no further need to search; an Exit For statement gets you out of the loop quickly.

With AutoCAD's Blocks collection still fresh in mind, consider the following example:

```
Dim objK As Block
For Each objK In Blocks
  If objK.Name = "WidgetA" Then
    objK.Delete
    Exit For
  End If
Next objK
```

In this example, the loop uses a nested If...Then structure to hunt for a Block object named "WidgetA" among all the Block objects stored in the Blocks collection. After — and only after — the right Block is found, the statements within the If...Then structure executes. *Execute* is the correct term, for the first of these statements deletes the Block. Mission accomplished. The loop isn't needed anymore, so Exit For terminates it, and the program moves on.

Chapter 11

The Instruments in VBA's Built-In Orchestra

. . . .

In This Chapter

▶ Avoiding unnecessary programming with built-in commands

▶ Formatting data painlessly with the Format function

▶ Converting from one data type to another

▶ Working with text strings

▶ Having fun with dates and times

▶ Using math and financial functions

. . . .

*B*efore you get rolling on writing your own procedures from scratch, be sure that you're not reinventing the wheel. Out of the box, every version of VBA comes equipped with a little arsenal of built-in commands that can blast through many common tasks. This chapter surveys the most useful of these ready-made weapons. I take up others elsewhere.

Finding Built-In Commands

VBA seems to have a bit of a conflict about its self-image. Oh, how desperately it wants to be seen as a truly *object-oriented* language. On the other hand, it realizes that some things you may want to do with your program don't fit so naturally into the object-oriented mold.

In a solution worthy of our elected representatives, VBA has shoehorned at least one naturally independent command into an object method, whereas it leaves other actions that seem appropriate for objectifying free, to be used on their own.

Keeping in mind, then, that an action may fall into an unexpected category, you get three types of VBA built-in commands that do useful work.

✔ **Statements.** Although the term *statement* usually encompasses a complete programming directive (see Chapter 7), VBA also refers to individual keywords for specific chores as statements. Some of these statement keywords function as complete statements in themselves. For example, the statement Beep sounds the computer speaker. (Don't go overboard with that one.) Other statement keywords must be used as part of a complete statement. For example, the ChDir (change directory) statement is useless unless you include with it an argument specifying the directory, or folder, to which you want to change:

```
ChDir("\Documents about Dreams")
```

✔ **Functions.** The built-in functions act just like the Function procedures I describe in Chapter 7 — that is, they return a value. Often, you use a function by assigning its value to a variable, as in this example with the Tan (tangent) function:

```
dblTangent = Tan(dblAnyOldAngle)
```

Functions also provide values in more complex expressions or in conditional statements, such as

```
If Tan (dblAcuteAngle) < 45 Then
```

✔ **Methods of built-in objects.** The curious one in this group is the Print method, the Debug object's only one. You use it to direct output to the Immediate window in the Visual Basic Editor, with a statement such as

```
Debug.Print(strMessageFromMars)
```

Although I don't see what benefits come from associating the Print command with an object, this method does perform a very useful role. I cover it further in Chapter 14. Note that although VBA itself does not encapsulate files as objects, you can use a software add-on to manage files and work with their contents using object-oriented techniques (see Chapter 17).

Table 11-1 lists examples of built-in VBA commands drawn from all three categories (statements, functions, and methods). The rest of this chapter explores some of the most generally useful of the built-in commands.

Table 11-1	Examples of Built-In Functions, Statements, and Methods	
Command	**Type**	**What It Does**
Randomize	Statement	Initializes the random number generator
Sqr (*number*)	Function	Returns the square root of *number*

Command	Type	What It Does
`Format (string)`	Function	Formats *string* according to your specifications
`Date`	Statement	Sets the system date
`Date`	Function	Returns the current system date
`Err.Raise`	Method of `Err` object	Generates a run-time error by ID number

Formatting Data

VBA's `Format` functions format any of the built-in data types for display or print purposes according to a pattern you specify. Via these functions, you can easily output a date variable — which VBA actually stores as an unintelligible number — as a short date (12/19/99), as a medium date (19-Dec-99), as a long date (Sunday, December 19, 1999), or in any of several other prefab date and time formats. You can perform similar tricks with numeric values and strings. `Format` actually converts the value you feed it into a new string, adding any characters necessary to produce the results you want.

Both VBA 5 and 6 offer the original `Format` function, while VBA 6 boasts four new related functions each tailored to specific kinds of data.

Working with the original Format function

The original `Format` function, available in both VBA 5 and VBA6, is the most versatile. It can handle just about any type of data, and its output is customizable — if none of the built-in formats will do, you can create your own formats at will.

Using the Format function in code

In simplified form, the syntax for the `Format` function is (the syntax shown here omits two optional and little-used arguments, both related to dates — you can read about them in the Help file):

```
Format(expression,"format")
```

The *expression* argument should contain an expression with the number, date, or string value you want to format (that is, output in a different form). This argument is required, of course.

The *format* argument is the argument that does the real work. As the example shown just below shows, you must surround the *format* argument in quotes

To use the Format function, assign it to a variable or to the Value or Caption property of a control on a UserForm. For example, the statement

```
lblDateMessage.Caption = "The date is " & _
  Format(Now, "Long date")
```

displays the text "The date is Tuesday, October 24, 2000" as the caption of a label control called lblDateMessage (assuming that today is Tuesday, October 24, 2000).

Using prefab formats with the Format function

Table 11-2 lists the named, built-in formats available for various VBA data types. Use them as the format argument in the Format function. Remember to enclose the format name you select (from the first column) in quotation marks.

Table 11-2	Named Formats for Use with the Format Function	
Format Name	**Description of Output**	**Example (Assumes U.S. Settings in Control Panel)**
Numeric		
General Number	Number with no thousand separators	2001.5599
Currency	Number with thousand separators and with two digits to the right of the decimal separator, with currency symbol	$2,001.56
Fixed	At least one digit to the left and exactly two digits to the right of the decimal separator (no thousands separators)	3390.10

Format Name	Description of Output	Example (Assumes U.S. Settings in Control Panel)
Standard	Number with thousand separators, at least one digit to the left and two digits to the right of the decimal separator	1,323.455
Percent	Number multiplied by 100 with two digits to the right of the decimal separator and a percent sign (%) at the right	12.54 %
Scientific	Number in standard scientific notation	1.23E+02
Boolean		
Yes/No	No if the value is 0, Yes otherwise	Yes
True/False	False if the value is 0, True otherwise	True
On/Off	Off if value is 0, On otherwise	On
Date/Time		
General Date	The date and/or time, depending on the value, formatted as specified in the Control Panel	3/15/98 5:27:45 PM
Long Date	The date formatted according to the Control Panel setting for the long date format	Sunday, March 15, 1998
Medium Date	The date formatted according to the Control Panel setting for the medium date format	15-Mar-98
Short Date	The date formatted according to the Control Panel setting for the short date format	3/15/98
	The time, including hours, minutes, and seconds, formatted according to the Control Panel setting for the long time format	5:27:45 PM
Medium Time	The time, including hours and minutes, in a 12-hour format with the AM/PM designator	05:27 PM
Short Time	The time, including hours and minutes, in the 24-hour format	17:27

Specifying custom formats

You can create your own custom format by assembling it from a variety of characters that have special meaning as part of the *format* argument. For example, you can use Format to display strings of text in all upper- or lowercase letters using a format argument of ">" or "<", respectively. I don't have space to list and describe all these special characters — you can find them by looking up the Format function in the VBA Help index, clicking See Also, and then looking for User-defined Formats. So as not to leave you completely unsatisfied, the following example shows a couple of custom date formats in action. Plus, it gives me a chance to illustrate another built-in VBA function called IIf.

```
MsgBox = "The time is " & Format(Now, _
"h:nn") & ". It's " & IIf(Format(Now, "a/p") = "a", _
"morning.", "after noon.")
```

If it's before noon when you run this code, the statement displays a string such as "The time is 9:07. It's morning." After noon, you get instead something like the message shown in Figure 11-1, which is the time message produced by the previous example statement. (By the way, the MsgBox function is covered in detail in the section "Displaying message boxes" later in this chapter.)

Figure 11-1:
A message
box.

Now for some explanation. In the first Format function, the *format* argument is "h:nn". The h outputs the hour, displayed in military time without a leading zero unless the time is after 10:00. After the colon, nn outputs the minute *with* a leading zero for times less than 10 minutes past the hour.

The second time Format is used, it's nested within the IIf function. Here, because "a/p" is the *format* argument, the function's result is simply "a" or "p," depending on whether the time is before or after 12 noon. Normally, you would use a/p as one component of a longer *format* argument. In this case, though, no one ever sees the result of the function. Instead, the IIf function uses the result.

Using the IIf function

IIf is a miniature version of an If...Then statement (covered in full in Chapter 12). The syntax goes like this:

```
IIf (expression, resultiftrue, resultiffalse)
```

In English, this function works like this: If expression is true, the function's return value is resultiftrue; if, however, expression is false, resultiffalse is the function's return value.

In the previous example, the expression to be evaluated is

```
Format(Now, "a/p") = "a"
```

So here, if the Format function returns a value of a, then this expression is True. If it returns any other value, including p, then the expression is False. VBA in turn determines the result of the IIf function based on whether the expression is True or False. If True, the IIf function returns morning; if False, it returns afternoon instead.

Working with VBA 6's new formatting functions

VBA 6 offers four Format-like functions designed for more specific tasks. These are FormatNumber, FormatDateTime, FormatCurrency, and FormatPercent. Like their parent, each of these Format offspring returns a string containing the formatted version of an original value. Because they give the results you probably want by default, they can be easier to use than Format itself. In brief, they work as follows:

✔ FormatNumber(number, NumDigitsAfterDecimal, IncludeLeadingDigit, UseParensForNegativeNumbers, GroupDigits): Returns the original value — the only required argument — as a formatted string. If you omit the optional arguments, FormatNumber formats number using the defaults specified on the Number tab of the Regional Settings applet in the Windows Control Panel. Assuming your system is set to English (U.S.), you get numbers such as 132,328.55. FormatNumber's optional arguments let you override the defaults for the number of decimal places, whether a zero appears to the left of the decimal point for fractional values, whether negative numbers appear in parentheses, and whether groups of digits are separated (for example, with commas).

✔ FormatDateTime(*date*, *format*): Converts a VBA date value into a formatted string. If you don't supply a *format* argument, the string is formatted according to the system settings for short date and long time on the Date tab of the Control Panel's Regional Settings applet. The *format* argument is a number (not a string as in the Format function), but you can specify it using named constants such as vbLongDate or vbShortTime.

✔ FormatCurrency(*number*): Returns *number* formatted as currency according to your Control Panel settings. Otherwise, FormatCurrency works just like FormatNumber, and takes the same optional arguments.

✔ FormatPercent(*number*): Multiplies *number* by 100 and adds a percent sign (.05 becomes 5.00%). FormatPercent takes the same optional arguments as FormatNumber. To drop the digits after the decimal point, use 0 as the *NumDigitsAfterDecimal* argument, as in FormatNumber (.05,0).

Converting Data

As I take pains to point out in Chapter 9, VBA automatically converts between different data types on the fly. The automatic conversions sure are convenient, and the results are usually exactly what you intended. The stress should be on the word *usually*, however.

When the automated conversions leave you unsatisfied, VBA stands ready with a raft of explicit functions for converting data types. Use them to

✔ Ensure that VBA performs the correct conversion.

✔ Perform conversions that VBA doesn't do automatically.

✔ Make your code self-explanatory (okay, *self-documenting*, if you want to sound like a Real Programmer).

The workhorse data conversion commands are a group of functions I refer to as the *C-type* functions. That's C for *convert*, not for the C programming language. VBA has one of these functions for every built-in data type aside from objects — CBool, CByte, CCur, and so on. For example, after execution of the statement boolMaybe = CBool(123), the boolMaybe variable contains the value True (any non-zero number has an existence, I guess, so that makes them all True).

Just realize that, aside from making the type of conversion explicit, these functions don't do anything that VBA's automatic conversions can't. (See Chapter 9 for specifics on the CDec function.)

The Fix and Int functions strip off the fractional part of any number you send them, returning a whole number. Unlike the CInt and CLng functions, they don't perform proper rounding — Int (4.989) returns 4, not 5.

These two functions differ only when used on negative numbers. With them, Int returns one integer less than the argument value, whereas Fix removes the decimal part of the argument. Int (-9.2) returns -10, for instance.

Working with hex and octal values

The Hex and Oct functions convert standard, base-10 whole number values into strings containing their hexadecimal or octal equivalents. You can't convert in the other direction in your code, but you *can* type in hex or octal literal values, letting the Visual Basic Editor convert them into decimal numbers automatically. The trick is to precede each hex or octal literal with a special code: &H for hex, &O (that's letter O, not number 0) for octal. After execution of the statement intBases = 10 + &O12 +&HA, the value of intBases is 30, just as it should be.

Converting between numbers and strings

Several VBA functions convert between numbers and strings. These include:

- ✔ CStr: CStr turns any non-object data you feed it, including numeric values, into the corresponding string. It adjusts its output according to the number (and date) display formats specified in the Regional Settings applet in the Control Panel. For example, in France, CStr(200.02) gives the string "200,02" as its output. Note that although the output *string* varies according to the regional setting, you must always enter actual numeric values using the format that prevails in the United States.

- ✔ Str: Converts a number into a string, but it always formats the string according to the U.S. custom, with a period as the decimal separator.

- ✔ **C-type functions for numeric data types:** These convert a string to the corresponding numeric value, but only when they recognize all the characters as legitimate within numbers. Again, this determination depends on the Control Panel settings. In France, CDbl ("200 ,02F") gives a result of 200.02; in the U.S., the same statement produces an error, but CDbl ("$200.02") works fine.

- ✔ Val: Converts the numerals in a string into a numeric value, stopping when it runs into a character that it doesn't recognize as numeric. Regardless of your Control Panel settings, the only characters it recognizes are numerals and the decimal point (period). It ignores spaces, tabs, and line breaks, however. The expression Val("28 190.43 12 by 14") gives 28190.4312 as its result.

> ✔ Chr: Converts a numeric ANSI value into the corresponding character. Use this function to place characters you can't type in your strings.
>
> ✔ Asc: More or less the converse of Chr, this function returns the numeric code of the first character in a string.

Con Text

VBA offers a rich collection of statements and functions for formatting text strings and extracting portions of them that you may find especially mesmerizing. In Table 11-3, I list all the string-related commands I could find.

Table 11-3	String-Related Statements and Functions	
Remember that literal string values (as opposed to variables containing strings) must be enclosed in quotation marks.		
Statement or Function	**Type**	**What It Does (for Statements) or Value It Returns (for Functions)**
Asc (*string*)	Function	Character code of first character in *string*
Chr (*charactercode*)	Function	Character corresponding to *charactercode*
Filter (*sourcearray, match, include, compare*)	Function (VBA 6 only)	An array containing only those strings in *sourcearray* that contain *match* as any part of the string. *Sourcearray* must be an array of string values. If the optional *include* argument is False, the function returns only those strings that *don't* contain *match*.
Format (*string*)	Function	See "Formatting Data" earlier in this chapter
Hex (*number*)	Function	A string containing a hexadecimal representation of *number*
InStr (*start, string1, string2*)	Function	A number specifying the position of *string2* within *string1*; the search begins at position *start*, which is an optional argument

Statement or Function	Type	What It Does (for Statements) or Value It Returns (for Functions)
InStrRev (*string1*, *string2*, *start*)	Function (VBA 6 only)	A number specifying the position of *string2* within *string1*, counting from the right side of *string1*; the search begins at position *start*, an optional argument.
Join (*stringarray*, *delimiter*)	Function (VBA 6 only)	One string that combines all the strings in *stringarray*, which must be an array of string data. By default, Join adds a space between each of the original strings, but you can specify a different *delimiter* character (surround a literal character in quotes).
Left (*string*, *length*)	Function	A string containing *length* number of characters taken from the left side of *string*
Len (*string*)	Function	The number of characters in *string*
LCase (*string*)	Function	A copy of *string* with all its characters converted to lowercase
LSet *stringvariable* = *string*	Statement	Assigns *string* to *stringvariable* without changing *stringvariable*'s length; aligns *string* on the left of *stringvariable*
LTrim (*string*)	Function	A new string containing a copy of *string* without any leading spaces
Mid (*string*, *start*, *length*)	Function	A new string containing *length* number of characters from *string*, beginning with the character at position *start*
Mid (*stringvariable*, *start*, *length*) = *string*	Statement	Replaces *length* number of characters in *stringvariable* with characters from *string*
Oct (*number*)	Function	A string containing the octal (base 8) value of *number*

(continued)

Table 11-3 *(continued)*

Statement or Function	Type	What It Does (for Statements) or Value It Returns (for Functions)
Replace (string, find start, count, compare)	Function (VBA 6 only)	A new string. Replaces *find* text with *replace* text within *string*. The *start*, *count*, and *compare* arguments are otional. Use *start* to specify the position where the search begins. Use *count* to specify how many times the *replace* operation is performed, assuming *find* text occurs more than once (by default, all occurrences of *find* get replaced).
Right (string, length)	Function	A string containing *length* number of characters from *string*, reading from the right side
RSet stringvariable = string	Statement	Assigns *string* to *stringvariable* without changing *stringvariable*'s length; aligns *string* on the right of *stringvariable*
RTrim (string)	Function	A new string containing a copy of *string* from which trailing spaces have been stripped
Space (number)	Function	A string containing the specified *number* of spaces
Split (string, delimiter, limit, compare)	Function (VBA 6 only)	An array of strings. This function breaks up the *string* argument into separate, individual strings. By default, it divides the original *string* at spaces, but you can specify a *delimiter* other than the space character (use quotation marks to specify a literal character as the delimiter). The optional *limit* argument specifies the maximum number of strings to return in the array.
StrComp (string1, string2)	Function	0 if the two strings are equal, -1 if *string1* is less than *string2*, 1 if *string1* is greater than *string2* (see Chapter 9 for information on string comparisons)

Statement or Function	Type	What It Does (for Statements) or Value It Returns (for Functions)
StrConv (*string, conversionmethod*)	Function	A new string based on *string*, prepared using the specified conversion method
String (*number, character*)	Function	A string of specified length containing a repeating sequence of *character*
StrReverse (*string*)	Function (VBA 6 only)	A string containing the characters of the *string* argument in reverse.
Trim (*string*)	Function	A new string containing a copy of *string* from which leading and trailing spaces have been stripped
UCase (*string*)	Function	A copy of *string* with all characters converted to uppercase

Don't be disappointed if you don't find a string function that does exactly what you want. Instead, think of them as building blocks — they often need to be nested to give you the final results you want.

For example, suppose that you have a list of full names stored as strings in this form:

```
"Guess, Helen Ms."
"Tran, Linda Dr."
"Wish, Ferd Mr."
```

(such a list should be stored as an *array* of strings, and I cover arrays in Chapter 13).

Removing characters at the end of a string with Len and Left

Suppose that someone has given you the job of removing the titles at the end of each string. Each name in the list is a different length, so a set formula won't help. However, if the string variable strOld contains the original name, the following statement would do the trick:

```
strNew = Left(strOld, Len(strOld) - 4)
```

If VBA read books instead of code, I could tell it to accomplish the same action by following these steps:

1. **Call the** Len **function to calculate the total length of the original string.**

2. **Subtract 4 from the result of Step 1 because a total of four characters is taken up by the title at the end of the string (including the space).**

   That action gives the length that the new string should be.

3. **Call the** Left **function, using this calculated new length as the second argument.**

   Left reads the number of characters specified by the second argument, from the string named in the first argument, returning only those characters.

4. **Assign the new, shorter string returned by** Left **to the** strNew **variable.**

Extracting characters from within a string

Working with your new list of names without titles, suppose that you are now asked to extract the first names and place them into a new list. You can accomplish your task with this statement:

```
str1stName = Mid(strNew, InStr(strNew, ",") + 2)
```

The Mid function extracts characters from anywhere in the string that you enter as its first argument. Its second argument tells Mid where in that string to start extracting characters. Here, this argument is an expression consisting of the InStr function plus 2.

For its part, InStr hunts in the specified string (the first argument) for another string (the second argument). In this case, the second argument is that comma that comes after the last name in your list. The value InStr returns is the position number in the first string at which it finds the second string — now you know where the last name ends.

You add 2 to the InStr value to bypass the comma and the space, locating the first character in the first name. Mid extracts the rest of the characters in the string as its result, unless you specify a third (optional) *length* argument.

Working with Dates and Times

In real-world programming, working with dates and times often assumes a major role. VBA cushions the ride with a panoply of statements and functions for finding out what day or time it is now, making date-related calculations, and extracting from a date variable the component of interest, be it the year, the day of the week, or the hour.

Table 11-4 lists these commands in summary form. I simplified some functions in the table by omitting optional arguments — you can get the dirty details in the VBA Help file. Following the table, a few of the most important date- and time-related commands receive more detailed attention.

To make use of this material, you need a working understanding of how VBA handles date and time data and how date variables work. All that occurs in Chapter 9.

Table 11-4   Date- and Time-Related Statements and Functions

Remember to enclose literal date values used as arguments within # characters (number signs) and string arguments such as date intervals inside quotation marks.

Name	Type	What It Does (for Statements) or Value It Returns (for Functions)
Date	Function	The current system date
Date (datevalue)		StatementSets the system date to datevalue
DateAdd (interval, number, datevalue)	Function	A new date value equal to datevalue plus number of the time or date periods represented by interval
DateDiff (interval, date1, date2)	Function	The number of the date or time periods represented by interval between date1 and date2
DatePart (interval, date)	Function	An integer representing the specified interval of date
DateSerial (year, month, day)	Function	The date specified by year, month, and day, which must be numeric expressions
DateValue (datestring)	Function	A date value corresponding to datestring
Day (date)	Function	An integer corresponding to the day of the month represented by date
Hour (time)	Function	An integer between 0 and 23, inclusive, representing the hour of the day corresponding to the specified time

(continued)

Table 11-4 (continued)

Name	Type	What It Does (for Statements) or Value It Returns (for Functions)
Minute (time)	Function	An integer between 0 and 59, inclusive, representing the minute corresponding to the specified time
Month (date)	Function	An integer between 1 and 12, inclusive, representing the month corresponding to the specified date
MonthName (month, abbreviate)	Function (VBA 6 only)	A string containing the name of the month corresponding to the month argument, which must be an integer between 1 and 12. If the optional abbreviate argument is True, the returned string is an abbreviation of the month's name.
Now	Function	A date value representing the current system date and time
Second (time)	Function	A whole number between 0 and 59, inclusive, representing the second corresponding to the specified time
Time	Function	A date value representing the current system time
Time	Statement	Sets the system time to timevalue
Timer (timevalue)	Function	The number of seconds since midnight
TimeSerial (hour, minute, second)	Function	A date value containing the time specified by hour, minute, and second
TimeValue (timestring)	Function	A date value containing the time corresponding to timestring (any date information in the string is discarded)
Weekday (date)	Function	A whole number representing the day of the week corresponding to date

Name	Type	What It Does (for Statements) or Value It Returns (for Functions)
WeekdayName (*weekday, abbreviate, firstdayofweek*)	Function (VBA 6 only)	A string containing the name of the weekday specified by the *weekday* argument, which must be an integer between 1 and 7. If the optional *abbreviate* argument is True, the returned string is an abbreviation of the weekday name. You can determine how VBA interprets *weekday* number by specifying a *firstdayofweek* argument using constants such as vbMonday, vbThursday, and so on.
Year (*date*)	Function	A whole number representing the year corresponding to *date*

A date with time

A handful of simple statements and functions let you work with the date and time stored in your computer's built-in clock, called the *system date and time.*

The Now function returns the current system date and time as a date variable, as in: datSeizeTheMoment = Now.

For work with the system time or the system date separately, VBA provides a pair of commands for each element. These are a bit confusing because each pair contains a statement and a function having the same name.

For example, to *retrieve* the system time as a VBA date value, you use the Time *function;* but to *set* the time, you use the Time *statement.* In other words, the Time keyword has different actions depending on the context.

```
datItsMyTime = Time ' Time function returns system time
Time (#3:15 AM#) ' Time statement sets the system time
```

The corresponding Date function and Date statement work the same way.

Calculating with dates

Time is a relative thing, right? The whole point of knowing the time or the date is so you can peg it compared to another time or a different date. Sometimes you want to know how far apart two times or two dates are. Or you want to know what the date will be, say, two years and three months from now. Several of VBA's date-related functions make math with dates and times reasonably simple.

Adding to and subtracting from dates and times

Use VBA's `DateAdd` function when you want to know what the date will be three years hence or what time it was an hour and 15 minutes ago. These calculations aren't hard for you to do yourself, but they require special handling because dates and times have so many different components and because their units aren't based on a straight decimal system (you have 7 days in a week, 60 seconds in a minute, and so on).

The `DateAdd` function has this syntax: `DateAdd (interval, number, startingdate)`.

The value it returns is the starting date (or time) to which the specified *number* of *interval*(s) has been added. Use a negative *number* if you want to subtract rather than add. Table 11-5 lists the codes available for the *interval* argument (remember to enclose them in quotation marks).

Table 11-5	Arguments Available for the DateDiff and DateAdd Functions
Argument (in Quotation Marks)	**Interval It Specifies**
yyyy	Year
q	Quarter
m	Month
y	Day of year
d	Day
w	Weekday
ww	Week
h	Hour
n	Minute
s	Second

For example, after this statement executes

```
datWhen = DateAdd ("s", -90, Now)
```

the `datWhen` variable contains a date value 90 seconds — a minute and a half — prior to the current time. If you then want to output only the time component of that value, you use the `Format` function with one of the time arguments, as in `Format(datWhen,"Medium time")`, as I describe in "Formatting Data," earlier in this chapter.

DateAdd doesn't steer you wrong by returning a non-existent date. If you add one month to the 31st of August, you get the 30th of September as your result. DateAdd is aware of leap years, too.

Note that you can't mix intervals in one pass of the DateAdd function. However, nothing is wrong with figuring what the date will be two years and three months from now by using DateAdd twice.

VBA provides two alternative functions for date and time calculations that *do* allow you to mix intervals: DateSerial and TimeSerial. Each function has three arguments.

```
DateSerial (year, month, day)
TimeSerial (hour, minute, second)
```

In each function, all three arguments must be included, and each should be an expression that gives an *integer* value (not a VBA date value). See if you can follow this code fragment, noting the calculation in the third argument:

```
intYear = 1999
intMonth = 12
intDay = 31
datNewMillenium = DateSerial (intYear,intMonth,intDay+1)
```

Of course, any or all of the arguments can be calculated.

Calculating the difference between two dates

Use the DateDiff function to figure how many intervals (years, months, weekdays, and so on) exist between two dates or times. Here's a sample:

```
lngHowLong = DateDiff ("m", #2/12/90#, #10/12/01#)
```

After this statement executes, lngHowLong — a long integer variable — contains the number of months between the two dates shown. DateDiff uses the interval codes for the first argument. In this example, the "m" tells the function to return months rather than years, weekdays, or some other interval.

Calculating a person's age

The following Function procedure uses the DateDiff and DateSerial functions to calculate a person's age in years. To prevent errors, you can improve the code by testing to be sure that the birthdate argument is actually a date value (use the IsDate function for this test) and by making sure that the birthdate isn't in the future.

```
Function WhatAge(dateDateOfBirth As Date)

Dim intAge As Integer ' use Long if you want ages > 255

IntAge = DateDiff("yyyy", dateDateOfBirth, Date)

' check to see if they've already had their birthday:
If DateSerial(Year(Date), Month(dateDateOfBirth), _
   Day(dateDateOfBirth))> Date Then
      intAge = intAge - 1
End If

WhatAge = intAge

End Function
```

Simple Interactions with the World

Because they more or less act as parasites on larger applications, VBA programs often don't require any user interface elements (dialog boxes, menus, and such). When triggered, a VBA program can swing into action on the document currently active in your application, adjusting what it does according to the contents of the document.

Obviously, though, plenty of programming situations still call for direct interaction with the ultimate user of the VBA program. VBA's UserForm tools give you the power to create a rich set of interactive windows for your users. But when less will do, less is better.

Two VBA functions, MsgBox and InputBox, provide the basic tools you need to talk to the program's users and let them talk back. Their basic duties are:

- ✔ MsgBox displays a message, of course, but it also lets you know which of two or more buttons the user clicked.
- ✔ InputBox displays a message and a text box where the user can type a response.

Displaying message boxes

The formal syntax for the MsgBox function is

```
MsgBox(prompt[, buttons] [, title] [, helpfile, context]).
```

As the brackets indicate, only the *prompt* argument — which specifies the message you want to display — is required.

Specifying the prompt

In its simplest form, the MsgBox function acts like a statement. All you do is type it on its own line, supplying the text you want displayed — the prompt — as the single argument, as in:

```
MsgBox "This is a test MsgBox."
```

When this line is executed, VBA displays the message box shown in Figure 11-2.

Figure 11-2:
A simple
message
box.

You can type parentheses around the prompt, but parentheses aren't required when a function is used as a statement.

The prompt can be a variable or any expression. As usual, VBA automatically converts numeric values and dates into displayable characters for you. The following code works fine:

```
intWishCount = 3
datWhen = Format(Now, "Short date")
strInfo1 = "As of "
strInfo2 = " wishes left."
MsgBox strInfo1 & datWhen & ", " & intWishCount & strInfo2
```

To display a message on more than one line, separate the lines by adding a carriage return character (ASCII value 13) to your prompt string, using the Chr function:

```
MsgBox "Here is line one." & Chr(13) & "Here is line two."
```

You can line up text on two or more lines in columns with Tab characters (ASCII value 9).

Creating fancier message boxes

Besides displaying text, a message box can show one of several icons and include buttons of several different types. You wrap up your choices for all these options as a single numeric value: the optional buttons argument.

By adding an icon, your message box can look a little spiffier than the unadorned box in Figure 11-2. The example in Figure 11-3 carries the critical message icon, which should generate a bit more excitement in the user.

The default message box has only an OK button, but you can add buttons labeled Cancel, Yes, No, Abort, Retry, and Ignore in various combinations. You can see a sample of these wares in Figure 11-3.

Figure 11-3:
A spiffier
message
box.

Calculating a value for the buttons argument

As with sundry similar arguments in other functions, you calculate the value for `buttons` by adding together constants representing the various available choices of icons and buttons. You can calculate the number yourself or create an expression using the named constants VBA has defined for this purpose. Table 11-6 lists each constant with its numeric value and purpose in life.

Table 11-6	VBA Constants for Message and Input Box Appearance and Behavior	
Constant	**Numeric Value**	**What It Does**
vbOKOnly	0	Displays OK button only
vbOKCancel	1	Displays OK and Cancel buttons
vbAbortRetryIgnore	2	Displays Abort, Retry, and Ignore buttons
vbYesNoCancel	3	Displays Yes, No, and Cancel buttons
vbYesNo	4	Displays Yes and No buttons
vbRetryCancel	5	Displays Retry and Cancel buttons
vbCritical	16	Displays Critical Message icon
vbQuestion	32	Displays Warning Query icon
vbExclamation	48	Displays Warning Message icon
vbInformation	64	Displays Information Message icon

Constant	Numeric Value	What It Does
vbDefaultButton1	0	Specifies the first button as the default
vbDefaultButton2	256	Specifies the second button as the default
vbDefaultButton3	512	Specifies the third button as the default
vbDefaultButton4	768	Specifies the fourth button as the default

Based on the table, the buttons argument in the function call for the Figure 11-3 message box should be 531. But who's counting? Typing the following statement is easier:

```
intA = MsgBox("Pick a button", vbYesNoCancel + vbCritical _
    + vbDefaultButton3, "VBA For Dummies")
```

Note that VbDefaultButton3, the third of the three constants in the expression for the buttons argument, sets up the third button, counting from left to right, as the default choice. In this case, that third button is Cancel. If you look closely at Figure 11-3, you can see that the Cancel button has the focus — it's highlighted by a dotted line, indicating that if you press the spacebar or Enter, it will be activated.

Who's got the button?

The point of displaying buttons in a message box is to give the user some choice about what action to take. In a message box, the users have nothing to type — they just click one of the buttons. Of course, you need a way to figure out *which* button.

That's easy because the MsgBox function returns an integer value corresponding to the button the user clicks. To minimize the strain on your memory, you can test the returned value against predefined named constants rather than arbitrary numbers. Here are the constants and their *real* values:

Constant	Value
vbOK	1
vbCancel	2
vbAbort	3
vbRetry	4

(continued)

Constant	Value
vblgnore	5
vbYes	6
vbNo	7

An If...Then statement works well to figure out which button was clicked, if your message box has only two buttons, as in this example:

```
If MsgBox ("Go on?", VbYesNo) = VbYes Then
  DoSomething
Else
  DontDoAnything
End If
```

With three buttons to test, you would need an If...Then...Else If statement.

Adding a title

By default, a message box displays the name of the VBA application you're using in its title bar (refer to Figure 11-2). You can substitute any title you like by supplying a string for the title argument when you call the MsgBox function — refer to Figure 11-3.

Obtaining user input

If you need to know more from the user than which of three options to pursue, the InputBox function may be adequate. Here's its formal syntax, minus the more advanced optional arguments:

```
InputBox(prompt [, title] [, default]).
```

As illustrated in Figure 11-4, the dialog box displayed by this function provides a text box, where the user is asked to type some piece of presumably crucial information. To bring that information into your program, just assign the return value of the InputBox function to a string variable:

```
strB = InputBox ("Seat preference?", "NYAir", "Aisle")
```

Figure 11-4:
A sample
input box.

Although an input box can collect a much wider range of information than a message box, its basic operations are actually simpler — you have no buttons and icons to fiddle with. The *prompt* and *title* arguments work just as they do in the `MsgBox` function. You can make it easier for the users by supplying a *default* response — if they like it, they just press Enter.

Working with Boolean values

The simplest way to toggle the value of a Boolean variable to its opposite is with the logical operator `Not`. All you need do is assign the results of the `Not` operation to the same variable. For example, the statement

```
boolBlinking = Not(boolBlinking)
```

makes the `boolBlinking` variable `True` if it started out `False`, and vice versa.

Fun with Math and Money

VBA comes chock full of prefab functions for manipulating numbers. These perform chores ranging from the very simple (such as returning an absolute value or a number's sign) to the staple computations of algebra and trigonometry. If the bottom line is sinking, VBA's healthy dose of financial functions may be just what you need to float the business boat again.

With a few exceptions, I don't cover the use of these functions individually. Again, I put them in the book just because they're so hard to dig out of the VBA Help file and you may otherwise miss them. Look over the listings to acquaint yourself with what's available and what isn't.

Math functions

Table 11-7 catalogs the VBA functions that are specifically math-related. When you're in the mood for math, don't forget to review the data conversion functions covered in "Converting Data," earlier in this chapter.

Table 11-7	VBA Math Functions
Function	*Value It Returns*
Abs(*number*)	The absolute value of *number*
Atn(*number*)	The arctangent of *number*
Cos(*number*)	The cosine of *number*
Exp(*number*)	The number *e* raised to the power of *number*
Fix(*number*)	The integer portion of number, similar to the Int function
Int(*number*)	The integer portion of *number*. The Int and Fix functions differ in their handling of negative numbers. Int returns the next lower (more negative) integer, whereas Fix simply drops the decimal portion of *number*.
Log(*number*)	The natural logarithm of *number* as a double
Rnd(*number*)	A random number as a single
Sgn(*number*)	1 if *number* is a positive number, 0 if it is 0, and −1 if it's a negative number
Sin(*number*)	The sine of *number*
Sqr(*number*)	The square root of *number*
Tan(*number*)	The tangent of *number*

Deriving other math functions

If VBA doesn't include the math function you seek, don't fret — you can usually put together an expression or Function procedure of your own that can get the job done.

If you're mathematician enough that you're calculating advanced trigonometric functions such as inverse cosecants, you don't need me to tell you how to use them. You may like to know, though, that the VBA Help file comes with a cheat-sheet summary of many such functions, with the expressions needed to calculate them. To see this, search for *derived math functions* in the Help index. The Help topic reminds you that, for example, the logarithm to base N of X can be calculated as = Log(X) / Log(N).

If you think you may ever reuse a math function derived from other functions, make it a permanent part of your VBA arsenal by wrapping it up into a Function procedure. After storing it in a module named something like MyMathFunctions, you can put it back to work any time the need for that computation comes up.

Rounding numbers

Rounding off a decimal point number is a common task, especially when you're working with currency values. Curiously, VBA doesn't offer a straightforward solution. However, the technique discussed here will solve your rounding problems.

VBA 6 has a Round function, not available in VBA 5, but it doesn't work reliably. For example, after VBA runs the statement

```
x = Round(2.505, 2)
```

the value of x is 2.5, not 2.51 as it should be. Don't use Round unless you're willing to put up with some incorrect answers.

However, there is a dependable, simple way to round off a number with too many decimal places: Use the Format function. Just Format the number in question using the custom *format* argument shown in the example code below (see "Specifying prefab and custom formats" earlier in this chapter for details on the *format* argument).

Here's an example of this technique in practice:

```
sngRoundedNumber = Format(sngUnRounded, "#,##0.00")
```

In VBA 6, you can use the FormatNumber function instead to get the same result as in:

```
sngRoundedNumber = FormatNumber(sngUnRounded, 2)
```

Both examples round sngUnRounded to two decimal places. To round to a different number of decimal places using Format, change the number of zeroes following the decimal point in the *format* argument. For example, the argument "#,##0.0" would round the number to only one decimal place. To change the number of decimal places using FormatNumber, just specify the desired number as the second argument.

Note that the variable into which you place the rounded value should be of type string, single, double, decimal, currency, or variant — don't use integers or longs, or you'll lose the fractional part of the result.

Suppose you want to round a value that doesn't have any decimal places so that it has fewer significant digits. The code you need is a bit more involved, but not by much, as is illustrated in the following example, which rounds the original number to two fewer significant digits:

```
sngRounded = Format(sngUnRounded / 100, "#,##0.") * 100
```

Note that the custom *format* argument for this task has no zeroes to the right of the decimal point. In addition, the code divides the unrounded number inside the Format function by a power of 10 and then multiplies the function result by that same power of 10. Select the power of 10 equal to the number of significant digits you want to drop. In the above example, the 2nd power of 10, or 100, produces the desired answer.

Working with random numbers

If the routine of life has dampened your spirits, liven up your programs by building in some unpredictability. Randomly generated numbers are useful when you're coding programs such as simulations of real-world problems, educational software, and games.

VBA includes two built-in commands specifically designed for generating random numbers. They are:

- ✔ **The** Randomize **statement:** Use it to prime the pump of VBA's random number generator. Used with no arguments, Randomize seeds the generator with the current system time. That way, you're guaranteed to get a different series of random numbers each time the code runs.

- ✔ **The** Rnd **function:** This is the function that actually produces your random numbers. It requires no arguments — you just set Rnd equal to a variable or use the function in an expression. Rnd returns a floating-point (single) value.

Floating-point numbers like those returned by Rnd are commonly used for statistical and scientific purposes. In more mundane situations, however, you usually need integer random values. You may want, for example, to write a procedure that selects the winning raffle ticket number. To convert the value returned by Rnd to an integer within a given range, use the following formula:

```
randomint = Int((high * Rnd) + low)
```

In the formula, the items *high* and *low* refer to the highest and lowest values in your series of numbers — if you specify them correctly, the formula always gives a result within that range.

The Raffle module on the CD-ROM is a complete little program that illustrates the formula and the use of random numbers in general.

Financial functions

VBA offers a load of built-in functions for calculating dollars-and-cents amounts such as payments on a loan (an *annuity,* technically speaking) or the return on an investment. Although I don't have space to cover them all in detail, I do go over the use of the Pmt function for figuring out payments on a loan.

Calculating payments on a loan or savings plan

Use the Pmt function to compute the payment you have to make (or someone else makes to you) on a fixed-rate mortgage or other loan or to put aside enough to meet a savings goal. Here's the Pmt function's formal syntax:

```
Pmt(rate, nper, pv[, fv[, type]]).
```

The first argument, *Rate,* defines the interest rate on the loan *per period.* You need to understand that the way you express the rate must correspond to the frequency of payments. If you'll be making monthly payments on an 8 percent mortgage, remember that 8 percent is the yearly rate. In this common situation, *Rate* should be an expression such as .08 / 12 (8 percent divided by 12 months).

The *nper* argument is an integer representing the total number of payments (it stands for *number of periods*) that must be made on the loan. For monthly payments on a 5-year loan, *nper* should be 5 * 12, or 60. Specify the total amount of the loan in the *pv* argument. This is the *present value.*

The remaining arguments are optional. If you want to calculate how much you should save to hit a financial target, use the *fv* argument to send the target amount as a *negative* number to the Pmt function — it stands for *future value.* (The interest rate you expect to earn would be your *rate* argument. If you've already saved something towards your goal, that amount would be the *pv* argument.) The *type* argument lets you specify whether payments are due at the end of each payment (in which case, it should be 0, the default) or at the end (give *type* a value of 1).

To use the Pmt function in your code, assign it to a variable of the double (floating-point) data type. Here are two examples:

```
dblPay = Pmt (.08/12, 360, 300000) ' Typical mortgage
dblSav = Pmt (.07/12, 120, 12500,-75000) ' Goal = $75,000
```

Putting bread and butter on the table

Table 11-8 summarizes VBA's cornucopia of financial functions. To make the table reasonably easy to read, I omitted optional arguments. Look up a function in the Help file for details on its arguments and a salient example.

Table 11-8	VBA's Financial Functions
Function	**Value It Returns**
DDB (cost, salvage, period)	The depreciation of an asset over period, based on the double-declining balance method
FV (rate, nper, pmt, pv)	The future value of an annuity of fixed interest rate rate, based on nper number of fixed payments, pmt (the amount of each payment, and present value pv of the annuity (rate and nper must be expressed in the same time interval, such as months)
Ipmt (rate, per, nper, pv)	The interest payment for a given period of an annuity based on periodic, fixed payments and a fixed interest rate
IRR (values())	The internal rate of return for a series of periodic cash flows (values() is an array of payments and receipts)
MIRR (values(), finance_rate, reinvest_rate)	The modified internal rate of return for the series of periodic cash flows (payments and receipts) listed in the values() array
Nper (rate, pmt, pv)	The number of periods for an annuity based on periodic, fixed payments and a fixed interest rate
NPV (rate, values())	The net present value of an investment based on a series of periodic cash flows and a discount rate
Pmt (rate, nper, pv)	The payment for an annuity based on periodic, fixed payments and a fixed interest rate
PPmt (rate, per, nper, pv)	The principal payment for a given period of an annuity based on periodic, fixed payments and a fixed interest rate
PV (rate, nper, pmt)	The present value of an annuity based on periodic, fixed payments to be paid in the future, and a fixed interest rate
Rate (nper, pmt, pv)	The interest rate per period for an annuity
SLN (cost, salvage, life)	The straight-line depreciation of an asset for a single period
SYD (cost, salvage, life, period)	The sum-of-years' digits depreciation of an asset for a specified period

Miscellaneous Built-In Commands

Even with all the tables and discussions presented in this chapter, this review of VBA's built-in commands is far from complete. I discuss some of these commands in later chapters, but I close this chapter with yet another table, Table 11-9, listing sundry commands that you may well find useful.

Table 11-9	Miscellaneous Built-In VBA Commands	
Name	**Function or Statement**	**What It Does (for Statements) or Value It Returns (for Functions)**
(Remember to enclose literal strings for items such as pathnames in quotation marks.)		
Working with Files on Disk		
ChDir(*pathname*)	Statement	Changes the active directory (folder), but not the active drive
ChDrive(*drivename*)	Statement	Changes the active drive
CurDir	Function	Current path (disk and directory name) as a string
Dir(*pathname*)	Function	The name of the first file or directory (folder) matching *pathname*, which may contain wildcards. Call the Dir repeatedly to obtain additional matching items.
FileCopy *source, destination*	Statement	Copies the disk file *source* to *destination*, which may include a path, a filename, or both
FileDateTime (*pathname*)	Function	Date value for the date and time when the file named by *pathname* was created or last modified
FileLen (*pathname*)	Function	Length of the disk file named by *pathname*, in bytes
GetAttr(*pathname*)	Function	An integer representing the attributes of the file or directory (folder) specified by *pathname*
Kill *pathname*	Statement	Deletes one or more disk files (wildcard characters are permissible in *pathname*)

(continued)

Table 11-9 *(continued)*

Name	Function or Statement	What It Does (for Statements) or Value It Returns (for Functions)
MkDir *pathname*	Statement	Creates (makes) a new directory
Name *oldpathname* As newpathname	Statement	Renames and/or moves a disk file, directory, or folder
RmDir ***pathname***	Statement	Removes a directory
SetAttr *pathname*, *attributes*	Statement	Sets chosen attributes of a disk file. The *attributes* argument represents a numeric value that is the sum of the values for each attribute to be set. VBA provides named constants for each of the available attributes.
Miscellaneous Commands		
AppActivate *title, wait*	Statement	Activates another running application. If the optional *wait* argument is True, VBA waits until your program has the focus before activating the application.
Beep	Statement	Beeps the computer speaker
Choose(*index*, *choice1, choice2*,) ...*choicen*	Function	The value of the item at position *index* (index must evaluate to a number) in the list of arguments *choice1, choice2, ...choicen*
DoEvents	Function	This function allows Windows to handle other events while in the middle of running your program. In VBA it always returns 0 (zero), so you do not need to assign its value to a variable — use it as a statement.
Environ (*envstring*) Environ(*number*)	Functions	The contents of an operating or system environment variable, specified by name *envstring* or numeric position *number*

Name	Function or Statement	What It Does (for Statements) or Value It Returns (for Functions)
RGB(*red, green, blue*)	Function	A whole number representing an RGB color value for the *red, green,* and *blue* components (you use the RGB value calculated by this function to set color-related object properties)
Randomize	Statement	Initializes the random number generator
Rnd(*number*)	Function	A random value; the *number* argument is optional
SendKeys *string, wait*	Statement	Sends the keystrokes specified in *string* to the active window as if typed at the keyboard. If the optional *wait* argument is True, the keystrokes must be processed before your program continues.

Manipulating the Windows Registry

Shell(*pathname*)	Function	This function attempts to run the program specified by *pathname*. It returns a number representing the program's ID if successful; otherwise, it returns zero.
DeleteSetting *appname, section, key*	Statement	Deletes an entry in the registry
GetAllSettings (*appname, section*)	Function	A variant containing a list of all settings for the specified *section* of application *appname* in the Windows registry (returned as a two-dimensional array)
GetSetting (*appname, section, key*)	Function	A single-key value from the specified *section* of application *appname* in the Windows registry
SaveSetting *appname, section, key, setting*	Statement	Stores a setting in the registry

(continued)

Table 11-9 *(continued)*

Name	*Function or Statement*	*What It Does (for Statements) or Value It Returns (for Functions)*
Output Formatting		
Spc(*number*)	Function	No useful return value; used to place the specified *number* of spaces in the output from the Print # statement or the Debug.Print method
Tab(*column*)	Function	No useful return value; positions output from the Print # statement or the Debug.Print method at column number *column* (or if *column* is omitted, at the next print zone)
Working with Variables		
IsDate(*variablename*), IsNumeric(*variablename*), IsObject(*variablename*) IsArray(*variablename*), IsNull(*variablename*), IsEmpty(*variablename*)	Functions	True if *variablename* is of the indicated type or value (such as Date or Empty); otherwise, False
Len(*variablename*)	Function	The number of bytes required to store the information contained in *variablename*
TypeName(*variablename*)	Function	A string representing the type of variable *variablename*, which must be a variant
VarType(*variablename*)	Function	An integer indicating the subtype of variable *variablename*, which must be a variant

Chapter 12

Controlling the Flow

In This Chapter

▶ Using control structures to control what happens

▶ Testing criteria with conditional expressions

▶ Making decisions with `If...Then` and `Select Case` statements

▶ Repeating code blocks with `For...Next`, `For Each...Next`, and `Do...Loop` statements

▶ Branching at will with `GoTo` statements

*C*ontrol structures are code statements that determine what the procedure will do next, based on some condition that is in effect at the time the code runs. VBA offers a healthy assortment of powerful control structures. This chapter takes these structures apart and demonstrates their use in practical examples (well, at least quasipractical examples).

Many of the examples in this chapter are available on the CD in its fullest form.

Controlling Wild Programs with Control Structures

Control structures fall into three main groups: conditional statements, loops, and the `With` statement. They work as follows:

✔ A *conditional statement* determines which branch of code to execute based on whether a condition is `True` or `False`. VBA conditional statements include `If...Then` (in several permutations) and `Select Case`.

✔ A *loop* repeatedly executes a block of code a fixed number of times or until some condition becomes `True` or `False`. When you know in advance how many times to execute a loop, use a `For...Next` loop. If your code needs to test some condition to see whether to continue running the loop, use the `Do...Loop` statement, which is available in multiple flavors. To repeat actions on the objects in a collection, use a `For Each...Next` loop, discussed in Chapter 10.

✔ The `With` statement allows you to perform multiple actions by using the same object without having to name the object in each action. The `With` statement is covered in Chapter 10.

Control structures lend clarity, organization, and . . . well, structure to your program. They make it relatively easy to trace the branches of the path that your program may follow as it runs.

Control structure anatomy

What makes a control structure a "structure" is the fact that it's not just a single statement, but a whole block of them. Your basic `If...Then` statement serves as a model for all control structures:

```
If a < b Then  ' "If a is less than b, then"
  b = a  ' "set the value of b equal to a"
  a = c  ' "and then set the value of a equal to c."
End If  ' "That's all—proceed with the program."
```

The skeleton of this structure is an opening statement that identifies its type and sets up a condition and a statement that tells VBA where the structure ends. Sandwiched in between is the meat of the structure — the statements that actually *do* something.

All control structures have this general outline, but in some of them, the structure's condition comes in the last statement rather than the first.

Nested control structures

When you're talking about control structures, *nesting* means placing one structure inside another, above the statement that marks the end of the first structure. VBA enters the second structure before it finishes executing the first. Nesting is a necessity for solving many complex, real-life programming problems. You can nest control structures to as many levels as you think necessary.

In the following example, a `Do While...Loop` structure is nested inside an `If...Then` structure, and another `If...Then` structure is nested inside the `Do While...Loop`:

```
If a < b Then  ' Start of outer If...Then
  Do While b > c  ' Start of nested Do While...Loop
    b = b - 1
    If c > d Then  ' Start of nested (inner) If...Then
      d = a
    End If  ' End of inner If...Then
  Loop  ' End of Do While...Loop
End If  ' End of outer If...Then
```

Use indents!

Consistent indenting is vital to writing understandable code. In the example in the preceding section, each pair of statements that defines a structure is indented by the same amount. Indentation makes it easy to see which End If statement belongs to which If...Then structure, for example. The statements that execute within a given structure are all indented by the same amount, so you can see that they are under the jurisdiction of that structure.

The Road Taken: Using Condition Expressions

Making choices is fundamental in software, as it is in life. Although they are simple in concept, decision-making control structures are among the most powerful programming tools at your disposal. "All" that these structures do is choose which of two or more different blocks of code to execute. But after one block executes and the other does not, you can say with Frost, "And that has made all the difference."

To decide whether to execute a block of code, three of VBA's control structures evaluate a *condition expression* that you write. These three include the Do...Loop looping structure, If...Then, and Select Case. I devote the rest of this section to the condition expressions used in all three of these structures. Two other decision-making control structures, For...Next and For Each...Next, don't use condition expressions.

How condition expressions work

If...Then, Select Case, and Do...Loop structures all decide what to do based on one simple test: Is the condition True, or is it False? The condition in question can be any VBA expression. (Remember that 0 is equal to False in VBA. All other values are considered to be True.)

Most often, condition expressions are built around a comparison operator that compares the values of two subexpressions. VBA's set of comparison operators are listed and discussed in some detail in Chapter 9. You can get the basic idea, however, by looking at the sample statements in the following table. Are the expressions in the table True or False? Only the control structure knows.

Expression	Translation in English
a < b	a is less than b.
b = c	b is equal to c.
colTBears("Henry") Is objCurrentBear	The object stored in the colTBears collection under the key "Henry" is the same one now referred to by the objCurrentBear variable.
sqr (1/x * 29.3234) >= CDbl (strNumber) + 12	The square root of the quantity 1 divided by x times 29.3234 is greater than or equal to the numeric value of the string variable strNumber plus 12.

Condition expressions without comparison operators

Although most condition expressions contain comparison operators, you're free to create conditions without them. Before I explain how this works, though, some background is in order.

I discuss this topic not to encourage you to write condition expressions without comparison operators, but because many programmers do. You commonly see such condition expressions in the code published in programming magazines and posted on the Internet. Until you live and breathe VBA, however, I suggest that you include comparison operators in your condition expressions for clarity's sake, even when they're not strictly necessary.

Now for the details. As you know, the value of a Boolean variable is always equal to either True or False. So the expression

```
boolUnder18 ' value can be only True or False
```

obviously works fine as a condition in a conditional statement, such as

```
If boolUnder18 Then
  GiveDiscount
End If
```

But because True and False have numeric values, you can use any numeric expression as a condition. These expressions are all valid conditions:

```
1234 ' Always True
0    ' Always False
True ' Always True
False ' Always False
intHowManyPets ' False if intHowManyPets = 0
lngA + lngB + lngC ' False if sum = 0
```

Object properties often represent Boolean (True/False) values, so expressions such as frmHelpWindow.Enabled are often tested as conditions, without comparison operators.

You can't use strings or objects as conditions by themselves; however, they work fine as components in expressions constructed with appropriate comparison operators.

Using logical operators in conditions

Introduced and listed in Chapter 9, logical operators evaluate two subexpressions separately as True or False and then combine them according to a set of rules to produce a final value — also True or False — based on a set of rules.

The most important logical operators — or at least the ones that are easiest to figure out how to use — are And, Or, and Xor. The following table shows how these operators work.

Operator	Returns True	Examples	Result
And	Only if *both* subexpressions are True	3*2 = 6 And 12 > 11	True
		2+2 = 4 And 4-2 = 1	False
Or	If *either or both* subexpressions are True	10 > 20 And 20 > 10	True
		5 < 4 And 6 < 5	False
Xor	If only one subexpression is True (False if both subexpressions are True or both are False)	5 + 5 < 9 Xor 5 + 5 = 10	True
		5 + 5 > 9 Xor 5 + 5 = 10	False

If you're so inclined, you can combine multiple logical operations in a single condition expression. Feast your eyes on this expression:

```
(a + b > 20 And c = 10) Or (objDoor.Open)
```

In English, this example can be translated as "This expression is true if either:

a + b is greater than 20, and also c = 10; or

the Open property of the objDoor object is False."

Unless you're so smart that you really don't need a computer, don't go overboard with logical operators in a single expression. Above all, use parentheses to clarify what the operators are comparing. In the preceding example, the parentheses around the objDoor.Open subexpression clarify that it is being "Or'd" with the first sub-expression.

Using If...Then Statements

By far the most commonly used conditional statements are If...Then and its variations, If...Then...Else and If...ElseIf. You can see lots of examples of If...Then statements in other chapters, but in this section they occupy center stage.

The basic form: If...Then

At its most basic, an If...Then statement executes a special block of code if the condition that you feed it is True, but simply does nothing if the condition is False. The syntax is:

```
If condition Then
(statements to execute if condition is True)
End If
```

For a simple example of a complete If...Then statement, refer to the "Control structure anatomy" section at the beginning of this chapter.

Heed these few points concerning If...Then statements:

✔ The condition is a condition expression of the type described earlier in this chapter in the section "The road taken: Using condition expressions." If the condition is True, VBA executes the statements between If... and End If. If the condition is False, VBA skips these statements, continuing with the next statement in your program following End If.

✔ Notice that the Then keyword goes on the same line as the If and the condition expression. VBA won't know what to think if you drop Then to the following line, and an error results (unless you use the underscore line-continuation character).

✔ Be sure to include the End If statement. Otherwise, VBA displays an error, because it can't identify which statement is the last in the block.

One-liners with If...Then

When an If...Then structure needs to execute a single statement only if the condition is True, you can put the entire thing on one line. In that case, an End If statement isn't required — in fact, it's illegal. The statement

```
If curPrice > 20 Then MsgBox "Warning! Price too high!"
```

functions identically to this structure:

```
If curPrice > 20 Then
  MsgBox "Warning! Price too high!"
End If
```

If...Then...Else statements

If you want your program to choose between two alternative blocks of code based on a condition, you need an If...Then...Else statement. In this case, one block is executed if the condition is True, and a completely differ-ent block is executed if the condition is False. Here's the syntax:

```
If condition Then
(statements to execute if condition is True)
Else
(statements to execute if condition is False)
End If
```

If the condition is True, VBA executes the first block of statements and then skips the rest of the structure to the line of code following the End If state-ment. If the condition is False, on the other hand, only the statements in the block following Else get executed.

In the following example, the condition expression checks to see if the con-trol in a UserForm is a command button. If so, the expression paints the button's background color red. All other controls are painted cyan (sky blue).

```
If TypeOf ctlCurrentControl Is CommandButton Then
  ctlCurrentControl.BackColor = &HFF& 'Red
Else
  ctlCurrentControl.BackColor = &HFFFF00 'Cyan
End If
```

In the example, you can assume that the ctlCurrentControl variable already holds an object reference to a particular control on the form. The TypeOf keyword allows you to check whether the object referred to by a variable or other object reference is of a specific type — in this case, a CommandButton object.

If...Then complexities: The introduction

Frequently, you need to test two or more conditions before you know what path your program should take. It's just like in real life. If you were writing a book about VBA, you may be thinking something like "If I finish by the deadline, and if I don't run out of money before then, and if the dollar holds its value against the peso, I can go to Mexico for two weeks in October. But if the dollar falls, I'll have to settle for Turlock."

Depending on the specific tests involved, you may need to include ElseIf clauses in your If...Then structure or to nest one or more levels of If...Then statements.

Complexities, Part I: Using If...ElseIf statements

Use the ElseIf keyword to test a new condition when you want to execute certain statements only if the first condition *isn't* True. The syntax is as follows:

```
If condition1 Then
(statements to execute if condition1 is True)
ElseIf condition2
(statements to execute if condition1 is False but
      condition2 is True)
ElseIf condition3
(statements to execute if condition1 and condition2 are
      both False but condition3 is True)
... (additional ElseIf clauses)
Else ' optional clause
(statements to execute if all the conditions are False)
End If
```

Only one ElseIf clause is required, but you can have as many ElseIf clauses as you like. The Else clause is optional, but if it is included, it must be the last one in the structure.

To put this monstrosity into action, imagine a program that helps you inventory your camera store's stock of film. A roll of film that has already expired shouldn't be counted. But if the film is still good, the program should add it to the inventory count for the correct type of film.

The following code fragment performs this job. The code assumes that you have an object that represents a roll of film and that the object has properties for expiration date, type of film, and color (versus black and white).

```
If objRollOfFilm.ExpDate < Date Then
  MsgBox "This film is no good."
ElseIf objRollOfFilm.Type = "Slide" Then
  intCountSlide = intCountSlide + 1
ElseIf objRollOfFilm.Color Then
  intCountColorPrint = intCountColorPrint + 1
Else
  intCountBWPrint = intCountBWPrint + 1
End If
```

The initial statement checks the `ExpDate` property of the object against the current date. If the date has already passed, the program displays a message box to that effect, and that's it. Only if the film is still good — in other words, if the first condition is `False` — is the first `ElseIf` clause executed. This clause looks at the film object's `Type` property. If this property is `"Slide"`, the count of slide rolls is incremented by the next statement.

If the film is some other type, however, the program skips to the next `ElseIf` clause, where the object's `Color` property is tested without a comparison operator (you can assume that this property can take only `True` or `False` as its value). If the value is `True`, the roll is counted as color print film. If the value is `False`, the `Else` statement near the end is the only place left to go — and the roll is counted in the black-and-white print category.

In an `If...ElseIf` structure, only the statements associated with the first `True` condition are executed. After those statements run, any remaining `ElseIf` and `Else` clauses are skipped.

Complexities, Part II: Nesting If...Then statements

Nested `If...Then` statements are sort of the opposite of `If...ElseIf` statements. Use these statements when you want to test a second condition to decide whether to execute a block of code, but only if the first condition is `True`. Nesting two `If...Then` statements is like saying, "If X is `True` *and* Y is `True`, I'm going to do A, B, and C."

You can nest `If...Then` statements of any variety — `If...Then...Else`, `If...ElseIf`, or garden-variety `If...Then` — in any combination. In schematic form, here's a pair of nested `If...Then` statements:

```
If condition1 Then
  If condition2 Then
  (statements that execute if both condition1 and
      condition2 are True)
  ElseIf condition3 Then
  (statements that execute if condition1 and condition3 are
      True but condition2 is False)
  End If  ' Ends the inner If...Then block
(other statements that execute if condition1 is True,
      regardless of condition2)
Else
(statements that execute only if condition1 is False)
End If
```

The following simple example of nested If...Then statements displays a congratulatory message box for high grades achieved with a minimum "full-time" class load:

```
If sngGPA > 3.5 Then
  If sngUnits > 10 Then
    MsgBox "You're on the Dean's List!"
  End If
End If
```

Complexities, Part III: Using logical operators in conditions

Using logical operators in condition expressions can be a more elegant alternative to ElseIf clauses and nested If...Then structures — but only when just one branch of a multiple-condition path has the statements that you want to execute.

Look at the code fragment at the end of the preceding section. You can accomplish exactly the same goal with a single If...Then statement, as follows:

```
If sngGPA > 3.5 And sngUnits > 10 Then
  MsgBox "You're on the Dean's List!"
End If
```

Conditional expressions constructed with logical operators have little value when you want to execute statements on more than one branch of the decision path. Try to consolidate this variation of the earlier example by using logical operators:

```
If sngGPA > 3.5 Then
  If sngUnits > 10 Then
    MsgBox "You're on the Dean's List!"
  Else
    MsgBox "You did well, part-timer!"
  End If
End If
```

The only solution I can come up with still requires two `If...Then` statements, which are just not nested:

```
If sngGPA > 3.5 And sngUnits > 10 Then
    MsgBox "You're on the Dean's List!"
End If
If sngGPA > 3.5 And sngUnits <= 10 Then
    MsgBox "You did well, part-timer!"
End If
```

Using Select Case Statements

`If...ElseIf` and nested `If...Then` statements are ideal for testing different expressions before deciding which block of code to execute. If, however, you need to test the *same* value against different conditions, a `Select Case` statement usually is the way to go. The syntax is

```
Select Case value
  Case test1
    (statements to be executed if value meets test1
       criteria)
  Case test2
    (statements to be executed if value meets test2
       criteria)
... ' additional Case clauses
  Case Else ' optional
    (statements to be executed if value meets none of the
       above criteria)
End Select
```

Testing conditions in Select Case statements

The `Select Case` structure doesn't directly use complete condition expressions of the type outlined earlier (see "The road taken: Using condition expressions"). Instead, you have to break up each condition into two parts, represented by `value` and `testn` in the syntax shown in the previous section. If the equivalent condition expression is

```
a + b > c
```

you can think of `value` as being the part to the left of the comparison operator (`a + b`) and `testn` as being everything to the right, including the operator (`> c`).

A sample Select Case statement

I definitely need to use an example to illustrate how a "real" Select Case structure may look. Here comes one now:

```
Select Case objRollOfFilm.Type
  Case "Slide"
    intCountSlide = intCountSlide + 1
  Case "ColorPrint"
    intCountColorPrint = intCountColorPrint + 1
  Case "BWPrint"
    intCountBWPrint = intCountBWPrint + 1
  Case Else
    MsgBox "Not a known type."
End Select
```

This code performs essentially the same job as the example that I use in the section on If...ElseIf statements earlier in this chapter (omitting the check for expired film). Since then, the hypothetical roll-of-film VBA object seems to have been modified — the black-and-white versus color information is now represented in the Type property, not in a separate Color property.

That being so, the program needs to work with only one value — the one returned by the Type property — but it must be compared with several possible alternatives. The Select Case statement is just what Dr. Dobbs ordered in this situation.

The example's first Case clause is equivalent to writing If objRollOfFilm.Type = "Slide" Then. That is, if the object's Type property is Slide, the program executes the next statement; if not, it moves on to Case clause number 2.

Notice, though, that the operator that you'd expect is missing from the tests in all three Case clauses. That's because in Select Case statements, equality is assumed to be the comparison that you're making.

The Case Else clause

If the value of the Type property isn't equal to the tests in any of the Case clauses, control falls to the Case Else clause, which is always the last one in a Select Case structure. In the above example, the result is the error message "Not a known type." A Case Else clause is optional because you may not want anything to happen if none of the criteria are satisfied. As in the example, though, it's often wise to include the Case Else clause, if only to alert you to unexpected values stored by your program.

More about Case clause tests . . . a lot more

The tests performed by the `Case` clauses in the previous example are sweet, simple tests of a single equality, as in "Is the `Type` property equal to such and so?" But you can do much more sophisticated testing with each `Case` clause.

This is easiest to illustrate with a numeric example. Suppose that your `Select Case` statement opens with the following line of code:

```
Select Case intPatientAge
```

In this example, the value being tested is an integer variable called `intPatientAge` that represents the age of a patient at a family-practice medical clinic. This value is the one to be tested in the `Case` clauses that follow. In the list below, I describe the kinds of tests you can make in `Case` clauses, and illustrate them with example clauses. Here's the list:

✔ You can test the value against a range, as follows:

```
Case 18 To 35
  Messages("YoungAdult").Print
```

Notice that you place the `To` keyword between the values that define the boundaries of the range. The range includes values and everything in between.

✔ You can test the value by using a comparison operator other than =, as follows:

```
Case Is > 65
  Messages("OlderAdult").Print
```

In this example, you're supposed to use the `Is` keyword before the comparison operator. Actually, you don't have to type `Is` — VBA puts it in for you if you omit it.

✔ You can perform multiple tests in the same `Case` clause, as follows:

```
Case 0 To 5, 15, Is > 55
  Messages("ImmunizationReminder").Print
```

Be sure to separate the tests with commas. By the way, a `Case` clause with multiple tests is equivalent to an expression built on a series of `Or` expressions — if the value passes *any* of the tests, the following statements get executed.

Repeating Yourself with Loops

Use a loop control structure to execute the same block of code more than once. Repeating one or more statements is a fundamental chore when you perform many mathematical computations, extract smaller data items from larger ones, and repeat an action on multiple items in a group.

VBA offers three main types of loop structures:

Loop Type	How It Loops
Do...Loop	While or until a condition is True
For...Next	A specified number of times
For Each...Next	For each object in a collection

When working with nested loops, remember this simple truth: The inner loop finishes looping before the outer loop.

Do-ing loops

The various versions of the Do...Loop statement all are designed to repeat a block of code indefinitely, until a condition is met. To determine whether to continue looping, a Do...Loop statement evaluates a condition expression of the type described in "The road taken: Using condition expressions" earlier in this chapter and used in If...Then statements.

Uses for Do...Loop structures are legion. These include:

- Displaying an error message repeatedly until the user makes a valid entry in a dialog box
- Reading data from a disk file until the end of the file is reached
- Searching for and counting the number of times a shorter string occurs within a longer one
- Idling your program for a set period
- Performing actions on all items in an array
- With If...Then statements, performing actions with multiple items that meet criteria in an array or collection (arrays and collections are detailed in Chapter 13)

Types of Do...Loop statements

VBA offers the `Do...Loop` in five flavors, all of which work very much alike. Here they are:

Statement	What It Does
`Do...Loop`	Repeat the block indefinitely, exiting when a conditional statement within the loop executes an `End Do` statement
`Do While...Loop`	Begin and repeat the block only if the condition is `True`
`Do...Loop While`	Execute the block once and then repeat it as long as the condition is `True`
`Do Until...Loop`	Begin and repeat the block only if the condition is `False`
`Do...Loop Until`	Execute the block once and then repeat it as long as the condition is `False`

The Do While...Loop statement

The prototypical `Do` structure is `Do While...Loop`. The syntax is

```
Do While condition
(statements that execute while condition is True)
Loop
```

When it encounters a `Do While` statement, VBA begins by evaluating the *condition*. If this expression turns out to be `False`, VBA ignores the rest of the loop, skipping to the program statement following `Loop`. But if the *condition* is `True`, VBA executes the statements in the block. When VBA reaches the `Loop` statement, it jumps back up to the `Do While` statement to test the condition again.

Typically, one or more statements in the body of the loop can change the value of the *condition,* so it may now be `False`. If so, VBA terminates the loop, skipping over it to the statement immediately following the `Loop` statement. But if the condition is still `True`, the loop statements again get executed.

The whole process repeats until at some point, the *condition* becomes `False`. In other words, there is no set limit on how many times the block of statements in the loop get executed. Assuming an infinite power supply and a computer that never breaks down, the loop repeats forever if the *condition* never becomes `False`.

A Do While...Loop example (two examples, actually)

The following example relies on two `Do While...Loop` statements to reverse the digits in a number selected by the user. It probably has no practical value — but it's cute, it runs in any VBA application, and it's short enough to illustrate how `Do` loops work.

```
Sub ReverseTheDigits()
Dim intOriginalNumber As Integer
Dim intOneDigit As Integer, strBackwardsNumber As String
Do While intOriginalNumber < 10
  intOriginalNumber = _
    InputBox("Type in an integer greater than 9.")
Loop
Do While intOriginalNumber
  intOneDigit = intOriginalNumber Mod 10
  strBackwardsNumber = strBackwardsNumber & intOneDigit
  intOriginalNumber = Int(intOriginalNumber / 10)
Loop
MsgBox strBackwardsNumber
End Sub
```

The example explained

The first `Do` loop checks the value of the number typed in by the user of the program to make sure that it's not a negative number and that it has at least two digits — otherwise, why bother reversing them? The first time the program encounters this loop, the value of the `intOriginalNumber` variable is zero because nothing has been assigned to it so far. Zero is less than 10, so the condition is `True`, and VBA enters the loop.

The loop contains one statement: an input box asking the user to type a suitable number. Once the number has been entered, the `Loop` statement sends VBA back to the top of the loop, where the number entered is checked. Only after a valid number has been entered does the loop terminate. (Notice that this example omits important validity checks, such as whether the number is an integer and whether it's not larger than the maximum value for an `Integer` variable.)

When VBA confirms a valid entry, it moves on to the next loop. The condition for executing this loop is that the variable containing the number must be greater than zero. Because a nonzero value is `True`, you can simply write `Do While intOriginalNumber` instead of `Do While intOriginalNumber > 0` — both versions work identically.

In the loop proper, a simple three-step procedure takes apart the digits of the original number, working from right to left, using the digits in reverse order to build a new string. You don't have to understand how this code works to figure out the loop, but it won't hurt you to know that:

✔ The first line uses the Mod operator to divide the number by 10 and assign only the remainder to the intOneDigit variable. Because you're dividing by 10, the remainder is the last (rightmost) digit of the original number.

✔ The second line takes the digit obtained by the first line and adds it to the end of the string under construction.

✔ The third line again divides the number by 10, this time keeping the result of the division in the original variable. The division effectively lops off the rightmost digit. Notice, however, that before the result is assigned to the variable, it is processed by the Int function. The Int function is necessary because, otherwise, VBA would round off the result — which could change the digits that were originally entered.

✔ As the loop loops, intOriginalNumber becomes 0 after all its digits have been processed (any digit divided by 10 is less than 1, and the Int function drops the fractional part of the result). In VBA-land, zero is False, so the loop ends, and the program displays the reversed number.

Other Do statements

Variations on the Do While...Loop are easy to understand once you get the basic form. This section discusses three of the alternative Do loops; see "When to use Do without While or Until" later in this chapter for the fourth.

Do...Loop While

The difference between the Do While...Loop and Do...Loop While statements is simple: Do While...Loop has the condition at the top of the loop, whereas in Do...Loop While, the condition comes at the end.

In a Do While...Loop structure, the loop is entered only if the condition is True the first time that the program reaches it. If the condition is False to start with, the statements in the loop never execute.

In a Do...Loop While structure, by contrast, the loop always executes at least once: the first time the program runs through the code. Only then is the condition tested, the loop repeating as long as the condition remains True. Use a Do...Loop While structure when the loop block contains a statement that sets a value in the condition before the condition gets tested.

Another situation that calls for a Do...Loop While structure is when you're performing an action on an item (such as a string or an array) that may have more than one element. If you already know that the item has at least one element, you want the loop statements to execute at least once and then repeat as many times as needed for the remaining components.

Do Until loops

The `Do While...Loop` and `Do Until...Loop` statements are functionally equivalent — that is, you can execute exactly the same statements with either one by modifying the condition expression to perform the opposite test. The `Do...Loop While` and `Do...Loop Until` pair are similarly complementary.

Pretend that you're Julia Child talking her audience through a recipe. You may say, "Keep whipping the batter as long as you see even the slightest little lump" or "Keep whipping the batter until it is perfectly smooth." Either way, you mean the same thing.

`Do While` and `Do Until` are similarly complementary. If the condition for a `Do While` statement is A = B, a `Do Until` statement with A <> B functions identically.

To Do or not to Do

At their most elegant, `Do` loops provide all the information that VBA needs to decide whether to execute the loop in the condition expression. Unfortunately, things aren't always so tidy in real-world programming. Sometimes, a change in a different condition occurring in the body of the loop demands a hasty exit, which is why VBA has an `Exit Do` statement.

Valid only in a `Do` structure, `Exit Do` summarily terminates the loop, passing program execution to the statement that comes after the loop. This example concatenates a string variable to an existing string, but if the variable contains more than one character, the loop terminates:

```
Do While strA < "Z"
  If Len(strA) > 1 Then
    Exit Do
  End If
  strB = strB & strA
  strA = GetNextCharacter
Loop
```

Normally, the `Exit Do` statement should appear in an `If...Then` or `Case Select` statement nested in the loop. That way, the loop runs normally unless some special or aberrant value occurs. You can also use `Exit Do` as a debugging device to bypass the loop temporarily, without having to comment out the code by placing a ' in front of each line.

When to use Do without While or Until

With standard `Do...While/Until...Loop` statements, you can test a condition at the beginning or end of a loop. But what if you want to test the condition somewhere *within* the loop?

In this situation, use a `Do...Loop` statement — without `While` or `Until`. This technique requires an `If` or `Select Case` statement nested inside the loop. One or more branches of the nested conditional statement include an `Exit Do` statement, allowing the program to terminate the loop when a specified condition is met.

Here's how a `Do...Loop` statement looks in schematic form:

```
Do
(statements to be executed with each pass of the loop)
If condition Then
    Exit Do
  End If
(more statements to be executed only if loop continues)
Loop
```

As you can see, this technique is appropriate when you want to execute some of the loop statements regardless of whether the condition is met. It's also useful if the loop should terminate under several different conditions.

Frequently, for example, you must validate a user entry based on several criteria. In the following example, a `Do...Loop` structure repeats the loop until the user enters a valid letter answer:

```
Sub GetAnAnswer()
strAnswer = InputBox("Enter your answer (A-E)")
Do
  If strAnswer = "" Then
    strAnswer = InputBox("You didn't enter anything." _
      & " Please type a letter between A and E.")
  ElseIf Len(strAnswer) > 1 Then
    strAnswer = InputBox("Your answer should be" _
      & " only one letter long. Please try again.")
  ElseIf strAnswer < "A" Or strAnswer > "E" Then
    strAnswer = InputBox("You typed an invalid" _
      & " character. Type a letter from A to E.")
  Else
      Exit Do
  End If
Loop
End Sub
```

The program executes the `Exit Do` statement only after all three validation criteria — expressed in the `If` and `ElseIf` clauses — have been met.

An alternative syntax that does exactly the same thing uses `Do While True` as the first line of the loop structure. Because `True` (the constant) is always a `True` value, the condition is always met, and VBA always enters the loop. Again, you need an `Exit Do` statement in the body of the loop to terminate the loop.

Repeating on count with For...Next loops

When you know how many times a loop should execute before the loop runs, use a `For...Next` loop. You specify how many passes VBA should make through the loop by supplying `start` and `end` values, which can be literal integers, variables, or even complex expressions. As the loop executes, a `counter` variable keeps track of the number of completed cycles. When the counter's value equals that of `end`, the loop is finished.

Simplified, the syntax of a `For...Next` structure is as follows:

```
For counter = start To end
(statements to be executed during each pass of the loop)
Next counter
```

Keeping it simple for starters, the following example procedure uses the Immediate window to display a message for each repetition of the loop (in the Visual Basic Editor, open the Immediate window by pressing Ctrl+G):

```
Sub CountToTen ()
Dim j As Integer
  For j = 1 To 10
     Debug.Print "This is pass " & j
  Next j
End Sub
```

In the above example, the `start` and `end` values are both literal numbers. When the loop begins, `j` is set to 1 — in other words, the value of `start` is assigned to the `counter` variable. Each time a loop cycle completes, the `Next j` statement increments `j` (raises its value by 1), and control shifts back to the beginning of the loop. When `j` finally equals 10, the loop terminates.

Important tips about For...Next loops

Keep your code easy to understand. Use 1 as the start value for a `For...Next` loop unless you have good reasons to choose another number.

Such good reasons do exist. One is when the value of the counter is used in the loop itself (not changed in the loop, mind you). If the loop takes some action based on consecutively numbered items, such as part numbers, you can use the actual values of the items as the `start` and `end` values. More commonly, you set `start` to 0 when you are working with arrays, as illustrated in the next section.

In the `Next counter` statement that ends a `For...Next` loop, the counter variable's name isn't actually required — the keyword `Next` by itself automatically calculates the next counter value and sends VBA back to the top of the structure. However, you should definitely train yourself to include the counter in the `Next` statement. That way, when you nest two or more `For...Next` loops, you can see at a glance to which loop a given `Next` statement belongs.

Do not change the value of the counter variable within a `For...Next` loop. Because the counter is just another variable, it's possible — and sometimes tempting — to write code that changes the counter value. Resist the urge. Fool with the counter, and the loop is likely to skip important steps or to go on infinitely.

Although you can specify the `end` value for a `For...Next` loop with a variable, changing the variable value after the loop starts doesn't affect execution of the loop. The loop still executes the number of times dictated by the original `end` value.

For...Next loops and arrays

`For...Next` loops are perhaps most useful for working with *arrays,* which are named storage bins for sets of data items. I cover arrays in detail in Chapter 13; still, this chapter's discussion of `For...Next` loops would be incomplete without mentioning the use of these loops with these important data baskets.

You can use a `For...Next` loop to fill an array with a set of calculated values, as in the following example:

```
Dim intArrayOfSquares (14) As Integer
For a = 0 to 14
  intArrayOfSquares (a) = a * a
Next a
```

The example code begins by declaring an array of 15 integer values (15, not 14, because VBA normally numbers the first item in an array 0). The code then uses a `For...Next` loop to assign a value to each item in the array, counting from 0 to 14. Notice that the variable `a` is used not only as the counter, but also as the array `index`, pointing to a numbered slot in the array.

Nested For...Next loops

Like other VBA control structures, `For...Next` loops can be nested within one another — or within other control structures — as deeply as you need to nest them. The following perfectly useless bit of code illustrates the concept:

```
Dim sngR ' R probably stands for random number
Randomize ' initialize the random number generator
For A = 1 To 5
 sngR = Rnd ()
 For B = 1 To 5
   Debug.Print sngR * Rnd ( )
 Next B
Next A
```

If you're observant, you can trace the steps that VBA follows to execute this code. Here they are:

1. **Preliminaries first.**

   The code starts by declaring a variable and initializing VBA's random-number generator.

2. **The outer** For...Next **loop starts.**

   VBA calls the Rnd function to assign a random number to the sngR variable.

3. **Then comes the inner** For...Next **loop.**

   This loop calculates five other numbers by repeatedly multiplying sngR by a new random value during each pass. The results appear in the Immediate window.

4. **The inner loop terminates after it completes all five calculations.**

   Now the outer loop takes over again. Obeying the Next A statement, VBA jumps back to the top of the outer loop.

5. **Steps 2 and 3 are repeated for four more passes of the outer loop.**

This example may be a trivial one, but it could be extended to perform Genuinely Useful Work. Suppose that you want to write a multimedia program that selects five CDs at random, playing five random selections from each one. Assuming that you know how to write the code that selects CDs and plays individual selections, the preceding example should get you started.

As discussed in Chapter 13, nested For...Next loops are also the key to working systematically with multidimensional arrays. Each loop corresponds to one dimension of the array.

Get out now with an Exit For

The Exit For statement provides a quick way to terminate a For...Next loop before the end of the loop has actually been reached. This statement is typically used within a conditional statement (If...Then or Case Select) nested within the main For...Next loop.

One use of the `Exit For` escape hatch is to test an array for invalid data, halting whatever process is underway if an aberrant value is detected.

Suppose that you learn that a malevolent genius inserted an array containing false information into your pricelist data. You happen to know that this evil-doer left his trademark behind. As you update the price information to reflect inflationary price hikes in each array, you want to be sure that the price data hasn't been tampered with. This code does both jobs at once:

```
For p = 1 To varArraySize
  If varPriceArray(p) = "Kilroy was here!" Then
    MsgBox "Infested data in this array!"
    Exit For
    End If
  varPriceArray(p) = varPriceArray(p) * sngCOLA
Next p
```

Custom steps

The complete syntax of the `For...Next` statement includes an optional `Step` argument in the first line of the structure, as in this example:

```
Sub ListOddNumbers
Dim strOddNumbers As String
For F = 1 to 33 Step 2
  strOddNumbers = strOddNumbers & F & " "
Next F
MsgBox "Odd numbers between 1 and 33 are:" & _
  Chr(13) & strOddNumbers
End Sub
```

In the example, the `For...Next` loop constructs a string out of all the odd numbers in the range defined by the `start` and `end` values. The counter variable F increases by 2 — the value of the `Step` argument — with each pass of the loop. Because the start value is 1, F is always an odd number, simplifying your programming task in the body of the loop.

In general, then, the `Step` argument tells VBA how to calculate the next value of the counter each time the end of the loop is reached. Normally, with no explicit `Step` argument, the counter is increased by 1. You can specify a different constant value to add to the counter, however, by listing a `Step` argument. You can even use a negative number as the `Step` argument if you want the loop to count backward.

Once again, try not to be too tricky. An unconventional `Step` argument can introduce hard-to-find errors, just because you're not used to working with it. So use an explicit `Step` argument only when the programming problem clearly calls for it — and even then, consider alternative solutions that may be less likely to trip you up.

Interrupting the Flow with GoTo

If your program is behaving in an unruly fashion, tell it where to go — by transferring execution to another location in the procedure. A GoTo statement, combined with a special label statement at the destination, allows you to hop at will from place to place within a procedure. A *label* is a statement that simply marks a location in your code. To enter a label, type its name (VBA naming rules apply) followed by a colon.

A GoTo example

In this example, a GoTo statement redirects program flow out of the main part of the function to the SpecialValue label when an unusual value is encountered:

```
Function GoToExample (ItemNumber As Integer)
 Dim intR As Integer
 Select Case ItemNumber
   Case 2412
     GoTo SpecialValue
   Case Is < CutOffValue
     DoSomething
   Case >= CutOffValue
     DoHardlyAnything
 End Select
 (statements that execute no matter what)
 GoToExample = intR
 Exit Function
SpecialValue:
 DoSomethingSpecial
 GoToExample = -intR
End Function
```

Notice the format of the SpecialValue label, which sits on a line by itself, followed by a colon. The colon is crucial — VBA gets indigestion and displays an error message if you leave it out.

GoTo caveats

Use of the GoTo statement is considered to be inferior programming form. The problem is that it creates *spaghetti code,* with the path of execution wandering all over the place. Spaghetti is hard to unravel, and code containing more than an occasional GoTo quickly becomes impossible to read. Whenever possible, use control structures to direct program execution.

Occasionally, however, a `GoTo` statement is the most practical way to get your program to do what you want it to. Your brain may be just too tired to come up with the intricate set of nested loops and conditionals required to implement a complex set of criteria. At such times, `GoTo` may cut through the maze. Just don't use it too often.

Chapter 13

Advanced Data Storage: Arrays and Collections

• •

• •

*W*ith any luck, you should by this point be comfortable working with variables to represent data of all types, from simple numbers and text strings to sophisticated and powerful objects. But the VBA built-in data types don't meet every need. Frequently, you need to work with similar chunks of information as a group. That situation calls for an *array* — a structured storage compartment for multiple data elements of the same type.

You can work with sets of various types of items in `Collection` *objects* that you create based on a built-in class supplied with VBA. Within some limitations, collections can have significant advantages over arrays.

Occasionally, you may find it convenient to create your own *user-defined data type*. As an individual variable, a user-defined data type is primarily helpful in clarifying your code; it allows you to refer to separate but related items as parts of an entire entity. But an array based on a user-defined data type can be a powerful device for working with groups of complex items.

Seeing A-rray of Hope

Suppose that you have a list of numbers representing prices, test scores, or the distances of certain astronomical objects from Earth. Imagine that you type that list on a piece of paper, with each item in a separate row. What you wind up with is a simple array. Here is an example:

Surefire winning lottery numbers

214236	545273	371453
891982	000000	941241

In a list of similar items, like this one, the individual items have unique values but otherwise lack special identifying characteristics. If you want someone else to ponder an item, you say something like, "It's the third item in the lottery-number list." VBA arrays work exactly this way.

Referring to the items in an array

Each VBA array has a name that corresponds to the title of a list on paper (like the one of lottery numbers at the beginning of this section). To work with an individual item in the array, you refer to it by the array name and an *index* — a positive-integer number specifying the item's slot in the array. The expression `intLottoArray(3)` refers to the third item (or fourth, depending on the numbering system in effect) in the array called `intLottoArray`. As you can guess, the `int` at the beginning of the array name tells you that this array is supposed to be an array of integer values. Therefore, it's a safe bet that the data stored in `intLottoArray(3)` is an integer.

Understanding array data

You should be clear about two key points regarding arrays:

✔ **You can create arrays of any data type.** VBA happily stores strings, dates, currency values, and all numeric data types in arrays.

✔ **An array can hold only one data type.** You can't build an array with separate slots for both Date and String data type values.

True as this second limitation may be, you can easily overcome it. As you know, the Variant data type can store any kind of VBA data, and arrays of Variants are perfectly okay. Information stored in a Variant consumes significantly more memory than it would if it were stored as a more specific data type, however, and this overhead can really add up with arrays of any size. Besides, a random assortment of different kinds of data stuffed into an array rarely makes sense.

On the other hand, working with related items of varying types in organized sets is common. That's the idea behind the typical database. In an address-book database, for example, each record represents a set of information items (such as name and address) about the same general topic (a person in your life). For this kind of data, creating a user-defined data type is the way to go — and you find out how to do so later in this chapter (see "Defining Your Own Data Types").

Using arrays of multiple dimensions

Before I get any deeper into working with the individual values stored in an array, I want to back up and consider arrays in general in more detail. One important concept to make room for somewhere is that arrays can have multiple *dimensions*. The simple list of lottery numbers in the example at the beginning of this section is a one-dimensional array. A table or spreadsheet with rows and columns corresponds to a two-dimensional array, as in this example:

Daily sightings of mud hens by three unnamed observers

12	2	21
4	9	3
11	0	0

Imagining arrays of three dimensions isn't much of a strain. Figure 13-1 shows a diagrammatic representation of one such three-dimensional array.

Although forming a mental picture of an array with more than three dimensions is tough, VBA has no trouble with them. VBA arrays can have up to 60 dimensions.

Declaring arrays

Like ordinary variables, arrays must be declared before you can use them to store data. Fortunately, declaring an array is just like declaring a variable, with one addition to the declaration statement. Here are some examples:

```
' Declare one-dimensional array of Date data:
Dim datTimeOfImpact (cdatMaxObservations) As Date
' Declare array of Currency data, but don't set its size:
Public curPriceQuotes () As Currency
' Declare four-dimensional array of Integer data:
Dim intArrayOfIntegers (34, 13, 29, 4) As Integer
```

As you can see, the obvious difference between declaring an ordinary variable and declaring an array is that you add parentheses following the name. The parentheses can be empty, as in the middle example. Alternatively, the parentheses can contain values specifying the size of each dimension in the array. (Notice that in the first example, a named constant supplies the size of the one dimension in the array.)

Figure 13-1:
This
diagram
represents
a three-
dimensional
array as
a set of
cubes, each
containing
a number.

Be sure to specify a data type when you declare an array by including the As Type part of the declaration. If you don't, VBA creates an array of Variants, which increases the memory requirements of your program and slows its operation. Arrays of Variants are permitted and may be the way to go in some situations, but you can declare them explicitly when appropriate.

The total number of individual data elements in an array is equal to the product of the sizes of each dimension. You already knew this fact, of course — but this point deserves a brief moment of your fully conscious attention. To figure the total number of integer data elements in the array `intArrayOfIntegers` (the third example in the set of sample array declarations at the beginning of this section), you would multiply $35 \times 14 \times 30 \times 5$. That little bitty declaration reserves space for an array consisting of 73,500 elements.

You may wonder why I say that the size of each dimension is one more than its value in the declaration statement (35 instead of 34 and so on). Read on for the answer.

Understanding array element numbering

Unless you specify otherwise, the elements in an array are indexed, or numbered, beginning with 0 — or, to put it slightly differently, element 0 is the first one in the array. For this reason, the value that you enter when sizing an array should be one less than the number of elements that you want to store. If the array is supposed to hold 10 elements, for example, enter 9 as the size.

When you later access the individual data elements in the array, you must keep this numbering system in mind. A reference to `intArray (1)` is actually a reference to the second element in the array.

If you don't like counting from 0, you can start numbering your array from a different number — which usually would be 1. To set things up so that VBA numbers all arrays in the current module starting from 1, place the statement

```
Option Base 1
```

in the module's declarations section (before any procedures). This statement affects only arrays in the same module, so you must include it in every module if that's how you want to number all your arrays.

You can also specify a numbering scheme for any dimension in an individual array. Here's an example:

```
Dim sngNumbers (55 To 75, 7 To 16, 99)
```

This example declares a three-dimensional array whose first dimension consists of 21 slots numbered from 55 to 75. The second dimension holds 10 slots starting with number 7, whereas the last dimension has 100 slots beginning with 0.

Declaring fixed arrays

If you specify the size of the array when you declare it, its size remains fixed; your program can't make the array smaller or larger later. To declare a *fixed array,* include the size of each of the array's dimensions in the parentheses in the declaration statement. The statement

```
Dim strHappyThoughts (9, 19) As String
```

declares a two-dimensional array that *always* holds 10 rows and 20 columns of string data (of course, the array doesn't actually store the data in rows and columns, but thinking of the array as a tabular list is helpful).

Fixing the size of an array when you declare it can be good practice if you know for sure that the array size won't change. That way, your code can't accidentally make changes in the array size. A potential disadvantage: After the array is declared, the memory that it occupies is reserved for the life of the program and can't be released for other uses.

Declaring dynamic arrays

Declare your array as a *dynamic array* if you

- ✔ Don't or can't know the size of your array before your program runs.
- ✔ Know that the array's size will change during the course of your program.
- ✔ Want to free the memory that it occupies for other variables when you're through using the array. A large array can use a great deal of memory, which you can liberate if the array is dynamic.

To declare a dynamic array, just leave out the array's size when you declare it. The statement

```
Dim dateBirthdays () As Date
```

prepares VBA for an array of `Date` data elements but doesn't actually create the array.

ReDim-ming dynamic arrays

A dynamic array can't hold any data until you actually create the array by specifying its size. Use the `ReDim` ("re-dimension") statement to do so, as in this example of a one-dimensional array:

```
ReDim dateBirthdays (intNumberOfBirthdays - 1)
```

Notice that the size of the array created by this statement is based on a variable, presumably one whose value has been determined by a previous sequence in the program. You have to subtract 1 from this value to adjust for the way that VBA starts numbering arrays from 0 — assuming you haven't changed the default numbering system as described in "Understanding array element numbering."

You must use the `ReDim` statement inside a procedure. You can re-`ReDim` a dynamic array as many times as you like, completely redefining the number of dimensions and their sizes. Just keep in mind that, ordinarily, resizing an array destroys its current contents. Also, you can't change the data type stored in the array except under special circumstances that are too complicated to explain here.

Preserving data when resizing an array

To hold on to some of the data when you resize an array, include the `Preserve` keyword in your `ReDim` statement. The following sequence of statements declares a dynamic array, creates it as a two-dimension array of specific size, and then makes the second dimension larger without destroying its existing contents:

```
Dim dblGalacticMasses () As Double
...
ReDim Preserve dblGalacticMasses (1 To 30, 1 To 50)
...
ReDim Preserve dblGalacticMasses (1 To 30, 1 To 100)
```

Actually, `Preserve` is of limited value — it doesn't allow you to change the number of dimensions in the array, and you can resize only the last dimension (you must still include the sizes of the other dimensions in the `ReDim Preserve` statement, however). Making the array smaller is legal, but if you do so, data in the deleted elements vanishes forever.

Addressing elements in an array

To work with a particular element in an array in your code, list the array name followed by the element's index in parentheses. The *index* contains an integer value for each array dimension. The expression strSayings (4,6), for example, uniquely identifies the string data at row 4, column 6 in a two-dimensional array of strings.

Remember that the numbers or values that you use in an index identify items in an array based on the numbering system that you specified when you declared the array. If you declare an array with the statement Dim strSayings (10, 20) As String, the expression strSayings (4,6) identifies the data at the fifth row and seventh column of the array. If the declaration was Dim strSayings (4 To 10, 6 To 50) As String, the same expression locates the data in the first row and first column.

Using array elements in code

With this system, you can use array data elements just as you would variables. You can

✔ Assign a value to an array element. The following example assigns a value to a single storage slot in a three-dimensional array of Currency values:

```
curBigDough(5,8,19) = 27.99
```

✔ Assign a value stored in an array to another variable, as follows:

```
datThatDate = datTheseDates(25,10)
```

✔ Use the value of an array element in an expression, as follows:

```
intA = 35 * (intB + intCounts(3,2))
```

Using variables in an array index

You're not restricted to literal values in the index, of course. Coding the index with variables is often crucial, as is allowing your program to decide which array element you need at the moment. The last line of the following program shows this method in action:

```
Sub FortuneTeller()
Dim strTodaysFortune(1 To 10)
Dim intUserChoice As Integer
strTodaysFortune(1) = "You become rich and famous."
strTodaysFortune(2) = "You will eat lunch with a stranger."
strTodaysFortune(3) = "Your stocks double in value!"
strTodaysFortune(4) = "You recall where you put your keys."
strTodaysFortune(5) = "A lovely bouquet arrives."
strTodaysFortune(6) = "You will skip lunch."
strTodaysFortune(7) = "All your dreams come true."
strTodaysFortune(8) = "You return overdue library books."
strTodaysFortune(9) = "No one sees your mismatched socks."
strTodaysFortune(10) = "You meet an old pal at fish market."
intUserChoice = InputBox("To see your fortune, enter a" _
   & " number between 1 and 10")
MsgBox strTodaysFortune(intUserChoice)
```

As an aside, this code would be greatly improved if you added statements to handle invalid entries by the user in the InputBox. Chapter 12 discusses the topic of validating data.

Finding the size of an array

Use the UBound function to discover how many slots are available in a given dimension of an array. UBound is especially useful when you're working with dynamic arrays, because you may not know how many elements an array contains at any given point in your program. The syntax is

```
UBound(arrayname, dimension)
```

The *arrayname* argument, obviously, is the name of the array you're working with, while the *dimension* argument is an integer that tells VBA which array dimension you're inquiring about. If you omit *dimension*, UBound returns the the size of the first dimension.

Assigning data to an array . . . in bulk

When you first create an array, the individual elements contain no valid information. At some point in your program, you need to fill those vacancies with some meaningful data. If you're filling multiple values at the same time, the most efficient way to do this is to use nested For...Next loops, one for each dimension in the array. The loop counter is usually a temporary variable declared in the procedure containing the loops.

The following little program illustrates this technique, filling a three-dimensional array with a consecutive series of integers starting with 1. Here's the code:

```
Const Size As Integer = 3
Dim dblMatrix (1 To Size, 1 To Size, 1 To Size) As Double
Sub ArrayFiller ( )
Dim I As Integer, J As Integer, K As Integer, X As Integer
X = 1
For I = 1 To Size
  For J = 1 To Size
    For K = 1 To Size
      dblMatrix(I, J, K) = X
      X = X + 1
    Next K
  Next J
Next I
End Sub
```

The nesting order for the loops determines the order in which data elements get filled. In turn, the order in which elements get filled often matters a great deal in determining their value.

Explaining how all this works in words alone is too complicated, so I'm going to use pictures. Refer back to the sample code at the beginning of this section. Imagine the three-dimensional array in the example as a cube, with little cubelets representing the slots for individual data elements. Figure 13-2 illustrates the thought experiment.

Notice that in the critical line of code `dblMatrix(I,J,K) = X + 1`, the variables `I`, `J`, and `K`, respectively, represent the first, second, and third dimensions of the array. In Figure 13-2, I arbitrarily labeled the cube's dimensions with these variables.

Now notice how those variables are used in the `For...Next` loops. The counter for the outermost loop is `I`; for the next loop, it's `J`; and for the innermost loop, it's `K`. The key point is that VBA runs through the loops starting from the innermost and working out. The two cubes in Figure 13-3 show two stages early in the filling of the array by the sample code.

What's happening is that while the innermost loop is looping, VBA holds the values of `I` and `J` constant. When the first pass of the innermost loop is complete, the `J` loop — the next one out — has its first chance to loop. This raises the value of `J`; then the innermost loop again runs through an entire cycle. The value of `I` changes only when `J` has looped three times. After `I` is increased, the next row of the array begins to fill (see Figure 13-4).

Figure 13-4:
The array's
second row
begins to fill
only when
the counter
for the
outermost
For...
Next loop
changes
value.

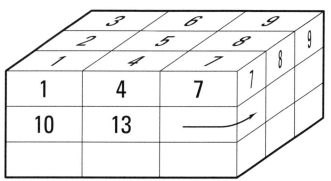

If you understand all this, you can see how changing the loops affects the values assigned to the array. Suppose that you reverse the nesting order of the loops, with K being the counter for the outermost loop. Here's how the code would read (notice that the variables are still in the same position in the assignment statement):

```
For K = 1 To Size
  For J = 1 To Size
    For I = 1 To Size
      dblMatrix(I, J, K) = X
      X = X + 1
    Next I
  Next J
Next K
```

The resulting array looks like Figure 13-5.

Figure 13-5:
This
diagram
illustrates
the order in
which the
revised
procedure
fills array
dimensions.

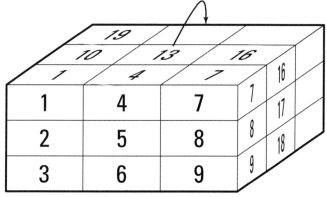

This array contains the same values as the first one, but the values are in different slots.

Copying one array to another

VBA 6 lets you assign the contents of one array to another with a simple statement such as

```
strCopyOfArray = strOriginalArray
```

The array on the left (the one receiving new contents) must be a dynamic array, but VBA ReDim's it for you automatically to match the dimensions of the array on the right. The receiving array must also be able to hold the type of data contained in the original array.

In VBA 5, you have to copy array data element by element, as in

```
' determine the size of the original array and ReDim the
'    second array to match
intArraySize = Ubound(strOriginalArray)
ReDim strCopyOfArray(intArraySize)

' perform the copy
For I = 0 to intArraySize
   strCopyOfArray(I) = strOriginalArray(I)
Next I
```

Managing Sets of Data with Collection Objects

When you need to manage sets of related information items, create a Collection object for the information. As I discuss in Chapter 10, VBA provides a generic Collection class for storage of just about anything. Based on this class, you can create as many Collection objects as you like. Although you can certainly use collections to store other objects, they can also hold just about any kind of data that VBA can handle.

A collection can store only a simple list of items, comparable to a one-dimensional array. But because collections are the most common types of arrays, they can do real service.

Weighing the trade-offs in using collections

When you're comfortable working with VBA objects, you may find that `Collection` objects are easier to use than arrays for handling sets of items. The `Add` and `Remove` methods make resizing the collection effortless; they are also much less likely to result in errors than repeatedly using `ReDim` statements in different parts of your program. (These advantages are especially significant when you must frequently add or remove individual items from the group.)

As a bonus, you can name individual items in the collection so that you can retrieve them by name later. This practice not only gives you an easy-to-remember handle for each element, but also makes accessing the data much quicker when your collection contains more than 100 elements.

One potential downside of using collections is the memory that they can consume. Collections use Variants to store all the information that they contain, and Variants use more memory than most other data types. In a large collection, the increased memory consumption can be significant.

But the most severe limitation of a generic VBA `Collection` object is that it can't store user-defined data types, which means that it isn't immediately suitable for work with database-type data (see the discussion of such data in "Defining Your Own Data Types" later in this chapter). You can overcome this limitation with some fairly simple programming, however. Besides, if you do serious database programming with VBA, you'll almost certainly be using the predefined database objects such as those provided in the Microsoft Jet (DAO) and ODBC libraries, instead of creating your own.

Creating Collection objects

Set up a `Collection` object in your program as you would any other object, using an `As` clause to specify the type of object. As you do with other objects, you can use either of two variations on the basic technique:

✔ You can declare a variable name for the object and then use a `Set` statement to create it. Notice that you must use the `New` keyword in the `Set` statement to create the new collection, as follows:

```
Dim colMixedBag As Collection
...
Set colMixedBag = New Collection ' Create collection
colMixedBag.Add "Howard, Ethel" ' Add a data element
```

✔ To have VBA create the object automatically the first time that you use the variable in your code, you can declare it with the New keyword, as follows:

```
Dim colSetOfStuff As New Collection
...
' The next statement creates the Collection while
' adding an integer to it.
colSetOfStuff.Add intStuffing
```

Adding data to a collection

After you create your collection, use its Add method to fill it with data, just as you would to add objects to your VBA application's built-in collections (see Chapter 10). The examples in the previous section show the Add method in action.

The complete syntax of the Add method is as follows:

```
Add (item[, key][, before index][, after index])
```

The *item* expression is required. This expression can be a literal value, a variable, an object reference, or a complex expression involving two or more of these components — anything that returns a value that VBA recognizes. The remaining terms in the Add method are optional; they're described in the very next section.

Assigning keys to items

Although you can always refer to an item in a collection by its index or "slot number," giving the item a meaningful name can be helpful. Supply the name as a string when you add the item to the collection, as follows:

```
colFinancials.Add 14323.44, "February sales"
```

The preceding statement adds the value 14323.44 to the colFinancials collection. At the same time, the statement creates a *key* (a name) for the item. String variables work fine, too.

A key isn't just easier to remember than a numeric index; it's the *only* reliable key for quick access to an individual item in a collection. Because of the way that the Add and Remove methods work, the positions of specific data items in a collection can change. If item 63 becomes item 29, you can still pull out its value if you know its *key* name.

The only way to assign a key is with the Add method. To assign a key to an item that doesn't have one or to change the existing key, you must Add the item all over again and Remove the original copy.

Adding an item at a specific location

Sometimes, organizing the items in a collection in a particular order is convenient. But if you can't add the items sequentially in the desired order, no problem — the Add method allows you to insert any item where you want it to go. Use the method's optional before and after terms for this purpose.

Suppose that you want to insert a new item just before the 35th item in an existing collection. Here's the statement that you may use:

```
colAnimals.Add strSpecies, before 35
```

The added item becomes the 35th member of the collection, pushing down all the subsequent members. (Unlike arrays, collections are numbered beginning with 1.) You can also use an existing item's key to tell VBA where to insert the new item, as in

```
colVegetables.Add strVariety, after "Tomato"
```

In this case, VBA searches the collection for an existing item whose key is Tomato, inserting the new item immediately after it.

Paint or get off the ladder — you can include before or after in an Add method statement, but not both.

Adding multiple items efficiently

You can use a For...Next loop to add multiple data items to a collection efficiently, similar to the way that you fill an array, as follows:

```
Dim X As Integer, Y As Integer
Y = 12
For X = 1 To 30
  colHouseOfValues.Add Y * X
Next X
```

Removing items

To state the obvious, the Remove method deletes an item from the collection. You can identify the object that you want to excise by its index number or by its key, as in these examples:

```
colMineral.Remove 2123
colMineral.Remove "Bauxite"
```

Remember that when you remove an item, VBA fills in the gap, so to speak. The index numbers of all the other items farther down in the list decrease by 1.

Count-ing your collection

Losing track of the size of your collection is easy, especially after you Add or Remove a few items. VBA's generic Collection object has only one property — the Count property — but it's vital. You can assign the property to a variable, as follows:

```
intCollectionSize = col20Questions.Count
```

You can also test it in a conditional expression, as follows:

```
If colPrices.Count > 1000
   MsgBox "We have too many entries!"
End If
```

In addition, you can use the Count property in a For...Next loop to perform some action on the entire collection, as follows:

```
Dim Z As Integer
For Z = 1 To colPrices.Count
   MsgBox "The price is " & colPrices(Z)
Next Z
```

A better practice, however, is to use a For Each...Next loop as described in Chapter 12.

Accessing items in a collection

To identify the specific item in a collection that you want to work with, you can use the item's index number or key (name), if it has one. For example, you might assign the value of a collection item to another variable, as shown here:

```
datBirthdate = colBirthdays("Sally Tran")
```

Unfortunately, you must keep track of the keys yourself — VBA doesn't provide a way to read the keys of an existing collection. And you can't modify an item's key without deleting the item from the collection and adding it again. Similarly, you can't place a new value in an existing collection item. The following assignment statement does *not* work:

```
colInventory(1465) = 119
```

Again, the only way to change a value in a collection is to remove the existing item and add a new one containing the new value. Dictionary objects, discussed in Chapter 17, overcome these limitations of collections.

Using collections for database-type data

As I said, collections based on VBA's generic `Collection` class have limited value because you can't store user-defined types in them. You can work around this limitation by assigning keys very systematically. In the following example, each pass of the `For...Next` loop creates a database record in the collection. The record contains three fields, each of which is added by means of a key formed by concatenating a simple identifier with the current record number. Here's the code:

```
Dim I As Integer, strName As String
Dim strPhone As String, strAddress As String
For I = 1 to Total ' I identifies the record number
  ' Obtain data for this record
  strName = InputBox ("Enter name for this record")
  strPhone = InputBox ("Enter phone for this record")
  strAddress = InputBox ("Enter address for this record")
  ' Add "fields" for this record to collection
  colDatabase.Add strName, "Name" & I
  colDatabase.Add strPhone, "Phone number" & I
  colDatabase.Add strAddress, "Address" & I
Next I
```

You can then retrieve the information stored in a particular record by the identifier and number, as in this obvious example:

```
MsgBox colDatabase ("Name2")
```

If you plan to write a program of any complexity to manage database-style information, don't base it on simple collection objects; they have too many limitations. One alternative is to use plug-in database-access components, examples of which are covered in Chapter 18. If you want to do the work yourself, you should create your own classes for custom data objects. These classes can contain any combination of data types that you like, which you can access as properties. In addition, you can build in code to ensure that the correct type of information gets stored in each element. Class modules are covered, albeit briefly, in Chapter 17.

Defining Your Own Data Types

Unless you're a mathematician, multidimensional arrays of the same data type are of limited value. On the other hand, bread-and-butter data-management chores often call for working with *different* types of items in sets. A simple way to manage such information in a VBA program is to create a *user-defined data type* to hold it.

The tired filing-card analogy (shown in Figure 13-6) is still the best metaphor for this sort of information, although personal computers have been around for so long now that I don't know whether anybody uses filing cards anymore.

Figure 13-6:
These 3 x 5 cards represent structured information like that you can store in VBA user-defined data types.

| Name: Says, Fran |
| Name: Smith, Francis |
| Phone: (209) 555-3366 |
| Position: Middle manager |
| Frame of mind: Distracted |

| Name: Best, France's |
| Name: Jones, Frances |
| Phone: (612) 555-9090 |
| Position: Database analyst |
| Frame of mind: Ebullient |

The garden-variety database represents the same arrangement in electronic form. A *database* consists of a set of records, each containing fields for individual items of information. The individual fields can contain different types of data (string, number, date, or what have you). Although the contents of an individual field vary from record to record, the field contains the same data type in every record.

Understanding user-defined data types

In VBA, a user-defined data type simply represents an amalgam of built-in data types of your choice collected under one roof, so to speak. After you define a user-defined type, you can declare variables of that type, just as you would declare variables of the built-in types.

An individual variable based on a user-defined type is comparable to a single filing card or to one record in a database. But to represent an entire set of filing cards or an entire database of records, you simply declare an array of a user-defined type.

Declaring a user-defined data type

Use the Type statement to declare a user-defined data type, as in this conventional example:

```
Type Personnel
   intEmpNumber As Integer 'Employee number
   strLastName As String
   strFirstName As String
   strAddress As String
   lngPhone As Long
   datDateHired As Date
End Type
```

This block declares a new user-defined type called Personnel. As the indented lines make plain, this type consists of three strings, a long integer value, and a date. (Notice that you must specify names for each of the elements when you declare the type; simply stating the elements' data types won't do.) When you declare a variable of your Personnel type, the variable automatically includes storage space for all five of these elements.

Notice also that a Type statement requires the End Type statement to close the block. If you leave out this last line, the compiler squawks at you.

Another key point: A user-defined type can be declared only at the module level (in the declarations section at the beginning of a module). You can't declare a user-defined type within a procedure.

Declaring variables of a user-defined type

Like the built-in data types, a user-defined type is merely an abstract concept until you actually declare a variable. There's nothing unusual about doing so; the standard syntax for declaring any variable applies. You can use the Public, Private, and Static keywords in declarations of user-defined-type variables. This example, however, which declares a single variable, is a standard Dim statement:

```
Dim usrOnePerson As Personnel
```

Notice that you don't have to declare the elements within the user-defined type. Although the Dim statement gives your new variable a name, the names of the individual elements are fixed when you declare the type.

To create an entire database of your user-defined type, declare an array with a statement such as

```
Private PersonnelDatabase(1 To 25)As Personnel
```

Working with information in a user-defined type

After you declare a variable of a user-defined type, you can start stuffing it with information. To do so, you must assign a value to each of the elements within the type. And to do *that*, you identify the element by the name of the variable, followed by a period, followed by the name of the element, as follows:

```
usrOnePerson.strLastName = "Smith"
```

If you're filling several elements at the same time, a `With` statement cuts down on the typing, as in this sample:

```
With usrOnePerson
  .strLastName = "Jones"
  .strFirstName = "Bob"
  .datDateHired = #12/9/48#
End With
```

Use standard array indexing to assign data to the elements in an array of a user-defined type. In this example, the index is given by a variable:

```
PersonnelDatabase(intENumber).strFirstName = "Sue"
```

Working with variables of a user-defined type as a whole

When a variable of a user-defined type contains a complete set of data, you can assign its contents to another variable of the same type — all at the same time, without messing with the individual elements that each variable contains. To assign the contents of the `usrOnePerson` variable to the second slot in the `PersonnelDatabase` array, use the following statement:

```
PersonnelDatabase(2) = usrOnePerson
```

This trick works great when you are saving or reading information to or from a disk file. You can save a database full of records on disk with code such as the following:

```
Sub WriteData()
Open "C:\Database\People.dat" For Binary As #1
For i = 1 To intDatabaseSize ' Loop for all records
  Put #1, , PersonnelDatabase(i)
Next i
Close #1  ' Close file--required step.
End Sub
```

Chapter 17 covers techniques for reading and writing disk files.

Chapter 14

Unbreakable Code: Debugging and Error Trapping

. . . .

In This Chapter

▶ A catalog of all the kinds of mistakes that can foul up your VBA programs

▶ Bug-fixing essentials

▶ How wonderful it is — as you're hunting bugs — to run in break mode

▶ All the debugging tools of the Visual Basic Editor, including the Step commands and the Immediate, Locals, and Watch windows

▶ How to use the Visual Basic Editor as a calculator in the Immediate and Watch windows

▶ Sophisticated error-handling techniques to ease the pain if run-time errors occur

. . . .

*W*riting VBA code is the easy part. Getting that code to run — and then to produce the expected results — is what takes real work. Hunting down and stamping out bugs is a crucial part of the coding process, and this chapter tells you how it's done in VBA. I also discuss error trapping, which enables a program to respond gracefully if something goes wrong while it's running.

What Can Go Wrong Does Go Wrong

Three main kinds of problems can beset the programs that you write in VBA or most any language. They are as follows:

✔ **Compile errors:** Syntax and other errors that prevent the program from running in the first place.

✔ **Logic errors:** Flaws in the program's design that cause it to do something you *don't* want it to do or not to do something you *do* want it to do. The program runs, but it doesn't run correctly.

✔ **Run-time errors:** These bring the program to a halt while it is running. Run-time errors can result from logic errors or can occur if the program encounters unexpected conditions. (See "Where run-time errors come from," later in this chapter.)

Of the three types, syntax errors are definitely the easiest to uncover and correct. I mention these errors only briefly, spending most of my time in this chapter on detecting and eliminating the other two types, which are the true bugs.

Fixing Syntax Errors

If you make the first type of mistake — a syntax error — the Visual Basic Editor helps you figure out what you did wrong before you try to run the program. As soon as you type something that the Editor can't figure out, it displays the line in red. Then, if you checked the box labeled Auto Syntax Check in the Editor tab of the Options dialog box (which you access by choosing Tools⇨Options), you get a message clarifying the problem as soon as you move the insertion point off the line. For example, if you type **If x = 3**, for example, but forget to type **Then**, the message is Compile error: Expected: Then or GoTo.

VBA doesn't catch some syntax errors until you try to run the program. In particular, VBA doesn't initially protest if you try to GoTo a nonexistent label or call a nonexistent procedure; you get a compiler error message only after you give the Run command.

Once you know you made the mistake, correcting syntax errors is relatively easy. If you have any doubt about the correct way to call or declare a procedure or function, name or declare a variable, create a new instance of an object, or use a control structure, consult the relevant chapters of this book or look up the item in the VBA Help system.

Entomology for VBA Programmers

After you get past all the compile errors and your program starts running, feeling an immediate wave of pride and relief is natural. But if the program reports that 2 + 2 = 22 or if all the text in your document turns chartreuse, you know that there's a mistake somewhere in your code.

These types of errors are examples of errors in program logic. The program is running and, in fact, is doing exactly what you told it to do; the problem is that what you *told* it to do with the code you wrote isn't what you actually *wanted* it to do. Your job is to track down exactly which statements led to the wrong outcome. This process is called *debugging* your program. The tools and techniques that you can use in your debugging campaigns are all cataloged in this section.

Of course, the same debugging techniques that you use to stamp out logic errors are vital in preventing the many run-time errors that result from logic errors. But because no program can anticipate every possible circumstance that it may face, you should still incorporate code for handling run-time errors in any program destined for other people to use.

Test, test, test

It's handy when errors announce themselves by displaying obviously wrong answers, turning things on the screen weird colors, or causing error messages to pop up. Unfortunately, many logic errors are more subtle, and many run-time errors occur only intermittently. Instead of assuming that your program is going to work properly after it's freshly hatched, budget plenty of time for testing it under different conditions.

Here are some testing suggestions:

- ✔ If the program is supposed to work with different documents, test it by running it with different documents. Try running the program while two or three documents are open in your VBA application — and while no document at all is open.

- ✔ See what happens if you run the program while the document window is in different states (minimized, maximized, or restored).

- ✔ Start the program while different items or groups of items are selected in the document window.

- ✔ If the program requires input from the user via an input box or custom form, make all kinds of typical and outlandish test entries to see what happens. If the required value is supposed to be an integer, try floating-point, date, and string entries to see how the program responds.

- ✔ If the program works with date or time values, see what it does with different dates (including February 29) and different times of day (including midnight). Feed various date or time values to the variables but also try running the program on different dates or at different times. You don't need to stay up late or wait for a leap year; just set the system clock to the test time or date temporarily.

As you test-run the program, look closely for evidence that something has gone wrong. Examine your document to ensure that it reflects all the changes that you wanted the program to make — and no others. Scrutinize for accuracy and correct format of any results that the program displays in dialog boxes or pastes into your document. Ideally, you should also check your variables while the program runs to make sure that no aberrant values occur. (I show you how to check your variables in the following section.) Obviously, if VBA reports a run-time error, you have a problem.

If you do find any mistakes, you need to start debugging in earnest. But if not, don't assume that mistakes aren't there. Remember — bugs are the most widespread and numerous animals on earth.

Take a break

The key to debugging a program is using VBA's break mode. In *break mode,* your program has begun running but is suspended at a particular statement in the code. Because the program is still live, you can inspect the current values of all the variables. Beginning from that point, you can use the Step commands to run the program one statement at a time, watching the variables change to see whether you're getting the expected results at each step in the process. Later sections of this chapter provide details on working with variables and the Step commands.

Figure 14-1 shows a VBA procedure in break mode. With the exception of a yellow highlight and arrow marking the next statement to be executed, the Visual Basic Editor looks almost exactly as it does while you're writing or editing code.

Figure 14-1:
A VBA
procedure
in break
mode.

In break mode, in fact, you can actually edit the code while your program is running, making changes or adding brand-new lines as whim or necessity dictates. This feature isn't at all a frill but a key debugging feature that you should train yourself to take advantage of — more on this topic in the section "Adding and editing code in break mode" later in this chapter.

Entering break mode

You can use a variety of techniques to put a program into the break-mode state of suspended animation. Here's the full list:

- ✔ Start the program in break mode from the outset by using the Step Into command. (See "Steppin' through code," later in this chapter.)

- ✔ Set a *breakpoint* on a line of code. After a running program reaches the statement at the breakpoint, it suspends execution and enters break mode.

- ✔ Place a Stop statement in your code. As the program runs, it enters break mode, ready to execute the statement following the Stop statement.

- ✔ Click the Break button, choose Run⇨Break, or press Ctrl+Break while the program is running. Use this technique to get back control of a run-away program that doesn't stop on its own. Where you end up when the program enters break mode is anyone's guess, but at least you can see what's going on after you get there.

- ✔ Create a Break When True or Break When Changed *watch*. The program enters break mode if the value of the watch expression becomes True or undergoes any change.

One other way that a program can enter break mode is if a run-time error occurs. VBA displays a dialog box describing the error (see Figure 14-2). Clicking the End button stops the program altogether, but clicking Debug puts it into break mode. You have some control over which run-time errors trigger break mode in the General tab of the Tools⇨Options dialog box.

Setting breakpoints

If you suspect that a section of code contains a logical error, place a break-point just before the miscreant statements. Figure 14-3 shows how the Visual Basic Editor represents a breakpoint on-screen — it's that big dot in the margin of the Code window.

With a breakpoint in place, you can run the program at full speed up to that point, bypassing code that (you hope) works correctly. When VBA gets to the statement that contains the breakpoint, it suspends the program. Once break mode is active, you can examine the variables and then use the Step commands to see how they change as VBA executes each dubious statement one at a time.

To set a breakpoint, all you need to do is click the margin of the Code window next to the target line of code. Using the keyboard, put the insertion point on the correct line and press F9.

Figure 14-2:
A dialog box
showing a
run-time
error.

Figure 14-3:
If you set a
breakpoint,
the Visual
Basic Editor
highlights
the line of
code before
the program
execution
that should
stop.

You can set breakpoints on as many executable statements as you like. However, you can't set breakpoints on comments, or on statements that VBA doesn't actually execute, such as variable declarations.

Keep in mind that VBA stops the program and switches into break mode after executing the statement just before the breakpoint. In other words, the statement at the breakpoint hasn't been executed yet and is the next to go after the program continues.

Clearing breakpoints

After you correct the errant code or give up on fixing it for now, you *clear* the breakpoint to remove it. Clearing a breakpoint enables VBA to execute that statement normally the next time that you run the program. The same techniques that you use to set a breakpoint — clicking the Code window's margin or pressing F9 — clear an existing one.

To deep-six all breakpoints, choose Debug⇨Clear All Breakpoints or press Ctrl+Shift+F9. Once you do that, the breakpoints are history; Undo can't restore them.

Knowing where you are in break mode

If a program is running in break mode, the Visual Basic Editor always high-lights the statement that is to be executed next. To make sure that you get the message, an arrow in the Code window's margin points to the selfsame next statement. Figure 14-4 shows you what you see (although the black-and-white image leaves much to the imagination).

Figure 14-4:
You can't miss the statement that's next in line for execution (as long as it's visible on-screen, anyway).

```
Phony macros for screenshots.xls - UserForm1 (Code)

UserForm                            KeyDown

        Salesperson.Locked = False
        Salesperson.SetFocus
        Exit Sub
ElseIf KeyCode = vbKeyReturn Then
        checktimes = checktimes + 1
        If (checktimes >= 2) And (cboMainItemEntry.Value
            QuantityForm.Show
            If QuantityHidden = "Cancel" Then
                checktimes = 0
                Exit Sub
            End If
            checktimes = 0
            Exit Sub
        End If

With ordersRS
    .Add (EnterQuantity)
    objects = .Count
End With
```

After you have the next statement on-screen, you can't mistake that highlight. But what happens if you start scrolling to other parts of your code or jump to the Code windows of other modules? You may have trouble finding the next statement again.

That's where the suitably named Show Next Statement command comes in. When you choose Debug➪Show Next Statement, the Visual Basic Editor whisks you straight to the statement in question. Another command lets you select a different statement as the next statement, but I cover that topic in "Choosing a different next statement," later in this chapter.

Using a breakpoint alternative: The Stop statement

Breakpoints are super-easy to use, but they have one drawback: They're temporary. If you're debugging a complex program, you may not be able to set things right in a single session. Because breakpoints aren't stored with your code, they're gone the next time you open the project in the Visual Basic Editor.

The Stop statement is the solution to this problem. Add this statement to your code wherever you want the program to switch to break mode. Like all code that you type, Stop statements are saved whenever you save the project.

Monsieur or Madame, do you crave an example? Allow me to oblige:

```
...
intDataFromMars = GetDataFromMars(1.5454)
Stop
MsgBox "The result is " & intDataFromMars / Z
...
```

After inspecting the example code, you can guess that the Stop statement is being used to probe suspect results displayed in the message box. When the Stop statement executes, it forces the program into break mode just after the intDataFromMars function procedure sets the value of a variable. You can now look at the values of both variables involved in the next calculation to see which of them seems to be out of line.

Getting out of break mode

After you're through with break mode, at least for the time being, you can tell VBA to resume normal program execution. Any of the commands that you can use to run a program in the first place work. In break mode, the Run menu item and toolbar button look the same and are in the same places, but their names are changed; both are now called Continue. F5 is still the keyboard shortcut. A Continued program pops back into break mode if it runs into another breakpoint or if any other of the conditions that activate break mode occur.

To stop running the program altogether, use the Reset command. You can find a Reset button and a Reset item on the Run menu. Pressing Alt+F4 stops any running Windows program, including VBA programs. However, you must make sure that you press Alt+F4 only while your VBA program is running, or you'll shut down the Visual Basic Editor, your VBA application, or whatever Windows program is currently active.

Steppin' through code

Like all good debuggers, the Visual Basic Editor allows you to run your program one statement, or step, at a time. Slowing things down in this way is a fantastic trick for catching the very point at which some logic error knocks a critical value out of whack.

To make the best use of this *step-execution* technique, you need a way to see the values of your variables as your program modifies them. The Editor's way-cool Auto Data Tips feature is always available for this purpose, but the Locals and Watch windows give you more details and enable you to change the values if the need arises. I cover all these features a bit later in this chapter.

So now about the three Step commands that you can use in the Visual Basic Editor: Step Into, Step Over, and Step Out. You can access all three commands via the Debug menu, as buttons on the Debug toolbar, or by way of these keyboard shortcuts:

Step Command	*Keyboard Shortcut*
Step Into	F8
Step Over	Shift+F8
Step Out	Ctrl+Shift+F8

I Stepped Into it this time

 The Step Into command is the one to use if you want to execute each and every statement in your program in correct sequence. Each time you invoke this command, VBA runs the next statement in your program and then returns to break mode, where you can see what changes have been wrought. Pressing F8 is the most efficient way to invoke the Step Into command.

This command gets its name because it steps into other procedures that your program calls as it runs. If the next statement calls a Sub or Function procedure, invoking the Step Into command opens the called procedure in the Code window, where you can step through it to see what it's doing.

 The Step Into command is available even if you're not already in break mode. If you want to step through the program beginning at the beginning, just give the Step Into command to run the first statement and enter break mode. Used in this way, Step Into runs the procedure containing the insertion point, always starting from the procedure's first line.

Stepping over and out

 The Step Over command (Shift+F8 is the keyboard shortcut) works just like Step Into, with the following two exceptions:

- ✔ Most importantly, Step Over doesn't step though the individual statements in a called procedure.
- ✔ You can't start running a program in break mode with Step Over.

If the next statement calls another procedure, Step Over runs the whole procedure in one gulp, going on to the following statement in the current procedure. That is great if you just want to see whether the procedure as a whole does anything goofy before you bother to check it out in detail. Stepping over a procedure is also a big time-saver if you're already fairly sure that the procedure works as it's supposed to.

The `Step Out` command (Ctrl+Shift+F8 is the keyboard shortcut) is a handy complement to `Step Into`. After you get inside the bowels of a called procedure, you may decide that everything is okay, or you may locate the error and fix it. More embarrassingly, you may just have clicked the Step Into button when you meant to click Step Over (a mistake I make regularly).

In any event, there's no point in hanging around to step through the procedure's remaining statements. Use the `Step Out` command to run the rest of the procedure at top speed. VBA returns you to the procedure from whence you came, highlighting the statement following the procedure call.

Major manipulations during debugging

In break mode, just because you're running your program doesn't mean that the program's course is fixed in stone. VBA is sophisticated enough to allow midcourse corrections. Specifically, you can edit the existing code and alter the sequence in which statements get executed.

Adding and editing code in break mode

The Code window's editing features are fully operational during break mode. You can type new statements, modify existing ones, or delete them altogether. But what's really special is that most of your changes work immediately, becoming part of the running program. For example, you can declare new variables and use them right away in calculations, perhaps in combination with existing variables. Some edits, such as changing a variable to a different type in its declaration, do bring the program to a halt.

Choosing a different next statement

Suppose that you're stepping through your code in break mode when you realize that the next statement contains a big mistake. Rather than execute the statement and send your program into a tailspin, you can choose to bypass it altogether until you've had a chance to make it right.

The Visual Basic Editor enables you to select a different statement almost anywhere in your code as the next statement, using either the keyboard or the mouse. You can jump forward or backward in the code. In addition to letting you skip over foul code, this also allows you to repeat statements until you're sure you understand how they work.

Just realize that variables retain the values that they have before you make the change. These values may well be very different from what they are when the program reaches the code in the normal sequence. If necessary, you can give the variables any value that you like by using the Immediate, Watch, or Locals windows, described later in this chapter.

Other ways to skip code

You have other options for skipping code that you know is broken. These methods work whether you're step-executing a program in break mode or editing the code before you run it. One approach is to type an apostrophe at the beginning of each line that you want to skip, thereby turning it into a comment. The only real drawback is that commenting — and later "uncommenting" — the code takes time. However, you can comment an entire block of code in a single step by selecting it and clicking the Comment Block button on the Edit toolbar (see Chapter 8).

Sometimes an even better way to skip over code is by using line labels in conjunction with temporary GoTo statements. When the following code runs, VBA completely skips all the statements between `GoTo AfterTheSkip` and the statement following the `AfterTheSkip:` label. When you're ready to run the skipped code again, just remove the GoTo statement or turn it into a comment ("comment it out").

```
. . .
GoTo AfterTheSkip
   A = B + C
   D = A + E/F
   G = B + D
AfterTheSkip:
   MsgBox "Today is " &
      Format(Now, "dddd")
. . .
```

If you can keep all that in mind, here's how to select a different next statement:

- ✔ Using the keyboard, move the insertion point to the line containing the statement, and then press Ctrl+F9 or choose Debug➪Set Next Statement.

- ✔ Using the mouse, drag the yellow arrow pointer in the Code window's margin to the new next statement (see Figure 14-5).

Seeing Data Tips

VBA's Auto Data Tips feature enables you to see the current value of any variable wherever it appears in your code. While you're in break mode, hovering the mouse pointer over any variable pops up the Data Tips window — a little box containing the name and current value of that variable. Figure 14-6 shows Auto Data Tips in action.

In case you don't see the Auto Data Tips box when you should, check to make sure that its box is checked in the Editor tab of the Options dialog box.

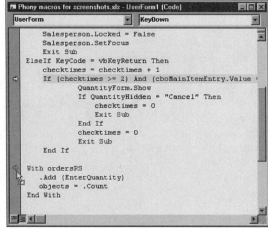

Figure 14-5:
Selecting a different next statement enables you to repeat blocks of code, the functioning of which you want to study.

```
Phony macros for screenshots.xls - UserForm1 [Code]
UserForm                                    KeyDown
        Salesperson.Locked = False
        Salesperson.SetFocus
        Exit Sub
    ElseIf KeyCode = vbKeyReturn Then
        checktimes = checktimes + 1
        If (checktimes >= 2) And (cboMainItemEntry.Value =
                QuantityForm.Show
                If QuantityHidden = "Cancel" Then
                    checktimes = 0
                    Exit Sub
                End If
                checktimes = 0
                Exit Sub
        End If

    With ordersRS
        .Add (EnterQuantity)
        objects = .Count
    End With
```

Figure 14-6:
The little Auto Data Tips box shows the value of the variable beneath the mouse pointer.

```
Phony macros for screenshots.xls - UserForm1 [Code]
UserForm                                    KeyDown
        Set QuantityForm = New EnterQuantityForm
    If KeyCode = vbKeyF12 Then
        Salesperson.Enabled = True
        Salesperson.Locked = False
        Salesperson.SetFocus
        Exit Sub
    ElseIf KeyCode = vbKeyReturn Then
        checktimes = checktimes + 1
        checktimes = 1 imes >= 2) And (cboMainItemEntry.Value =
                QuantityForm.Show
                If QuantityHidden = "Cancel" Then
                    checktimes = 0
                    Exit Sub
                End If
                checktimes = 3
                Exit Sub
        End If
    With ordersRS
        .Add (EnterQuantity)
        objects = .Count
```

You can use a different Editor feature to display the type and scope of a variable, although not so automatically. Place the insertion point in or beside the variable name and then press Ctrl+I to bring up a Quick Info box containing that information. You don't need to be in break mode to use this feature, which is especially helpful if you're working in the middle of a long program whose variables were declared at the top. Figure 14-7 shows the sort of information that you get.

Figure 14-7:
Displaying a
Quick Info
box for a
variable.

Immediate Gratifications

Press Ctrl+G to display the Immediate window, as shown in Figure 14-8. The
Immediate window enables you to do two things:

- See the values of calculations and variables by using the `Debug.Print`
  method.

- Execute individual code statements directly without running them inside
  a procedure. To execute a statement in the Immediate window, just type
  it and then press Enter.

So what good are these talents, you ask? Allow me to list the benefits:

- You can use the Immediate window as a crude calculator. Type an
  expression such as the following:

```
Print (27 * 398) + 1414
```

Then press Enter and you get the result . . . well, immediately (refer to
Figure 14-8). If you work in the Immediate window, you don't need to
specify the `Debug` object.

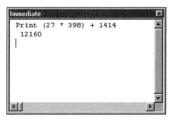

Figure 14-8:
The
Immediate
window in
action.

✔ You can route intermediate values of variables and expressions at various points in a running program to the Immediate window by placing the `Debug.Print` method in the program's code (not in the Immediate window itself). After the program terminates, you can quickly check to see whether it produced the correct results without displaying a message box for each value. Figure 14-9 shows an example of this technique.

✔ During break mode, you can display the value of any variable or object property in the Immediate window by using a `Print` statement or change the value by typing a standard assignment such as this:

```
intTheirNumber = 25
```

You can also call `Sub` and `Function` procedures just as you normally would. Notice that, during break mode, statements that you execute in the Immediate window can access only those variables, objects, and procedures that are within the scope of the procedure that's currently executing in the program. In other words, executing a statement in the Immediate window produces the same effect as typing it in the running procedure and executing it there.

Figure 14-9:
Output from
a program
that uses
the
Debug.Print
method.

From the Interesting Facts Department: You can drag selected text from the Code window to the Immediate window, which means that you don't need to retype long expressions or variable names if you want to use them there (if you don't hold down Ctrl as you drag, the code is moved, not copied, to the

Immediate window). The F1 key works in the Immediate window as it does in the Code window, displaying Help on whatever keyword the insertion point lies within. Auto Data Tips do not function there, however.

Keeping an Eye on the Locals (Window)

If you have room to display it, the Locals window should be on your screen at all times when you're debugging a program in break mode. Bring the Locals window into view by clicking its button on the Debug toolbar or by choosing View➪Immediate.

As shown in Figure 14-10, the Locals window automatically displays all the variables that are accessible in the current procedure, showing their names, values, and data types. The Visual Basic Editor updates the information each time that you execute a statement, so what you see in the Locals window always reflects the current values.

Other collapsed items

The program's individual variables

Collapsed item for module-level variables

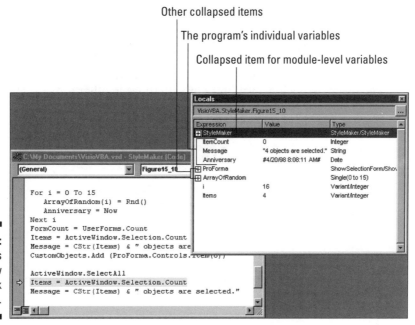

Figure 14-10: The Locals window during break mode.

Local mechanics

As are most Visual Basic Editor windows, the Locals window is dockable by default but can also be displayed as a free-floating separate window. Chapters 5 and 6 cover the basics of working with Editor windows.

If you can't see all the information in a column, remember that you can re-size the columns. Position the mouse pointer over a column separator in the gray column header just above the main part of the window. After the pointer becomes a double-headed arrow, drag to the left or right to change the widths of the adjacent columns.

If you look back to Figure 14-10, you can see that some rows list individual variables, while others show items such as arrays, variables of user-defined type, and objects. Such items have no values of their own; instead, they hold variables and other "container" items. After you begin running a procedure, the Locals window lists them in collapsed form; you can't see the subsidiary items that they contain. To expand a collapsed item, click the boxed plus sign to its left. (See Figure 14-11 for examples of expanded items.)

Only variables declared (implicitly or explicitly) in the currently running procedure appear already expanded at the top level of the Locals window's hierarchy. To see module-level variables that are accessible to all procedures in the current module, expand the first item in the Locals window. This item always pertains to the module in which the current procedure is running. You can't work with global variables or with those in other projects in the Locals windows.

Why edit variable values?

Before I tell you how to change a variable's value, you probably should know why you might want to. Here are some good reasons:

- ✔ A previous line of code contains an error that assigned an incorrect value to the variable. You've caught the mistake, but you want to continue stepping through the program. Before you go on, change the variable's value to what it should have been so that the mistake won't affect subsequent statements.

- ✔ You want to test various alternative values for the variable without changing your code. You can use the Set Next Statement command to repeatedly pass through the same stretch of code, entering different values in the Locals window each time.

- ✔ The values that the program uses as it runs in real life aren't currently available to it. The program may read information from a database or the Internet, for example. In this case, you can supply simulated values via the Locals window.

How to edit variable values

Okay. To change the value of a variable in the Locals window, follow these steps:

1. **Click twice (but don't double-click) directly over the variable's current value in the window so that only the value is highlighted.**

   Clicking elsewhere in the same row simply selects the entire line.

2. **Type the new value.**

   If you're typing a string value, you must include beginning and ending quotation marks. Similarly, enclose date literals with pound-sign (#) characters.

3. **If you change your mind, you can cancel your entry and restore the preceding one by pressing Esc; otherwise, press Enter to confirm it.**

   The Editor won't accept an invalid value, and you may get an error message telling you what was wrong with your entry.

You can edit any variable's values, including those of individual members of arrays and user-defined types. Just realize that you must expand the array or user-defined type variable before you can get to its member data elements. With an object variable, you can't change the object that's assigned to it, but you can edit the object's properties (except the read-only ones). Again, you must expand the object to see the editable items. Figure 14-11 shows expanded array, user-defined type, and object variables.

Figure 14-11:
The Locals window for the same procedure shown in Figure 14-10, but items that were collapsed there are now expanded.

The Watch Window: Key Debugging Tool

After you've mastered the Locals window, working with the Watch window is a piece of pie. This window works in essentially the same way, the obvious difference being that *you* get to pick out which values it displays. Figure 14-12 shows the Watch window in action.

Figure 14-12:
The Visual
Basic
Editor's
Watch
window.

Watches				
Expression	Value	Type		Context
66 sngArrayItem	2904.3	Single		
66 FormCount	2	Integer		Figure15_12
66 intTempCounter	52	Integer		Figure15_12
66 frm1		FormAnOpinion/FormAnOpinion		Figure15_12.FormVariableDem
_Default	"??□□□□□□(	String		Figure15_12.FormVariableDem
BackColor	-2147483633	OLE_COLOR		Figure15_12.FormVariableDem
BorderColor	-2147483630	OLE_COLOR		Figure15_12.FormVariableDem
BorderStyle	fmBorderStyle	fmBorderStyle		Figure15_12.FormVariableDem
Caption	"All of the abo	String		Figure15_12.FormVariableDem

REMEMBER

Use the Watch window when you're debugging large programs in which many different procedures manipulate global variables. By adding these global variables to the Watch window, you can track their current values, no matter what part of the program you're currently stepping through.

The Watch window appears automatically as soon as you define a *watch expression.* (See the sidebar "What else is different compared with the Locals window" for a discussion of watch expressions.) If you want more room on-screen, however, you can put the window away by clicking the close button in the top-right corner.

Adding watch expressions

If you like having options, you'll love the Watch window. Prepare to be overwhelmed by how many ways you can add watch expressions.

No matter which technique you eventually use, you should start in the Code window by selecting the variable or expression that you want to watch. When I say "selecting," I mean selecting the entire item as you would in a word processor, by highlighting it with the mouse or arrow keys.

However, if you want to watch only an independent variable (in other words, an item that's not an object property or an element in a user-defined type), you don't actually need to select the whole thing. Putting the insertion point in the variable name will do.

What else is different compared with the Locals window

Besides the fact that what appears in the window is up to you, the Watch window differs from the Locals window in two other important ways:

✔ Each line in the Watch window lets you track the value of any valid VBA expression, not just an individual variable. Expressions such as (X - Y) > 15, "The color is " & strColor, or even 2 + 2 are perfectly acceptable. That's why entries are called watch expressions.

✔ Because the Watch window can track variables from any module or procedure in the project, it adds a fourth column labeled Context. This column describes the scope in which the window displays a value for the variable or expression. If you're executing a procedure outside the defined context, all you see is <Out of context>.

Now for that "overwhelming" list of techniques. You can add a watch based on the selected expression by:

✔ Right-clicking the selection and choosing Add Watch from the shortcut menu to display the Add Watch window.

✔ Choosing Debug⇨Add Watch, which also displays the Add Watch dialog box.

✔ Clicking the Quick Watch button in the Debug toolbar, or choosing Debug⇨Quick Watch. The Editor shows you a confirmatory message describing the watch expression that you're about to add, but you can't change anything.

✔ Dragging the selection to the Watch window. This method creates the watch without any intermediate steps.

If you're a diehard do-it-yourselfer, you don't actually need to select anything in the Code window. You can just click the Add Watch button and then type in the expression of interest from scratch in the Add Watch dialog box.

Working with the Add Watch window

Figure 14-13 shows the Add Watch window, which appears after you choose Debug⇨Add Watch or choose Add Watch from the Code window's shortcut (right-click) menu. In this window, you define the details of your watch expression.

Figure 14-13:
The Add
Watch
dialog box.

The Expression field is, of course, where you specify the expression that you want to watch. If you selected the correct variable or expression before you started, you shouldn't have to change anything, but you can if you want.

The Context section of the dialog box lets you define the procedures in which the Visual Basic Editor actually calculates and displays the value of the watch expression. The values of the Procedure and Module choices are initially set to the procedure in which the variable appeared when you added the watch. If you want to see the value while a different procedure is running, select it by name. If that procedure is in a different module, you must first select its module and then choose the procedure.

If you want the variable value to remain visible no matter which procedure in a given module is executing, choose (All Procedures), the first item on the Procedures list. And if you want to see the value *always* — throughout the entire program — choose (All Modules) from the Modules list. The broader the scope that you choose, the longer VBA takes to calculate and report the value. Still, being able to track a variable wherever you are in the program is often worth the short wait.

For a normal watch expression, leave the Watch Type set to Watch Expression. I explain the other choices a bit in "Using watch expressions to define break-points," around the next bend.

Editing watch expressions

The easiest way to modify an existing watch expression is to type changes in the Expression column of the Watch window. Click the line containing the expression to select it; then click the expression itself to highlight it. You can then edit the expression to taste.

As you can in the Locals window, you can change the value of a variable while the program is running. However, you can't change the Context setting for a watch expression in the Watch window. Instead, you must open the Edit Watch dialog box, which is a spittin' image of the Add Watch box. Edit Watch is a choice in the Debug window and on the shortcut (right-click) menu for the Watch window. After the dialog box opens, you can make changes to the expression's context or type or to the expression itself, just as when you originally defined the watch.

Using watch expressions to define breakpoints

The larger a program gets, the harder it is to keep track of which procedures and statements are changing which variables. Often, you suspect that a variable's final value is incorrect, but you're not sure where to look for the code that caused the problem. In this situation, a breakpoint based on a watch expression can be a lifesaver (or at least a code-saver).

Using the Watch Type option buttons in the Add Watch or Edit Watch dialog box, you can set up the following two types of these automatic breaks:

✔ You can have your program automatically enter break mode as soon as it executes any statement that changes an expression to a nonzero value. (In VBA, remember, 0 is False, and everything else is True.) Choose Break When Value Is True for this type of breakpoint.

✔ You can automatically enter break mode immediately after the program executes any statement that changes the value of an expression. Choose Break When Value Changes for this type of breakpoint.

Their special talents notwithstanding, these "breaking" watch expressions still function as ordinary watches in the Watch window. You can distinguish watches of different types, however, by the differences in the little icons to the far left of each item. You can sort of see them if you squint real hard at Figure 14-14, but on the screen they're easy to pick out.

After a watch-based breakpoint is triggered by a value change, VBA suspends program execution and enters break mode. In the Code window, the statement that caused the change is the one just before the highlighted next statement. The watch expression that triggered the break is highlighted in the Watch window so that you know which one did it (refer to Figure 14-14).

Figure 14-14:
A "break
when value
changes"
watch
expression
on variable
intItHappened
has just
dropped the
program
into break
mode.

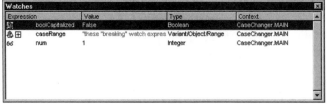

Trapping Wild Bugs with On Error and the Error Object

If something goes unexpectedly wrong while a program is running, the result is often catastrophic. VBA brings the program to a grinding halt, displaying a run-time-error dialog box to give you the bad news about what went wrong — tersely. You saw this box before, back in Figure 14-2. Your clickable choices are End (to terminate the program), Debug (to enter break mode), and Help (to display a Help topic about the specific error that you've run into).

None of these options are particularly appealing, especially if you're running the program for real instead of while you're testing it. It would be far less jarring if your program could detect the error and correct it — or at least sidestep it — before VBA muscles in with that ominous run-time-error message. Failing that, you might at least present the user with a more congenial message.

All this is possible but requires you to add your own error-handling code. This section tells you how.

Where run-time errors come from

As I previously mentioned — but will repeat here since it was so long ago — run-time errors can occur for the following two reasons:

✔ A serious error in your program's logic produces a situation that VBA can't deal with. To haul out the customary example for one more performance, suppose that you have written a statement in which a value gets divided by a variable. If your code assigns a value of zero to that variable, you're sunk; dividing by zero is strictly forbidden, and trying to do so gives your computer a seizure, so VBA stops the program.

✔ Some unforeseen circumstance sideswipes your program. A required connection to a database file, network server, or Internet site may be cut off, for example, so your program can't retrieve the values that it needs to do its work.

Either way, the outcome is the same. Protect your program and your users by writing your own error-handling code.

How error-handling code works

To prevent VBA from dealing with run-time errors and to take care of them yourself, you must adorn each procedure with an *error handler* — a block of code whose sole purpose is to step in if an error occurs. If something goes wrong as the procedure runs, VBA transfers program execution to the error handler. The code in the error handler can figure out what type of error has occurred and take whatever steps you think that the situation warrants.

How to write error-handling code

To add error-handling code to a procedure, you must do three things:

✔ Add an `On Error` statement at the beginning of the procedure to tell VBA where the error-handler code is.

✔ Type an `Exit Sub` or `Exit Function` statement following the body of the procedure, just before the error-handler code.

✔ Write the code for the error handler itself, preceded by an identifying label.

All three steps are vital. Without the `On Error` statement, VBA doesn't know that the error handler exists.

Writing On Error statements

The `On Error` statement enables the error handler by telling VBA where to find the error handler in the procedure code. The full statement has the syntax `On Error GoTo label`, where `label` is a label elsewhere in the procedure identifying the first line of the error handler's code.

Here's how the `On Error` statement looks in a procedure:

```
Sub ErrorHandlerDemo()
On Error GoTo ErrorHandler
  MamaVariable = DoThisFunction (X,Y,Z)
  PapaVariable = DoThatProcedure
  BabyVariable = MamaVariable + PapaVariable
' Stop the procedure here if no error has occurred:
  Exit Sub ErrorHandler:
(error handling code goes here)
End Sub
```

You should know about two other forms of the `On Error` statement, which work as follows:

- ✔ `On Error GoTo 0` disables error handling from this point forward in the procedure and clears the `Err` object. Use it at a point in your procedure after a previous `On Error GoTo label` when you want to turn off your own error-handling code in favor of VBA's default screech-to-a-halt system.

- ✔ `On Error Resume Next` causes VBA to ignore the line that caused the error and to continue execution with the following line of code. Obviously, ignoring an error won't make it go away. `On Error Resume Next` is primarily useful when your code uses objects from the host application or other components you didn't create — an advanced VBA skill introduced in Chapter 17.

Adding an Exit statement to the procedure

An error handler is part and parcel of the procedure in which it appears, which means that VBA executes the code in the error handler every time the procedure runs. Obviously, this situation isn't right. You want the error handler to run only if an error occurs and at no other time.

To prevent the error handler from running except when it's supposed to, all you need to do is add an `Exit` statement immediately before the error-handler code, as shown in the example in the section "Writing `On Error` statements," earlier in this chapter. If you're writing a `Sub` procedure, the `Exit` statement should be `Exit Sub`; for a `Function` procedure, it should be `Exit Function`.

Writing the error handler

The error handler itself requires several components:

- ✔ A label showing where the error handler starts
- ✔ Code to determine the type of error that occurred

> ✓ Code to deal with the error
>
> ✓ Optionally, a statement to resume execution of the main part of the procedure

Adding a label

To identify the start of your error-handling code, enter a standard VBA label as the first line of the error handler. (Remember that a label is a single word followed by a colon.) As I explain earlier in this chapter, the `On Error` statement for the procedure directs execution to this label if an error occurs. In this example, `ThisIsTheErrorHandler` is the required label:

```
...
ThisIsTheErrorHandler:
...
  (Error handling statements)
...
End Sub
```

As illustrated in this example, error-handling code almost always belongs at the very end of a procedure — thus, the `End Sub` terminates the error handler.

Getting information about and dealing with the error

The body of your error handler has two main tasks: checking to see what type of error has occurred and doing something about it. Although these chores differ conceptually, they go on almost simultaneously in practice.

The standard method for learning what has gone wrong is using VBA's `Err` object. If you know that a particular variable has a tendency to go haywire, you may want to check it directly to see whether its value is out of bounds before you look at the `Err` object. Otherwise, the `Err` object is the ticket.

The `Err` object is always available in every VBA program. You can use it directly, without creating an instance of it first. VBA automatically stores information about the most recent error in the `Err` object. All that your code must do is retrieve the `Err` object's properties, which include `Number` and `Description`.

The `Number` property simply tells you the number of the current error. You can assign this property to a variable or use it directly in a conditional statement, as in this example:

```
Sub YetAnotherFineMess()
On Error GoTo ImTryinToThinkButNothinHappens
...
(error prone statements)
...
Exit Sub
```

```
ImTryinToThinkButNothinHappens:
Select Case Err.Number
  Case 7 ' Out of memory error
   (code for handling error number 7)
  Case 11 ' Division by zero error
   (code for handling error number )
  ... (and so on)
  Case Else
   (code for handling all other errors)
End Select
End Sub
```

In the above example, the Select Case statement checks the Number property against a series of values for which you've written specific error-handling statements. Such statements may perform the following tasks:

✔ Inform the user that something is wrong and ask for instructions via an input box or custom form

✔ Try again to get valid data from a source that was unavailable earlier or try an alternative source

✔ Change an errant value to a valid one, recording in a file or via a message box that data had to be changed by brute force to make the thing go

Effective use of the Number property requires that you know what each error number means. I don't have space to catalog the possibilities. In some VBA applications — such as those in the Office 97 suite — you can find information about the most common errors in the Trappable Errors topic of VBA Help. Locate this topic by typing **trappable errors** in the Help window's Index tab. I haven't been able to find a similar topic in the Office 2000 Help system.

If your code can't deal with an error, or if you don't want to take the trouble, you can still avoid the standard VBA run-time-error message by using the Err object's Description property. The following example displays a genteel error message based on the text string supplied by the Description property:

```
strMyErrMessage = "I'm sorry to inform you that " _
  & "something has gone amiss in this lovely " _
  & "program. According to VBA, the cause of the " _
  & "trouble is "
MsgBox strMyErrMessage & Err.Description
```

Some VBA applications provide additional objects and functions that provide information about application-specific problems. Microsoft Access, for example, offers a separate Error object.

Resuming program execution

After your error handler completes its work, you have a choice: Do you want the procedure to pick up where it left off when the error occurred, or do you want to transfer program execution back to the procedure that called the one where the error occurred?

Place the Resume statement in your error handler if you want to jump back into the current procedure. The Resume statement comes in several flavors:

✔ Simply typing **Resume** on its own line transfers control back to the procedure at the statement that caused the error. You should use this version of the statement if your error handler corrected values used in that statement so that you know an error can't occur again.

✔ To skip the statement that caused the error, add a Resume Next statement to your error-handling code instead. Execution continues at the statement immediately following the one that caused the error.

✔ To jump to a particular point in the procedure, enter a Resume label statement after the error-handling code. Here, label refers to a label somewhere in your procedure but *not* to the label that identifies your error handler. If you use this version, of course, you must also add the label to the procedure.

Part IV

Designing Active Forms

The 5th Wave   By Rich Tennant

All through high school he wouldn't talk to anyone - hardly said a word. Now he's graduating from an Ivy League college with an advanced degree in communications.

In this part . . .

In stand-alone versions of Visual Basic, the form is the only access point for interaction with a program while it runs. Forms tend to be less critical in VBA programming because you can tack your VBA programs onto the user interface of the underlying VBA application.

Even so, plenty of situations in VBA programs call for custom dialog boxes, and this part of the book covers all the skills that you need to construct them. Chapter 15 introduces the basics of form design and working with controls. The bonus online chapter — "Control Fetishes" — focuses in detail on the individual controls, and when and how to use them in your forms. Even with a gaggle of cool controls, however, a VBA form can't do anything productive until you write code for the form and its controls. That minor part of the form-design cycle is the subject of Chapter 16.

Chapter 15

Laying Out VBA Forms

● ●

In This Chapter

▶ Running and printing forms during the design process

▶ Inserting a new form and filling it with controls

▶ Using the Properties window — the easy VBA way to set properties

▶ Surveying the most important form and control properties

● ●

*W*ith VBA, you can design fine-looking windows, be they control centers for custom applications or simple subsidiary dialog boxes. Compared with writing code — or even with writing decent English sentences — laying out a UserForm is a piece of cake. Still, some work is involved, and you can get in trouble in a few places if you're not forewarned. This chapter walks you through all the basic steps of the form-design process. Topics covered in the chapter include planning the form, creating it in the Visual Basic Editor, adding controls, and working with form and control properties.

Getting Started with Form Design

Knowing a few pieces of background information before you start laying out your forms is helpful. Knowing this stuff really does help the process go faster and more smoothly.

Running forms

As you lay out a form, you can "run" (display and activate) it whenever you like. Two steps are required:

1. **Select the form window.** Click on the form's window. Alternatively, you can click inside the Code window associated with the form.

2. **Display the form.** Press F5 or click the Run toolbar button, shown in the margin above.

When you run a form, it appears on the screen over your VBA application (that is, the Visual Basic Editor disappears for the moment). You can then test the form by clicking its controls to see what happens. Just keep in mind that if the form is part of a larger program, it may not work right if you run it in isolation.

A form's window must be selected before the form will run. In the Visual Basic Editor, selection handles around the perimeter of a form remain visible even when you click on another Editor window. The form may appear to be selected, but it won't run automatically when you press F5. If the Macros dialog box unexpectedly pops up, cancel it and then click any part of the form before you try to run it again.

To stop a running form that you haven't equipped with a Cancel button, you can click the Close button at the far-right end of the form's title bar. Alternatively, press Alt+Tab to get back to the Visual Basic Editor and click the Reset toolbar button.

You must be working in the Visual Basic Editor and use the technique described above to run a form on its own. However, the goal of creating a form is to run it from your VBA application. To do this, you must trigger the form from other VBA code, as discussed in Chapter 16, and then run that code with the techniques given in Chapter 4.

Forms and controls are objects — and they must be programmed

Just to remind you, forms and controls are full-fledged VBA objects, which means that they have properties, methods, and events. Forms are different from other objects in one respect: you can set the properties of forms and controls in dialog boxes, without having to program. Keep in mind, however, that you must write code for every control, with the exception of some label and frame controls. Forms themselves often require code, too. Be sure to account for this in your thinking about what needs to be done to complete your project. Chapter 16 covers the programming side of the form-design process.

One quick information item about forms in Microsoft Access: Although Access uses the standard VBA language for the code you write, and although Access has forms with controls that look and work just like the ones in other VBA applications, Access forms are not standard VBA forms. The properties of Access controls are quite different from those of regular VBA controls, and you can't exchange a form that you design in Access with one that you create in another VBA application.

Planning forms for your program

Laying out forms in VBA is fun and easy, but designing those forms requires some thoughtful planning when you're constructing real programs. Remember that your forms are part of a larger software entity that has a practical mission to accomplish. So before you start fiddling with the forms, spend at least a little time on the following steps:

1. **Define a mission statement for your program.**

   This step applies even if the program has no forms, but you want to hold the overall goal in mind while you plan your forms.

2. **List the specific tasks that the program's forms have to perform in support of that mission.**

   What information does the form have to display for the user to respond to, what information is needed from the user, and what input should the user have in deciding how the program operates? You must translate these tasks into elements of the form.

3. **For each task, decide which type of control makes the most sense.**

   Are you asking the user to make a selection among mutually exclusive options? If so, you need a set of *radio buttons* (option buttons), but if the options can be set independently, checkboxes are the way to go. (See the bonus Web chapter at www.dummies.com/bonus/vba/ where I go over the common control types and how they're best used.)

4. **Decide where to place each control on the form.**

   Base your decision on the task's importance, how often it needs to be performed, and which tasks are related (so you'll know which other controls this one should be grouped with).

5. **With all these details clarified, you can sketch out your forms, at least mentally.**

   Avoid overloading a single form with too many controls. Judicious use of tab (multipage) controls can help keep the number of forms down, but be ready to add extra forms to the project to avoid clutter and keep them easy to read.

6. **After you take care of all this practical stuff, *then* considering the frills makes sense.**

   Will a different font on certain buttons — or special rocketship spinner controls — really make it easier for the user to get the job done? Carefully used, variety in colors, fonts, or graphics definitely perks up the interest level, but too much variety is a distraction.

I'm not saying that you should spend endless hours in abstract planning. In fact, after you have a rough idea of what you're trying to accomplish, it usually helps to play around with a tentative form design, test it, and then see what works and what doesn't. All I'm suggesting is that if you start throwing together forms with no plan at all, you're likely to find that they need major revisions later.

Printing forms during the design process

As you work on laying out forms for a VBA project, it sometimes helps to have paper copies that you can carry around with you as you think about the project. Printed forms are great for scribbling tentative design revisions, and you can pass them around to potential users or other programmers for their reactions.

To print a project's forms in the Visual Basic Editor, follow these steps:

1. **If you want to print only one form, select the form in the Project Explorer; if you want to print all the forms in a project, select any form, module, or other component for that project.**

2. **Choose File➪Print or press Ctrl+P.**

3. **In the little dialog box that appears, check the Form Image box.**

4. **Uncheck the Code box unless you also want a printout of the form's code.**

5. **Choose Current Module if you want just the current form printed or Current Project if you want to see all the forms on paper.**

6. **Choose OK to start printing.**

Laying Out a New Form

As Figure 15-1 illustrates, a new form provides a blank canvas for your dabblings in user-interface design. You can alter the form's size and position onscreen, give it a different color, and fill it with the controls that make it do productive tricks.

Before you create a new form, be sure that the correct project — the one where you want the form to live — is active. Open the project's document in the VBA application, then switch to the Visual Basic Editor. If the application permits you to open more than one document at the same time, or if it uses template documents, use the Project Explorer window to select the correct project. (Chapter 7 discusses the Project Explorer.)

Figure 15-1:
A brand-
new
UserForm.
Notice the
Toolbox and
its controls.

Creating the form

Create a new VBA form by choosing Insert⇨UserForm from the Visual Basic
Editor's main menu system or from the Project Explorer's shortcut (right-
click) menu. The new UserForm appears in its own window, accompanied by
the Toolbox (refer to Figure 15-1), a special toolbar containing the controls to
attach to your UserForms.

Adding controls from the Toolbox

When the empty canvas of a new UserForm is onscreen, it's time to start
adding controls — the little doodads on the form with which people interact.
Controls come from the Toolbox.

The Toolbox appears automatically when you create a new UserForm, unless
you previously closed it. The Toolbox graciously hides itself when you click
any non-form window but pops up again when you click the UserForm
window. If the Toolbox isn't visible when you need it, however, choose
View⇨Toolbox to call it forth.

To add a control to your form, follow these steps:

1. **Click the Toolbox icon for the control that you want to add.**

2. **Move the mouse pointer over the form.**

   The mouse pointer becomes a cross, showing the icon of the control that you selected.

3. **Click and drag the mouse over the part of the form that you want the control to occupy (see Figure 15-2).**

4. **Release the mouse button.**

   The control appears on the form.

Normally, VBA reverts back to the arrow mouse pointer for selecting objects as soon as you finish adding a new control. If you want to add two or more of the same type of control to a form, double-click the icon for that control in the Toolbox. When you're through, click the arrow icon to stop adding controls.

Figure 15-2:
Adding a new toggle-button control to a UserForm.

Working with Form and Control Properties

Because VBA forms and controls are objects, they have properties that determine their appearance and behavior. And, as with all object properties, you can examine and change the properties of forms and controls in your code.

For these objects, however, you don't *have* to write code. Instead, the Visual Basic Editor's Properties window allows you to easily control many critical characteristics of forms and controls without programming per se. As your programs get more sophisticated, you'll want — in fact, you'll *beg* — to set properties in code. Even then, though, the Properties window is still the easiest way to control the initial settings for form and control properties.

The Properties window is shown in Figure 15-3. If the Properties window isn't already on-screen, display it by choosing View➪Properties Window or by pressing F4.

Figure 15-3: The Properties window for a VBA form.

Touring the Properties window

The Properties window is especially cool for two reasons:

  ✔ It automatically shows the properties of whatever you selected in the UserForm window (a particular control or the form itself).

✔ You can work with the properties for any item on the form by choosing the item from the drop-down list at the top of the Properties window. Figure 15-4 shows the drop-down list in action.

Figure 15-4:
The drop-down list at the top of the Properties dialog box lets you see and change properties for any item on a form, or the form itself.

Notice that the display at the top of the window always shows the name and type of the item whose properties you're currently working with.

The bulk of the Properties window is divided into two tabs. Both tabs display exactly the same set of properties, but the Alphabetic tab lists them according to annual income (not really), whereas the Categorized tab divides them into related groups.

Whichever tab you choose, the window works the same way. To the right of the property names, each individual property has a *field* where you can change the property's setting.

Getting Help on properties

If you can't figure out what a given property is for or what settings work, just ask for Help. Click the property's field and press F1 to display the relevant topic from the VBA Forms Help file.

Changing property settings

Depending on the individual property, you change the setting in its field in one of three ways:

✔ By typing a new setting

✔ By choosing the new setting from a drop-down list

✔ By choosing the new setting in a dialog box

Some properties allow you to either type a setting or choose it from a list.

You can't tell whether a property has a drop-down list or a dialog box until you click the property field. When you do, a button appears in the field; then you can click this button. (The button has a downward pointing arrow for drop-down lists or three little dots for dialog boxes; refer to Figure 15-3 for an example.)

Don't forget to select the right item

Before you add controls to a form, the form itself is the only item listed in the Properties window. As soon as you add one or more controls, however, you need to start paying attention to which item (the form or one of its controls) is selected. VBA is quite conventional in indicating a selection. Just as you might expect, little square *handles* appear on the corners and sides of the selected item.

One way to select an item in the first place, of course, is just to click it. But that procedure can be a bit tricky.

For one thing, even though you can look at the form and see which item is selected, you can easily think that you clicked the right item, go to the Properties window and start changing things, and then realize that the wrong item was selected after all. I don't have any great secrets on avoiding this problem. Also, if the form is crowded or (especially) if you stacked controls on top of one another, clicking the item that you want to work with can be hard.

For these reasons, I suggest that you make it a habit to select form items in a different way — via the drop-down list at the top of the Properties window. The selection handles appear around the selected item's perimeter just as if you had clicked it. If you prefer the direct click-it method, at least practice glancing at the display at the top of Properties to make sure that you selected the right item.

Working with Key Form and Control Properties

Many properties of forms and controls work identically across different objects and specific properties. For example, you use very similar techniques to change the size of a form and its controls. All of the color-related properties work the same way whether you're setting the color of the form's background or that of a control's text. This section covers the most important format-related properties that are common to forms and controls.

When you create a new form, get in the habit of making the following property settings for the form, before you add any controls:

Step to Take	Property to Set	Comments
Name the form	(Name)	You use the name to refer to the form in your program. Choose a terse name that nevertheless describes its function.
Assign a caption to the form	Caption	The caption is the text that appears in the form's title bar. Choose a caption that will help the user identify the form's purpose.
Specify a default font	Font	
Select a default text color for the form's control	ForeColor	
Specify the form's background color	BackColor	

These properties are discussed in more detail in the following sections.

The Name is not the Caption

As you may know by now, every object in a VBA program has a name, and forms and controls are no exception. But an object's name doesn't appear anywhere on the form. Instead, you use the name to refer to the object in your code — if, for example, your program needs to activate one of the object's methods or to change one of its other properties.

And yes, forms and controls do have a `Name` property. If you think about it, this fact is sort of odd — you need the name to refer to the object in the first place. But if you're using a `For Each` loop to access the forms in the `Forms` collection or the controls within a form, the program can obtain a valid object reference without knowing the name of the object in question.

Anyway, the main point is that the name you choose for an object is the name that you use in your code when you want to do something with the object. A form or control name must be a valid VBA name (no spaces or punctuation characters allowed; see Chapter 8). And the name should describe the object's function in your program.

The *caption* of a form or control is something else again. A form's caption specifies the text that appears in its title bar, while a control's caption — if the control has one — specifies the text on the surface of the control. You can change the `Caption` property by typing a new text string in the corresponding field of the Properties window. In the case of controls, you can click once to select the control and then click again to edit the caption directly on the control. (Don't double-click the control — that action takes you to the Code window.)

Modal versus modeless forms

The classic example of a *modal* form is the typical dialog box: When the dialog box is active, you can't work with any other part of the program; you have to close the dialog box in order to work with a different dialog box or directly with a document. Likewise, when a modal form is active, the only parts of your VBA program that can run are the procedures belonging to the form itself. The form can respond to events, but the rest of your program is suspended and the underlying application itself is off limits to the user — until the form is closed.

VBA 6 gives you a choice between modal and *modeless* behavior for each dialog box. By default, the form's `ShowModal` property is `True`, meaning the form is modal. Change it to `False` if you want users to be able to switch back and forth between this form and other open forms. When the `ShowModal` property is `False`, your program — the one that displayed the form — continues running actively while the form is visible.

Users of your program won't be able to move between forms unless *all* the open forms are designated as modeless. As soon as your program opens a single modal form, the remainder of the program is suspended until the user closes that form. If the program shows other forms before the modal one, they remain visible on the screen but can't be activated until the modal form gets closed.

All forms in VBA 5 are modal. VBA 5 forms don't have the `ShowModal` property.

Sizing and positioning forms and controls

Before you do any serious design work on a form, be aware that like any self-respecting graphics program, the Visual Basic Editor has a grid. The *grid* defines imaginary magnetic lines, vertical and horizontal. When you move or resize any item on a form, the edges automatically snap into place along the nearest grid line. I save details on the grid for the "Aligning and grouping controls" section of the bonus chapter at www.dummies.com/bonus/vba/. But you should know that the grid can save you work if you set it up to suit your own project.

Okay, now with that out of the way . . . the easiest property to change in a form or control is its size. Although you can set the `Height` and `Width` properties in the Properties window, it's easier to just grab the item by one of its handles — the little boxes that appear on the corners and sides of the item when it's selected. I know that you know how to do resize items already; every Windows program that allows you to resize graphical shapes, from Paint on up, uses this system. But here's how to do the drill:

- Drag a bottom or right *side* handle to size the form in one dimension
- Drag the *corner* handle to size the form in both dimensions simultaneously

Sizing forms with the mouse

Notice that only white handles work for sizing — and that most of the handles for a form are black. The black ones don't do anything except set off the form smartly. Forms are always pushed up against the top-left corner of their windows. You can't move a form in its window. But don't worry about this — a form's position in the window doesn't affect its position on-screen.

Sizing by the numbers

You can also size a form or any of its controls by using precise numeric measurements; just change the `Height` and `Width` properties in the Properties dialog box. Key "point": values for these properties are given in points, a *point* being 1/72 of an inch.

Controlling a form's position on-screen

You have full control over where the form initially appears on-screen when you run your program (or when you run the form by itself, which you can do to test it). The StartUpPosition property is the key.

The default value for this property is 1 - CenterOwner. This specifies that the form should appear in the center of the VBA application's window, regardless of how big it is or where on the screen it's located (well, unless the window is partially off the screen, in which case, your form pushes itself all the way to the edge, but never farther than that). If you want your form to appear in the middle of the screen, no matter what the VBA application is doing, set the StartUpPosition property to 2 - CenterScreen instead. To set the position yourself, choose 0 - Manual and then type values for the Left and Top properties, too.

Positioning controls

To change a control's position within a form, just drag the control wherever you want it to go. If you're a stickler for details, you can type numeric position values for the Left and Top properties.

Choosing colors

The ForeColor and BackColor properties specify the foreground and background colors, respectively, for forms and controls. Note that for controls, the ForeColor property determines the color of text displayed on the control. It isn't available for controls that have no text. For forms, this property specifies the default ForeColor setting for new controls you add to the form, as well as the color of the grid (visible only when you're designing the form).

All color-related properties work the same way. When you click the arrow button for a color property, you get a cute little color menu, which, despite its small size, is complete with two tabs. Figure 15-5 shows you what I mean.

The System tab, shown on the left in Figure 15-5, allows you to choose colors from the Windows system palette — in other words, based on the settings in the Windows Control Panel for the items listed. When you choose an item such as Desktop or Button Face from the list, VBA automatically adjusts the color property whenever the system colors change in the Control Panel.

The Palette tab, shown on the right in Figure 15-5, allows you to choose a color from a menu of preset choices. VBA transfers the numeric value for the color that you pick to the property field. Simple enough.

Figure 15-5:
This illustration shows both tabs of the VBA Color Selection dialog box.

Selecting fonts

Although the default text that VBA paints for you on forms and controls looks swell, you have free rein to choose alternative typefaces. In fact, you can select any of the fonts that are installed on your system for any text item displayed in a form, via the Font property of Form objects and most controls.

A form's Font property doesn't actually change anything in the form itself. The font for the form's caption, which appears in the title bar, is controlled by your Windows system settings via the Control Panel. Instead, you use the form's Font property to set the default font for controls that you add to your form.

This fact leads to a tip: If you want to use a nonstandard font throughout the form, set the *form's* Font property and be done with it. That way, you don't need to change the Font properties of every control individually.

To select a font for a form or an individual control, locate the Font property in the Properties window, click the corresponding field, and then click the little three-dot button to the right of the field. This button displays the no-surprises Font dialog box shown in Figure 15-6.

Become your own color designer

If none of the color choices in either tab suits you, you can choose a custom color from any of those available on your system. The trick is to right-click on any of the color squares on the bottom two rows of the Palette tab. When you do, the dialog box shown in the figure appears.

Although you can type numeric values for Hue and Saturation settings, don't bother. Instead, just drag the mouse around in the main part of the dialog box until the color you want appears in the Color/Solid area at the bottom right. If all you see is white or black, adjust the luminosity setting represented by that vertical bar at the far right of the dialog box. Just drag that little arrow located to the right of the bar toward the bar's middle. The luminosity setting controls the lightness or darkness of the colors available in the dialog box.

When you're happy with the color, click Add Color to close the dialog box and select the

chosen color for whatever form or control property you're working with. The next time you display the Palette tab, the color you chose appears in one of the squares on the bottom two rows.

Figure 15-6: Use this dialog box to choose the default font for a form or for text on any control.

You should consider two potential downsides if you're thinking about using alternative fonts. The practical concern applies if you intend to distribute your program to other people; in that case, those people must have the same fonts that you used installed on their systems. If they don't, Windows chooses substitute fonts, and who knows how those fonts will look? The other caveat is simply esthetic: Fancy fonts and mixtures of typefaces draw attention to themselves and away from the purpose of the form.

Trés chic with special 3-D effects

If you go in for the faux 3-D look, check out the SpecialEffect property, which is available for forms and some controls. Chosen from a drop-down list, settings other than 0 (for flat) impart a subtle but definite impression of depth to the target object. Figure 15-7 demonstrates the three special effects that you can use.

Figure 15-7:
A form with all the available options for the Special Effect property.

Easy mouse tricks

Several VBA properties allow you to control what users see when they're just doodling, allowing the mouse to linger here and there on-screen. No event programming is required!

Customizing the mouse pointer

In really classy professional software, the mouse pointer changes when it passes over certain parts of the screen. As a really classy professional yourself, you deserve to have this impressive feature in the VBA programs that you write.

And you can, just by setting a property or two. Here's how:

1. **Select the form or control for which you want special mouse-pointer treatment.**

2. **Locate the** `MousePointer` **property in the Properties window and click its field.**

3. **Choose a pointer option from the drop-down list.**

All but one of the choices in the drop-down list correspond to the Windows mouse pointers that you set in the Windows Control Panel (specifically, the Pointers tab of the Mouse applet). With these choices, the actual pointer that appears when the program runs depends on which graphic is currently assigned to that type of pointer in the Control Panel.

When you assign a custom mouse pointer to a *form,* your pointer appears in the entire form, including all its controls (except those for which you assign a different pointer).

Using mouse pointers of your own design

Maybe you want a skull and crossbones to appear when the mouse pointer crosses a forbidden control — no matter what, regardless of the Control Panel settings. Or perhaps a more prosaic image, such as a classic desk clock, suits you better (see Figure 15-8).

Figure 15-8:
A custom
mouse
pointer
hovering
over a
VBA form.

As long as you have a suitable graphic, converting it into a custom mouse pointer is no big deal. Follow these steps:

1. **Draw a new icon or crib one from a clip-art collection.**

   The graphic should be saved in the standard Windows icon format in an .ico file.

2. **Follow the three steps detailed in the previous section, "Customizing the mouse pointer," setting the** MousePointer **property to** 99, for fmMousePointerCustom, **in Step 3.**

3. **Click the** MouseIcon **field.**

4. **Click the dialog-box button (the one with the three dots).**

   VBA displays a Load Picture dialog box, which you can use to locate and open your mouse-pointer graphic.

Adding ToolTips to controls

Your VBA forms can even have ToolTips — those little text messages that appear when the mouse pointer hovers over a control for a second or two. ToolTips are a great way to inform the user unobtrusively about the function of a control. And, yes, ToolTips are available only for individual controls, not for the form that houses them.

To add a ToolTip, just type the appropriate text in the field for the ToolTip property. Figure 15-9 shows an example of the result that you can expect.

Adding a picture to a form or control

Because you can't restrain your artistic impulses forever, the time will come when you want to grace a form or its controls with pictures. In addition to adding colorful variety to dull text windows, you can use pictures as icons on command buttons, check boxes, option buttons, and frames, among other controls. Figure 15-10 shows a few examples.

The Image control — which is the only one in the Toolbox with a little picture on it — isn't the only control to which you can add pictures. An Image control is essentially just a label without a caption. You can use a label control to hold a picture, if you prefer, removing its caption if you don't want to display text on the control.

Don't worry that working with graphics is beyond the skill of a beginning programmer. Once again, VBA makes the process almost trivially easy. Follow these steps:

1. **Click the form or control that deserves a pretty picture.**

2. **In the Properties window, click the** Picture **property for the selected object.**

Figure 15-9:
What does
that button
do, anyway?
The telltale
ToolTip
tattles.

3. **Click the dialog-box button (with three dots) that now appears in the** Picture **property's field.**

4. **In the Load Picture dialog box, locate the desired picture file and then click Open to add it to the object.**

   The picture appears in the selected form or control.

Figure 15-10:
Pictures
added to a
VBA form
and several
of its
controls.

5. **Use the** PictureAlignment, PictureSizeMode, **and** PictureTiling **properties (if they're available for the object that you're working with) to adjust the picture to your taste. Here are details on each of these properties:**

- Options for the PictureAlignment property allow you to control whether the picture sits right in the center of the object or is snuggled into a corner.

- Options for the PictureSizeMode property allow you to stretch the picture so that it fills the entire form or control (fmPictureSizeModeStretch); shrink it until the entire picture fits into the object (fmPictureSizeModeZoom); or leave it at normal size, cutting off any part that doesn't fit (fmPictureSizeModeClip).

- The PictureTiling property has only two options: True (meaning that VBA duplicates the picture as many times as necessary to fill the object) or False.

Removing a picture using the Properties window

After you fool around with pictures in your forms for a while, you may decide that a Spartan look is better after all. To remove a picture from a control or form, click the field for the Picture property in the Properties window, and then press the Delete key. No other method works — not pressing Ctrl+X, not pressing the spacebar or typing, and definitely not pressing the Backspace key.

Editing Controls: The Basics

Before you go bananas with the fancier formatting commands for controls, be sure that you know the basics. I discuss how to size and move controls by using the mouse or via their properties in "Key form and control properties" earlier in this chapter. In this section, other simple editing techniques come to light.

Cutting, copying, and pasting controls

As a card-carrying Windows program, the Visual Basic Editor allows you to cut, copy, and paste controls individually or in groups. The standard Windows menu commands and keyboard shortcuts apply. In addition, you can use the Cut, Copy, and Paste buttons in the Editor's Standard toolbar for one-click access to these functions. (These buttons look just like the ones in Microsoft Office.)

The only thing special about these commands has to do with Paste. When you paste a control from the Clipboard, VBA deposits it in the center of the form, even if that part of the form isn't currently visible. If you select a frame or multipage control before doing the paste, however, the control goes into the center of that item. (Frames and multipage controls are discussed in the bonus online chapter at www.dummies.com/bonus/vba/.)

Deleting controls

You can delete one or more selected controls without placing them on the Clipboard by pressing the Delete key or choosing Edit⇨Delete. Notice that the Backspace key does not work for this purpose, as it does in some other programs.

Selecting multiple controls

You can select a group of controls and then move, resize, cut, or copy them as a unit, or apply other formatting commands as described later in this chapter. This is also a great way to efficiently set properties they have in common to the same values. To select multiple controls, you can use these methods:

- ✔ Draw a selection rectangle around the controls that you want to include in the group by clicking the Toolbox arrow pointer and dragging diagonally over the controls. If any part of a control is included in the rectangle, that control is included in the selection.

- ✔ Click the first control in the group and then Shift+click a control at the other side of the selection area. All controls between the two that you clicked are included in the selection.

- ✔ Ctrl+click individual controls to add them to or remove them from the selection.

After you select a group of controls, you can move, resize, cut, or copy them as a unit and apply other formatting commands, as described later in this chapter. Selecting controls as a group is also a great way to efficiently set properties that the selected controls share to the same values.

Undoing changes

You usually can reverse the effects of the last formatting change involving controls by using the Undo command (Ctrl+Z). Undo doesn't work after you resize a form, however, nor does it reverse changes that you make in the Properties window.

Working with the grid

The *grid* is an array of horizontal and vertical lines that crisscross your forms. The grid has two functions:

- ✔ **To visually guide you as you place controls with the mouse.** The visual grid comprises those dotted lines that you've probably seen in your forms.

- ✔ **To automatically align controls to the grid as you move or resize controls.** No matter how you move the mouse, the edges of your controls always snap into alignment along one of the gridlines. This ensures a reasonable consistency in your form layout, although it limits your flexibility.

The two functions work independently. You can turn off the visible grid and leave automatic alignment on, or vice versa.

Setting grid options

To control the way that the grid works, choose Tools⇨Options. When the Options dialog box appears, click the General tab to reveal the panel of choices shown in Figure 15-11.

Figure 15-11:
Change grid settings in the General tab of the Options dialog box.

Confining your attention to the top-left part of the dialog box, you can see the few simple grid-related options. They are:

- **Show Grid.** Clear this checkbox to turn off the visual grid — those dotted lines in your forms. This option doesn't affect automatic alignment to the grid.

- **Width** and **Height.** These two text boxes allow you to control the size of your grid in the horizontal and vertical dimensions independently. The Width setting controls the distance between each pair of vertical gridlines, which in turn affects the horizontal position of controls. Similarly, the Height setting is for the horizontal gridlines but pertains to vertical position.

- **Align Controls to Grid.** When this box is checked, the "snap to grid" function is in force. Clear the box to give yourself complete freedom to position and size controls to any measurements that you please. Again, the visual grid *can* be on when this function is off.

Formatting Controls

Generally people are affected by intangibles such as symmetry, consistency, and general neatness. You want to help users of your forms stay focused on what they're trying to accomplish, rather than distract them with a disorganized jumble of controls.

Fortunately, VBA provides a stable of tools that help you achieve this goal easily. Although laying out a well-organized form still takes some manual labor, the Visual Basic Editor's automatic formatting features can handle much of the work.

Using the Format menu

The Visual Basic Editor's Format menu (see Figure 15-12) is the control center for commands that affect the layout of controls in a form. Getting on intimate terms with the menu and its multiple submenus serves you well during the process of form design.

Using the UserForm toolbar

When you're working with a form in the Visual Basic Editor, the UserForm toolbar comes in handy. If the toolbar isn't already visible, display it by right-clicking any toolbar and then choosing UserForm from the shortcut menu. Figure 15-13 shows how the UserForm toolbar looks in its floating configuration.

Figure 15-12:
The Format menu in the Visual Basic Editor.

Figure 15-13:
The UserForm toolbar offers buttons for common control formatting commands.

Bring to Front   Make Same Size
Group   Align
Ungroup   Center
Send to Back   Zoom

Most of the buttons on the UserForm toolbar correspond to items on the Format menu. Some of them are split buttons — the ones with little down arrows to their right — providing multiple options. If you click the main part of one of these split buttons, VBA immediately activates the option that was last used. To select a different option, click the little arrow and choose the option from the list.

Grouping multiple controls

Although it's fairly easy to use the mouse to select multiple controls on the fly, this method isn't ideal when you want to work repeatedly with the same set of controls as a unit. By combining all the controls into a *group,* you don't have to reselect the same controls every time you do something to them, and you eliminate the possibility of selection mistakes. Figure 15-14 shows examples of grouped controls.

Creating a group is simple. Just follow these steps:

1. **Select all the controls that you want to include in the group.**

2. **Click the Group button in the UserForm toolbar or choose Format⇨Group.**

Figure 15-14:
Several
groups of
controls.
Notice
that the
selection
rectangle
extends
around all
the controls
in the group.

Grouping lets you apply formatting commands that normally work on single controls to groups as a whole. If you want to even out the spacing between three rows of buttons, for example, you can convert each row into a group, select all three groups simultaneously, and then choose the Horizontal Spacing⇨Make Equal command (see "Adjusting horizontal and vertical spacing" later in this chapter).

Arranging controls on top of one another

Although it's usually best to avoid overlapping controls, such a design can be vital when you need to change the contents of a form while your program runs. If you set each control's `Visible` property to `True` or `False` as necessary, the program can keep all but one of the overlapping controls invisible at any one time (see Chapter 16 for more information on this technique).

Inside the Visual Basic Editor, however, every control is always visible — unless, that is, it's buried underneath other controls on the form. When this happens, you can use the Order commands in the Format menu to rearrange the controls.

Here are suggestions for using the Order commands:

- ✔ If you can get to a tiny piece of a buried control, click there to select the control, and then choose Format⇨Order⇨Bring to Front to place the control on the top of the pile. Have at it.

- ✔ If the control that you want to work with is completely covered by the ones on top, click the topmost control to select it, and then banish it to the bottom of the pile by choosing Format⇨Order⇨Send to Back. Repeat this process until the control that you want is on top.

- ✔ If you're arranging controls that will actually overlap while the program runs, you may need to use the Format⇨Order⇨Bring Forward or Send Backward commands to order them just so. These commands move the selected control by one position in the pile.

Formatting multiple controls

Many of the more advanced commands on the Format menu only work on multiple controls, or on selections that include two or more groups. This section describes each of these commands, after an important digression about which selected item has the power in the relationship.

Control and domination

No, this section isn't a sudden kinky detour. In some formatting commands involving multiple controls, one control serves as the reference point for the command. This control is the *dominant control,* in VBA lingo.

When you use the Format⇨Make Same Size command to make uniform a set of selected controls, for example, VBA copies the chosen dimension (height, width, or both) from the dominant control to all the other controls in the set. Likewise for the Align command — the other controls in the set line up with the dominant control, which doesn't move. The effects of the Horizontal and Vertical Spacing commands (also on the Format menu) also depend on which control is dominant.

In Figure 15-15, you see that only one of the selected controls is outlined in white sizing handles. That's the dominant control, whose handles are always white. Other controls in the selection have black handles around their margins.

As you already know, you can select a group of controls in one of two main ways: by dragging a selection rectangle around the entire group by using the Toolbox arrow pointer or by Shift+clicking or Ctrl+clicking each control, one by one. What you haven't seen so far is how to set the dominant control while you're using these techniques. The following table shows how:

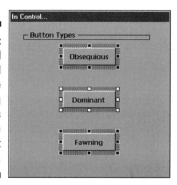

Figure 15-15:
The control surrounded by white sizing handles is the dominant control.

Control Selection Strategy	Selection Technique
Choose the dominant control by dragging a selection rectangle	Begin dragging the selection closer to the target control than any other
Choose the first control you click as the dominant control	Shift+click to select each control in the set
Choose the last control you click as the dominant control	Ctrl+click to select each control in the set
Choose a different dominant control for an existing selection	Ctrl+click the chosen control *twice*

Aligning controls

Even with the grid on, it's common to find that controls that ought to be in a straight line or column actually are staggered. Instead of laboriously lining the controls up by hand, enlist the Visual Basic Editor's Align commands to do the work for you. You can bring the midline or any edge (top, bottom, left, or right) of each selected control into alignment along either a vertical or horizontal axis.

Follow these steps to align a set of controls:

1. **Select the controls, taking care to choose the one control that should remain in place as the dominant control (refer to the preceding section).**

2. **Choose Format➪Align and then choose a specific type of alignment from the submenu.**

Alternatively, you can click the Align button in the UserForm toolbar (if it indicates the correct type of alignment) or click just beside the button proper to display the same list of alignment options that appears in the menu.

Making controls the same size

The three <u>M</u>ake Same Size commands on the Format menu automatically adjust all selected controls to match the size of the dominant control in the selection. You can bring instant conformity in width, height, or both dimensions. The three commands can also be found on a split button on the UserForm toolbar.

Adjusting horizontal and vertical spacing

The Format menu's Horizontal Spacing and Vertical Spacing commands can each change the space between two or more controls in four different ways. Three of these options are most useful — and one is available only — when the selection includes at least three controls. Here's how the choices work:

- ✔ **Make Equal:** Evens out the space between three or more selected controls. The controls at either end of the selection stay in place, while the controls in between move. This command isn't available if only two controls are selected.

- ✔ **Increase** and **Decrease:** Add or remove space between the selected controls by an amount equal to one grid unit for the dimension that you're working with. The dominant control stays in place while the others move.

- ✔ **Remove:** Moves controls so that there is no space between them and their edges touch. The dominant control doesn't move.

Making other formatting choices

For the most part, the other options on the Format menu work on individual controls as well as groups. After selecting one or more controls, you can use

- ✔ **Center in Form** to center the items either vertically or horizontally. Notice that if you selected two or more controls, this command brings all the controls to the midline rather than centering the set as a unit (group the controls first if you want the latter result).

- ✔ **Arrange Buttons** to place one or more selected command buttons at the bottom or right edge of the form. Although Arrange Buttons operates when other controls are included in the selection, only the command buttons move.

✔ **Size to Fit** to have VBA resize the control(s) to fit whatever text they currently contain. This command is a one-shot affair — it does not set the `AutoSize` property to `True` — so the size remains constant if you later change the text in the control.

✔ **Size to Grid** to move the edges of the selected control(s) to the nearest gridline.

The Visual Basic Editor lacks a command for distributing controls evenly along a row or column. You can approximate this command easily enough, however, by following these steps (all the commands mentioned are on the Format menu):

1. **Arrange the controls with the mouse so they're about where you want them to be.**

2. **Select the controls and activate the A̲lign⇨T̲ops command (or any other horizontal alignment option).**

3. **With all the controls still selected, activate the H̲orizontal Spacing⇨Make E̲qual command.**

4. **Group the selected controls (activate the Group command).**

5. **Activate the Center in Form Horizontally command.**

The preceding steps assume that you're distributing the controls along a row. To distribute the controls vertically instead, substitute the vertical version of each command in Steps 2, 3, and 5.

Chapter 16

Form Programming

. . . .

. . . .

*A*dding controls to a form is a piece of cake, but getting them to do your bidding takes a little more brain power and programming work. This chapter cuts through the complexities of the form programming process.

If You've Got It, Flaunt It!

Once you've decided to include custom forms in a VBA program, the first and most fundamental programming problem is how to get your forms on the screen to begin with. You can construct the most beautiful, elegantly organized form ever, but if nobody gets to see it, so what?

Since a VBA program can fall back on the user interface of the underlying application, the program doesn't automatically display a form when it runs. In this respect VBA is different than its cousin Visual Basic, in which the program *is* the form, in essence. At any rate, in a VBA program, you must add code to display a form so that it becomes accessible to users.

You can always display a form in the Visual Basic Editor by viewing the form in its UserForm window. There, although the form's controls are inert, you can see and edit the form's layout as discussed in Chapter 15 and the bonus chapter on the Web at www.dummies.com/bonus/vba. You can also run a form manually in the Visual Basic Editor by selecting it and pressing F5. Running a form activates the controls, but they probably won't work properly because the rest of your VBA program isn't running. What I'm talking about in this section, however, is having your program display the form.

Loading and Showing Forms

Displaying a VBA form is a two-step process:

- ✔ Loading the form into memory.
- ✔ Showing the form on the screen.

You can use a single VBA statement to perform both steps. However, you may sometimes find it useful to separate the steps over two distinct statements.

Show-ing windows

The ticket to displaying any form is to execute its Show method. If the form is named FormICa, all you need to type is:

```
FormICa.Show
```

Note that Show is a method of the UserForm object, so you append it to the form name following a period. If the form in question isn't already loaded into memory, the Show method loads it and then displays it. If the form is loaded but hidden, the Show method just makes it visible.

Loading a form without displaying it

Use the Load statement to load the form into memory before you actually display it on the screen. Load is not a method, so the syntax is backwards compared to Show, as in:

```
Load FormAlDeHyde
```

Why load a form without displaying it? Well, if your program uses numerous or complicated forms, this can make your program seem faster to the user. Loading a form takes much longer than displaying it. Since a program of any complexity performs lots of miscellaneous initialization procedures (such as reading data from files, calculating initial variables, and creating objects), a waiting period is typical when the program starts up. If you load your forms at that time too, users won't notice the wait as much as they might later on. The only disadvantage of preloading your forms is that they consume memory that you may need for other purposes.

Making changes in your form before you display it

You can also load a form — without the Load statement — by entering code statements that manipulate a property or method of the form, or of one of its controls. This technique allows your program to make changes in a form before displaying it on the screen. True, the Visual Basic Editor's Properties window allows you to control exactly how the form looks and acts without any programming, but consider this point: you often don't know how the form (or its controls) should look or act until your program is running.

As a simple example, suppose you want the form's caption to display the date and time. Since you can't predict when someone is going to run your program — and since you probably expect it to run more than once — you need to let VBA figure out the current date and time for you. This simple sample does the trick:

```
Sub DisplayDateCaptionedForm ()
    DateCaptionedForm.Caption = Now
    DateCaptionedForm.Show
End Sub
```

Using a similar approach, you could have the form use a label or text box control to display information about whatever is currently selected in your VBA application. Figure 16-1 shows what you get by running the following VBA procedure in Visio, coupled with an appropriate form:

```
Sub DisplayShowSelectionForm()
    Dim ItemCount As Integer, Message As String
    Items = ActiveWindow.Selection.Count
    Message = CStr(Items) & " objects are selected."
    ShowSelectionForm.lblCountOfItems.Caption = Message
    ShowSelectionForm.Show
End Sub
```

Notice the line of sample code that alters the property of a label control in the target form:

```
    ShowSelectionForm.lblCountOfItems.Caption = Message
```

Technically, you can't access a form's properties or methods until it has been loaded. You don't need to write an explicit statement to do so, however. VBA automatically loads the form into memory as soon as it encounters a statement that refers to one of the form's properties or methods. Referring to a property or method of one of the form's controls has the same effect.

Figure 16-1:
This
program
figures out
what to
display in
the label
caption just
before you
show the
form.

Altering a form with the Initialize and Activate events

The example in the preceding section demonstrates one way to make
changes in a form before displaying it — from within a standard procedure in
a regular module. But there's more than one way to skin a cabbage. In this
case, your alternatives are the form's own Initialize and Activate events.
Code that you place in these event procedures runs automatically when the
corresponding event occurs. Decide between the two events as follows:

   ✔ Use the Initialize event for code that should run only when VBA first
     loads the form.

   ✔ Use the Activate event for code that should run every time the form is
     displayed (including the first time).

Writing code for event procedures is discussed in the section "The Main
Events" later in this chapter.

Referring to forms using variables

Although your code can refer to a form object directly by name, you may prefer to use a variable. If the form has a long name, this can cut down on your typing. It can also help your code run faster when your program displays forms from different projects.

Because forms are objects, the techniques for working with object variables described in Chapter 10 apply. The following procedure illustrates the process. Note that you must declare a form variable based on a specific form, not as a generic UserForm.

```
Sub FormVariableDemo()

Dim frm1 As FormAnOpinion
Set frm1 = FormAnOpinion

' Alter properties and invoke methods via the variable:
With frm1
 .Caption = "All of the above"
 .Show
End With
End Sub
```

Technically, the Set statement creates a separate copy or *instance* of the form, assigning it to the variable you've chosen. You can use this technique to display multiple copies of the same form, each having its own values in its controls. You must use the New keyword with the Set statement to create additional instances of a form. Here's how it's done:

```
' declare form variables
Dim frmOne As MultiForm
Dim frmTwo As MultiForm
' fill each variable with a separate instance of the form
Set frmOne = MultiForm
Set frmTwo = New MultiForm ' use New keyword here
' display the two instances of the form
frmOne.Show
frmTwo.Show
```

Hiding a visible form

Use a form's Hide method to close the form so your program can return to the VBA application's document or activate another form. A statement such as

```
FormErly.Hide
```

does the trick. But you can't use the `Hide` method just anywhere in your program. If the form is modal, you must place the `Hide` method in an event procedure belonging to the form itself. As discussed in Chapter 15, when a modal form is open, the only procedures that can run are those tied to the form. Remember that all VBA 5 forms are modal, and that VBA 6 forms are modal by default. In VBA 6, you can hide modeless forms from other parts of your program.

And by the way, when you do use the `Hide` method in an event procedure belonging to the form you're hiding, you don't need to use the form's name. VBA is smart enough to know that the `Hide` method belongs to the form, so when placed within an event procedure belonging to any form, a simple

```
Hide
```

always works to hide that form.

Most often, the `Hide` statement belongs at the end of the `Click` event procedure for an OK, Cancel, or Close command button. For examples, see "Adding a Close or Cancel button" and "Programming the OK button" later in this chapter.

Hiding the form does not remove it from memory. You can redisplay the form at top speed any time you need it with the `Show` method.

Removing a form from memory

If you know that your program won't be needing a form again, you can destroy the form altogether, removing it from memory. In a small VBA program, you have no real need to do this, but when your program becomes large and memory is at a premium, unloading unneeded forms makes sense.

Just as when you load a form, you use a statement, not a method, to unload a form from memory, as in

```
Unload FormAtion
```

Unloading a form also removes it from the screen, if it was visible.

If you know that a form won't be needed again, you can substitute the `Unload` statement for the `Hide` method in the form's event procedures that close the form (see the previous section). In that situation, `Unload Me` is equivalent to `Unload formname`, since the `Me` keyword always represents the current form object.

Unlike the Hide method, however, Unload works with modal forms that aren't currently active on the screen. You can unload any form, including a previously hidden modal form via an Unload statement placed in the main part of your program — that is, in a procedure that isn't tied to a form.

The Main Events

When you activate a Sub procedure that doesn't display forms, your code has full control of what the program does and when it does it. Once a form is on the screen, though, your program enters a much more passive state, watchfully waiting for instructions from the user. As the user presses keys or moves or clicks the mouse, each such action generates a software event. In turn, your program registers each event, checking to see whether the form's code contains an event procedure tied to that event. If not, the event passes through your program without a trace. But if the form does have a corresponding event procedure, the program springs to life, faithfully running the procedure.

An event procedure can do anything that any ordinary procedure can. It can calculate variables, manipulate object properties and methods, and even load and display other forms. After the event procedure finishes running, control returns to the form. The program goes back to waiting for the next event to occur.

Common events

VBA forms and their controls are capable of detecting and recognizing a wide variety of events. (In VBA lingo, when you say that an object "has" events, you mean that the object can detect and recognize those events.) Forms and controls share many events, but each of these objects has a different set of events. Table 16-1 lists commonly useful events.

Table 16-1	Selected Events for Form and Control Objects	
Event(s)	*Objects It Applies to*	*When It Occurs*
Activate	Forms	Each time the form is activated (receives the focus)
AddControl	Forms, frames, and multipage controls	When a control is added to the object while the form is running

(continued)

Table 16-1 *(continued)*

Event(s)	Objects It Applies to	When It Occurs
AfterUpdate	All "action" controls except command buttons (not labels, pictures, frames, or multipage controls)	After VBA has registered a new value for the control, just before exiting the control to move to another one
Change	All action controls except labels and command buttons; also mulitpage and tabstrip controls	When the Value property of the control changes
Click	Forms and all control types	When the user clicks the mouse over the object
DblClick	Forms and all control types	When the user double-clicks the mouse over the object
DropButtonClick	Combo and text boxes	When the drop-down list drops down (when the user either clicks the drop-down button or presses F4)
Enter	All control types	Just before the control receives the focus from another control on the same form
Error	Forms and all control types	When an error occurs and error information can't be returned to the program
Exit	All control types	Just before the focus moves from the current control to another one on the same form
KeyUp, KeyDown, KeyPress	Forms and all control types	When the user presses or releases a key
Layout	Forms, frames, and multipage controls	When the object's size changes
RemoveControl	Forms, frames, and multipage controls	When a control is removed from the object while the form is running

Event(s)	Objects It Applies to	When It Occurs
Scroll	Forms, frames, multipage controls; and text, combo, and list boxes	When the scroll box is repositioned
Zoom	Forms, frames, and multipage controls	When the object's magnification (Zoom property) changes

Event Procedures Gotta Have Code

As Table 16-1 shows, a form or control *can* respond to many events. But when does a form actually respond to a specific event? Only if the form or control in question has an event procedure for that event. Event procedures have to come from somewhere — they come from you. Writing code for an event procedure is called *trapping* the event.

Writing and editing event procedures

Writing an event procedure is just like writing any other VBA code. You just have to know where to put the statements. Code for an event procedure — and any other code associated with a specific form — belongs in that form's Code window in the Visual Basic Editor. Therefore, event procedures for all the controls in the form, as well as for the form itself, go in the form's Code window. So before you start tapping out new statements, follow these three steps:

1. **Display the Code window for the form.**

   Double-clicking the form or control is the quickest way to do so. Alternatively, you can select the form and choose View➪Code from the shortcut (right-click) menu for the form or control you want to work with. Pressing F7 also works when the form is selected in its UserForm window.

2. **In the Code window, select the object for which you're writing the event procedure.**

   Choose the object from the Object drop-down list in the top-left corner of the form's Code window (see Figure 16-2).

3. **Select the event for which you want to write code.**

   This time, use the Procedure drop-down list in the top-right corner of the Code window.

Figure 16-2:
Selecting a control in a form's Code window in preparation for writing an event procedure.

As soon as you choose an event from the Procedure drop-down list, VBA whisks you directly to the event procedure for that event in the Code window. If no code has been written for this event procedure, VBA creates a new procedure skeleton for you, courteously placing the insertion point on a blank line between the opening procedure declaration and the closing statement (see Figure 16-3). If the event procedure already contains code, VBA simply places the insertion point in the top line of the existing code.

Figure 16-3:
A brand-new event procedure skeleton in the Visual Basic Editor.

Event-procedure syntax

As Figure 16-3 shows, the basic syntax for an event procedure is exactly the same as for ordinary Sub procedures that you write in VBA modules. The only thing unique about an event procedure is its name.

For the event procedure to function at all, its name must consist of the name of the object (the form or control), followed by an underscore character and then the official VBA name for the event. Observe these examples through heavy lenses:

```
Private Sub cmdCalculateSquareRoot_Click()
End Sub

Private Sub UserForm_Activate ()
End Sub

Private Sub sclVolumeControl_Change
End Sub
```

Type-it-yourself event-procedure declarations

You don't have to worry about naming an event procedure. That's because
VBA creates the procedure declaration for you when you select the event in
the form's Code window.

When to change an event procedure's name

The one time you can get into trouble with an event-procedure name is when
you change the name of the associated object after you create the event procedure. VBA doesn't change the name of the procedure automatically, so you
must go back to the Code window and modify the event procedure name to
match the control's new name.

Suppose you've written an event procedure for the Click event of a button
that VBA automatically named CommandButton1. At this point, the procedure
name is CommandButton1_Click. Now you belatedly give the button a more
descriptive name, such as cmdTakeOutTheTrash. Unless and until you
change the name of the original event procedure to
cmdTakeOutTheTrash_Click, the button just sits there, mute and unrespon-
sive, when the form runs, no matter how many times you click it.

Because VBA doesn't remove the procedure when you change the button's
name, you only have to rename the procedure, not retype it from scratch.
Alternatively, you can start a new event procedure for the button, and use the
Cut and Paste commands to move the code from the original procedure to
the new one.

Click here . . .

In Windows, the Click is the quintessential event. You click icons to select
them; text documents to position the insertion point; menus to open them;
and buttons to trigger them, activating whatever function they perform.
Because clicking is so integral an activity in the Windows user interface, you
definitely want your VBA forms to respond to mouse clicks. For most types of
controls, however, you don't have to write any code to make them do tricks
when clicked (I explain why in "When not to write event procedures"). Of
course, you *do* have to write code for the most important control of all, the
command button.

Making Private events Public

Event procedures are special because VBA triggers them automatically when the appropriate events occur. But because an event procedure is otherwise just a regular VBA procedure, you can call it from other code just as you would any other procedure. By simply listing the event procedure name as a separate statement, as in

```
cmdDoTricks_Click
```

you trigger the procedure, in essence tricking VBA into thinking that the event has occurred.

Event procedures are `Private` by default — that is, when VBA creates an event-procedure declaration, it automatically adds the `Private` keyword at the beginning of the declaration. Because event procedures are `Private`, you can run the procedure only from other code associated with the same form.

Nothing stops you, however, from erasing `Private` and typing `Public` instead. You can then call the event procedure from any other part of your program. One caveat: The form must be loaded into memory before you can call any of its `Public` procedures (the form doesn't have to be visible onscreen).

Every command-button control definitely must have a `Click` event procedure, if you want the button to do anything when someone clicks it. The following event procedure simply counts and displays the number of times the user clicks the button:

```
Private Sub cmdCountClicks_Click()
' Declaring the intCount variable as Static preserves
'    its value between calls to the procedure
Static intCount As Integer
intCount = intCount + 1
cmdCountClicks.Caption = "You clicked this button " _
    & intCount & " times."
End Sub
```

This code is fairly straightforward. Each time the event procedure runs — which should occur only when the user clicks the button — the value of the `intCount` variable increases by 1. This value is then used in a string that sets the button's `Caption` property. By the way, declaring the `intCount` variable as `Static` tells VBA to retain the variable's value between passes through the event procedure. If you declared `intCount` with a `Dim` statement, VBA would reinitialize the variable to each time. Here's an event procedure for a button named `cmdMoveThisForm`:

```
Private Sub cmdMoveThisForm_Click()
Move(Left -24), (Top -24)
End Sub
```

In case you're curious, whenever the user clicks the button, this event procedure moves the entire form 24 units up and 24 units to the left. In the procedure's one line of action code, the Move method appears without an object reference; VBA assumes that it refers to the main object of the form, the form itself. If you wanted to move the button instead of the form, you would have used cmdMoveThisForm.Move to specify it as the target object. In the same way, Left and Top are assumed to be properties of the form because no explicit object reference was given.

These two examples are fairly trivial; still, they illustrate the fact that event procedure code looks and acts like any other code.

When not to write Click event procedures

Most VBA controls that you can place in a form have (recognize) the Click event. Except in the case of command buttons, however, it's usually neither necessary nor wise to write event-procedure code for the Click event, even when you want the control to respond to mouse clicks. The reason: These controls respond to clicks automatically and in the way that you want them to.

Suppose you place some option buttons in a VBA form. When you run the form, clicking a button selects the one that you clicked; no programming is required to make this happen. In like fashion, VBA handles clicks of a toggle button or check box automatically. VBA knows to alternate the control between its two possible states (out or pushed in for toggle buttons cleared or checked for check boxes). For its part, a text-box control automatically responds to clicks by positioning the insertion point at the spot where you click.

What VBA can't do — and what you have to do by writing code — is transfer the setting of the control to your program. What text did the user type in the text box? Is the check box checked or cleared? Which option button in the group is selected? Your program won't know unless you write code to collect and use this information.

The key is the control's Value property, which contains the current setting for any control that can assume different states or hold data. You can read the Value property each time it changes by writing an event procedure for the Change event. Alternatively, you can simply read the Value property after you hide the form. See the section on the Change event and "Handling Common Form Programming Tasks" for more information on these techniques.

Click events in UserForms

Even forms themselves have Click events. In practice, of course, most forms are mainly just backdrops on which you place the buttons, text boxes and other controls with which the user interacts. But if you want it to, an entire form can act as one big button, so that clicking it anywhere makes something happen in your program.

Just type the code for the actions you want carried out, inserting it into the Click event for the form, as in:

```
Private Sub UserForm_Click()
...(event code goes here)
End Sub
```

Notice that the names of all event procedures for a form as a whole start with UserForm, no matter what name you have given to the form. If you do write a Click event procedure for a form, be aware that VBA triggers the procedure only if the user clicks the part of the form that isn't covered by any controls. Other mouse-related event procedures work similarly.

Writing code for the Change event

For controls such as scroll bars, spin buttons, option buttons, check boxes, and toggle buttons, Change is the main event. These controls do respond to mouse clicks and key presses, but they do so automatically. VBA and Windows handle the dirty details of changing a control's appearance and adjusting its setting according to which key presses or mouse actions occurred.

Give the poor user some feedback

When users click the up-arrow button at the top of a scroll bar or spinner, they deserve some sort of feedback. How much has the value increased by virtue of this click? For that matter, did the user actually manage to click the button?

Trapping the event allows you to write code to provide that feedback. As discussed at the end of the bonus chapter on the Web at www.dummies.com/bonus/vba, the simplest way is by displaying the Value property of the changed control as the caption of a label control elsewhere on the form. If you like, though, you can include in the Change event procedure statements that play an animated graphic or a sound clip.

You may want your program to respond not to the mouse click itself, however, but to the setting change that it caused. In that case, you should write code for the Change event. The Change event occurs whenever a change occurs in the value of the control (that is, when the control's Value property changes). It doesn't matter whether this change results directly from the user's mouse click or typing, or whether it occurs because some other procedure manipulates the control's Value property in code statements.

You may also want your program to respond to changes in a control's value when the user finishes working with the control. In this case, write code for the control's AfterUpdate event, which is triggered when the focus moves to another control.

An event procedure can do more with a control's new value than just display it, of course. It can also

- ✔ Check to see whether the value meets certain criteria
- ✔ Make calculations based on the value, taking other actions depending on the calculated results
- ✔ Use the control's value to manipulate some other setting, such as the volume of your computer's speaker

Detecting keystrokes

Use the KeyPress, KeyDown, and KeyUp events to respond to the user whacking away at the keyboard. The KeyPress event is good for reading ordinary "typeable" keys — letters, numerals, and punctuation marks — when you're processing entries typed into a text box or combo. It can also recognize many Ctrl+<key> combinations and the Backspace key. Later, I show you how you can validate or change typed characters by using the KeyPress event procedure — see "Screening out or changing individual characters."

The KeyDown and KeyUp events, by contrast, detect just about any key combination you throw at them, including convolutions such as Alt+Shift+Ctrl+F9. Although they're harder to work with than KeyPress, these events give you more flexibility for creating keyboard shortcuts. For example, you can write a KeyDown event procedure to have the Ctrl+Left Arrow and Ctrl+Right Arrow combinations lower and raise the value of a scroll-bar or spin-button control by 10.

Handling Common Form Programming Tasks

Once you understand how event procedures work you can put your knowledge to work in building dialog boxes that work the way you want them to — and the way users expect them to. In this section I've collected a set of tips covering many of the common scenarios in dialog box construction.

Adding a Close or Cancel button

At a minimum, most dialog boxes have one all-important command button: the one that removes the dialog box from the screen. Depending on the way the rest of the dialog box works, this button is typically captioned Close or Cancel, but captions such as Exit, Finish, All Done, or Give Up would also be appropriate. Every form you make needs such a button.

By convention, both Close and Cancel buttons simply hide or unload the form, without doing much else. Here's how to tell which of them your form should have:

✔ Use a Close button for a form that just displays information or performs tasks immediately, without changing program settings or modifying variables that will be used later in the program.

✔ Use a Cancel button on a form that does change variables or program settings. When the user clicks the Cancel button, the dialog box closes without recording those changes — everything stays the way it was before the dialog box was displayed. The form should also have an OK button that confirms any changes that are made.

Easy event procedures for Close and Cancel buttons

Like any other command button, a Close or Cancel button needs a `Click` event procedure to do its job in response to a mouse-click. In most situations, this event procedure requires only a single statement, as in these two examples:

```
Private Sub cmdClose_Click()
    Hide ' Object reference to current form implied
End Sub

Private Sub cmdCancel_Click()
```

```
    Unload frmOptions
End Sub
```

Either type of button can use either the Hide method or the Unload statement, of course. The differences between these two ways to close a form are discussed in the "Hiding a visible form" and "Removing a form from memory" sections earlier in this chapter.

Of course, event procedures tied to Close or Cancel buttons can do other tasks before closing the form. One simple example would be a statement displaying a message box asking if the user really wants to close (or cancel) the dialog box:

```
Private Sub cmdCancel_Click()
    Message = "Do you really want to close the " _
        & "dialog box and cancel all the changes " _
        & "you've made?"
    If MsgBox(Message, vbYesNo) = vbYes Then
        Hide   ' Hide only if the user clicked Yes
    End If    ' Otherwise do nothing
End Sub
```

The keyboard alternative

Remember to tie the Close or Cancel button to the Esc key. People are used to pressing Esc to back out of a dialog box, and you shouldn't disappoint them. You don't need to add a KeyPress event procedure — simply setting the button's Cancel property to True in the Property window does the trick.

Programming the OK button

Imagine you're staring at a typical dialog box. When you click the OK button, you expect the program to accept the current entries in the box as final, making the specified changes in the program's appearance, behavior, or data. The form should then remove itself from the screen.

Gratify these expectations by writing a Click event procedure for the OK button. All the code has to do is transfer values from the form's controls to variables in your program, or use the controls' values in conditional statements. The final line in the procedure should be the form's Hide method or an Unload statement. In the following examples, txtCName and txtCAddress are text boxes. The first two statements transfer their contents to corresponding program variables. Next, the program checks the status of the tglSend toggle button and, if it's on, runs a procedure called SendBillToCustomer. Finally, it hides the Form.

```
Private Sub cmdOK_Click()
    strCustomerName = txtCName.Value
    strCustomerAddress = txtCAddress.Value
    'check toggle button status
    If tglSend.Value = True Then
        SendBillToCustomer
    End If
    Hide
End Sub
```

Validating Entries

One of the most common tasks performed in event procedures is validation of entries the user makes via a control. Often, a program can only accept certain values. However, the user is free to enter any text in a text or combo box, and to pick almost any number via a slider or spinner.

The solution is to add validation code to an event procedure for the control. The code looks at the user's entry, evaluating it to see whether it meets your criteria. If so, the code can store the value or pass it along to another part of your program. If not, you can display a message box or another form informing the user of the problem (see Figure 16-4). Alternatively, the code might convert the entry into an acceptable one—say, by capitalizing the lowercase letters.

Figure 16-4:
I used a Change event procedure to check the entry in the text box and display this error message to the user.

Code for validation routines

Validating the value of a control requires you to write If...Then statements, Select Case statements, or both. This simple example checks a spin button for an unacceptable value:

```
Private Sub spnVolumeControl_Change
    If spnVolumeControl.Value = 13 Then
        MsgBox "13 is not an acceptable setting."
    End If
End Sub
```

Events you can use to validate user entries

Performing validation at any of four points in the cycle of user and form inter-
actions can make sense. Each of these validation points corresponds to a
different event procedure on the current control or the form as a whole, as
shown here:

When Validation Takes Place	Event Procedure to Use
Each time a key is pressed	KeyPress event for the control (to evaluate the one key just pressed)
Each time the value of the control changes	Change event (to evaluate the entire value)
When the user finishes working with the control but before moving to another	BeforeUpdate (allows the update to be canceled, returning the user to the control)
When the user closes the form	Click event for the form's OK or Close button

How to choose a validation event

It's up to you to decide which event procedure to write for validating user
entries, based on such factors as:

- Whether the validation code runs quickly or slowly
- Whether you want to hassle users at the moment that they create an invalid value or wait until they finish the entry before checking it
- Whether you base the validation on entries in more than one control

In the simple case in which you want to validate the entire value of a control
each time it changes, use a Change event procedure. The following sections
discuss alternatives.

Screening out or changing individual characters

In text box or combo box entries, you may not want to allow certain individual characters anywhere in an entry. Use a `KeyPress` event procedure to screen them out as the user types them. The following code rejects all characters except letters and numerals:

```
Private Sub txtSerialNumber_KeyPress(ByVal KeyAscii _
    As MSForms.ReturnInteger)
' this whole block is the condition:
If Chr(KeyAscii) < "0" Or _
    (Chr(KeyAscii) > "9" And Chr(KeyAscii) < "A") Or _
    (Chr(KeyAscii) > "Z" And Chr(KeyAscii) < "a") Or _
    Chr(KeyAscii) > "z" _  Then

    MsgBox "Invalid character!"
    KeyAscii = 0 ' Throw out the character

End If
End Sub
```

Okay, I admit that the condition in the statement is rather lengthy, but it does the job. Once the `If...Then` statement detects an invalid character, it displays a message to that effect. Then comes the statement; `KeyAscii = 0`. `KeyAscii` is an argument to the `KeyPress` event procedure, so it works like a local variable in the procedure. Changing its value changes the character code sent to the text box. Since the text box itself won't accept a character code of 0, the character typed by the user vanishes without a trace.

Changing the `KeyAscii` value also lets you change an invalid entry into a correct one. For example, you could use the following event procedure to display and store all letters typed by the user in upper case:

```
Private Sub txtSerialNumber_KeyPress(ByVal KeyAscii _
    As MSForms.ReturnInteger)
KeyAscii = Asc(UCase(Chr(KeyAscii)))
End Sub
```

The conversion statement requires three nested functions. Since `KeyAscii` is a numeric character code, you must first convert it to a string with `Chr`, then make it uppercase with `UCase`, and finally convert it back to an integer with `Asc`.

Delayed validation with the BeforeUpdate event

If you want to revalidate the control's value every time it changes, write an event procedure or use event procedures like those discussed in the previous section. Sometimes, however, it's preferable to postpone validating the entry until the user finishes working with it. Some people appreciate being allowed to correct their own mistakes before passing an entry off to the program for a final check — it makes them feel like you're giving them some credit in the intelligence department.

Another reason to put off validating an entry is in cases when the validation code takes a long time to run. If you must compare an entry with items stored in a database or (yikes) somewhere on the Internet, you don't want to make users wait for your program to look up the acceptable values every time they type a key or click the mouse.

To check a control's value after the user indicates that work is complete, write a BeforeUpdate event procedure. These events occur when the user clicks the mouse on a different control, presses Tab, or presses the keyboard shortcut for another control. VBA detects the BeforeUpdate event just before leaving the original control, which gives you an opportunity to cancel the update and remain there, forcing the user to fix the problem. This example shows how to use the Cancel statement:

```
Private Sub txtSerialNumber_Change
    If len(txtSerialNumber.Value) > 5 Then
        MsgBox "Your entry is too long. Try again."
        Cancel
    End If
End Sub
```

Waiting until the form closes

Sometimes it makes sense to postpone validation for a control until the user clicks the OK button to close the entire form. You could do this if the validation criteria depend on the values of other controls. If you go this route, place the validation code in the OK button's Click event procedure.

Suppose that you design a form that allows the user to specify the dates of important upcoming events. The form also has a list box that allows the user to indicate how far in advance of each event he wants to be notified. If the user plans a meeting for tomorrow but asks to be notified two days before the event, you may decide to raise a red flag only when the user clicks OK. That way, the user doesn't have to make entries in the two controls in a particular order to avoid error messages.

Part V

The Part of Tens

WITH OBJECT-ORIENTED PROGRAMMING, I UNDERSTAND THE "ENCAPSULATION" AND "INHERITANCE" PART PRETTY WELL. IT'S THAT DARN "CLUTTERMORPHISM" THAT STUMPS ME.

In this part . . .

This short but succulent dessert section tickles the palate with a host of VBA delights. After nibbling on the samples introduced here, you're sure to want bigger bites.

Chapter 17 introduces a variety of advanced programming techniques that can make your VBA programs really sing. Topics include storing and retrieving information from the Windows registry, tapping the capabilities of other applications and components, reading and writing disk files, and adding more ActiveX controls to the Visual Basic Editor Toolbox. Chapter 18 surveys a flock of other VBA resources you should know about, including magazines, Web sites, and third-party programming tools.

Chapter 17

Ten (Minus Three) Really Cool Things You Can Do with VBA

*I*f you've already read most of this book, you're a real VBA hotshot. Because you don't need much hand-holding, this chapter introduces a grab bag of potentially crucial skills in a hurry. I can't claim that I cover these rather advanced topics thoroughly, but you should be able to do productive work with the information provided here — and it will serve as *hors d'oeuvres* for the big feast of advanced VBA topics you'll soon devour.

Storing Stuff in the Windows Registry

Although you can use little disk files to save and retrieve settings and other variables between, the Windows registry is specifically intended for such housekeeping chores. VBA provides all the tools you need to create registry keys, place data in them, and retrieve that information later.

Use the SaveSetting statement to save an entry in the registry. The SaveSetting statement automatically creates the key you specify if it doesn't already exist. The syntax is

```
SaveSetting appname, section, key, setting
```

The *appname, section,* and *key* arguments are names corresponding to levels in the registry hierarchy. All the registry settings for a single VBA program should go in one main registry branch named for the program (use the *appname* argument to identify this branch). You can divide the settings into sections and keys any way you want, using names for any of these arguments that suit you.

If you call your program "Random quotes" and want to add a registry setting that determines how often to pop up a dialog box containing a random quote, you can use a statement like this:

```
SaveSetting "Random quotes", "Options", "Poptime", "6"
```

The final argument, "6", specifies the actual data you want to store in the registry. Figure 17-1 shows the result of running this line on the registry.

Figure 17-1: The Windows registry after a custom key has been added.

You use a similar function, GetSetting, to retrieve values from the registry. In the syntax shown here, the first three arguments are required, but the *default* argument is optional:

```
GetSetting (appname, section, key, default)
```

You can use the GetSetting function when you want to answer the question, "What's the current value stored in this registry key?" To use the GetSetting function in your code, assign it to an appropriate variable (a string or variant), as in

```
sngTiming = GetSetting ("Random Quotes", "Options", _
    "Poptime")
```

The optional *default* argument lets you specify the value GetSetting should return if it can't find the key you specified.

VBA provides two other registry-related commands:

✔ The GetAllSettings function returns a list of key settings and their respective values in the form of a two-dimensional array of strings.

✔ The DeleteSetting statement lets you delete the registry value as well as the key itself.

Exposing Themselves (Accessing the Objects of Other Applications)

A software world of dazzling variety lies just outside the confines of your particular VBA application — and you're free to travel there with VBA. An ever-increasing number of applications incorporate the COM object model, brazenly exposing their objects so that you can access them in your own programs (see Chapter 1 for theoretical background on COM).

As a relatively simple example, suppose you want to base a Visio organization chart on personnel data stored in your Microsoft Outlook folders. If your VBA skills extend to creating shapes and connections in Visio, your only new challenge is writing code to pull in the information "live" from Outlook.

Outlook itself doesn't include the full-scale VBA development environment (the Visual Basic Editor), but it does expose its objects through COM. After you connect to Outlook in VBA, you can use those Outlook objects in your program just as if they were native to your "home base" VBA application.

Understanding the basics of cross-application programming

This rule may be obvious: You can use the objects of another application only if that application has been installed on your system. If that requirement is met, working with objects from another COM-based application requires three preliminary steps:

1. **In the Visual Basic Editor, add a reference to the external application's object library.**

2. **Declare variables for the objects you plan to use in the program.**

3. **Create (instantiate) the objects using the** `CreateObject` **function.**

I have more to say about each of these steps in the next three sections.

Adding a reference to the foreign object model

To inform the Visual Basic Editor about an external application's objects model, you add and activate a *reference* to the application's *object library*. In the Visual Basic Editor, choose Tools➪References to open the References dialog box.

Outlook's object library should already be listed in the dialog box, assuming you've already installed Outlook on your computer. You have to find it in the Available References list, checking its box to activate it and make its objects accessible. If the object library you want to use isn't listed, add the reference to the list yourself by using the Browse button.

Declaring external objects

Use standard VBA syntax to declare variables for objects from external applications. Use the Object Browser or the external application's Help file to learn which objects it makes available. The following statements declare variables for the Outlook objects required in the example program (the CD-ROM that comes with the book includes this code and the related fragments that follow in one complete module).

```
Dim objOutlook As Outlook.Application
 Dim objOLNamespace As Outlook.NameSpace
Dim colFolders As Outlook.Folders ' collection of folders
Dim objPeopleFolder As Outlook.MAPIFolder
Dim colPeople As Outlook.Items ' collection of contacts
Dim objPerson As Object ' one individual contact
Dim strName As String
```

Creating the external object

Declaring the objects announces your intention to use them. You must then actually create the objects you need with `Set` statements inside a VBA procedure.

The key to creating an object belonging to an external application is the CreateObject function. CreateObject starts the application, which in turn creates the object. The function's return value is a reference to the object, which you can assign to the appropriate variable. To start the application with a specific file or document, use the GetObject function instead.

Here's a sample procedure for the Outlook-Visio example — it instantiates the needed objects:

```
Sub PeopleDiagram()
Set objOutlook = CreateObject("Outlook.Application")
Set objOLNamespace = gobjOutlook.GetNamespace("MAPI")
Set colFolders = gobjOLNamespace.Folders ' all folders
Set objPeopleFolder = colFolders.Item("Personal Folders")
' redefine variables to drill down into folder hierarchy
Set colFolders = objPeopleFolder.Folders
Set objPeopleFolder = colFolders.Item("Contacts")
Set colPeople = objPeopleFolder.Items
' Call a Sub procedure that puts the Outlook data to work:
    ChartAName
End Sub
```

Note that in many situations — including this example — you need the CreateObject function only once. After you create the external application's object, you can access any of its properties and methods. In this case, as is common, those properties include other objects (here, the Folders collection, the Personal Folders and Contacts folders, and the collection of items within the Contacts folders).

Applications you run from within your code via the CreateObject function start up in hidden form — you can't see them on the screen. This is great when you want to use an application's data in your own program without distracting the user. However, sometimes you want to see the application in its usual form. Depending on the application, you may have to activate a Display method or set a Visible property to True, as in

```
objPeople- Folder.Display
```

Using the external objects

At last, you're ready to roll — you can now use the external application's objects in your code, just as if they came from your VBA application. Here's an example of how you might use this technique in Visio to create an organization diagram labeled with the names in the Outlook Contacts folder.

```
Sub ChartAName()
For each objPerson in colPeople
  strName = objPerson.FullName
  ... (code to build Visio diagram from this data)
Next
End Sub
```

The sample code on the CD-ROM doesn't include this procedure because I can't be sure you have Visio. Instead, the PeopleDiagram procedure just displays a message box for each contact in the Outlook data. (Of course, you may not have Outlook either, but if that's the case, the example doesn't work for you at all.)

Managing Database Data with VBA

If you plan to use VBA to work with data stored in "real" databases, such as Microsoft Jet (the database format used by Access), SQL Server, or dBase files, you need help, friend. That help comes in the form of an object library. A database object library turns databases and their components — tables, queries, and reports — into proper objects with properties and methods. Because the database is packaged as a set of objects, you don't have to muck around with the details of the database's structure. Additionally, you can use the same set of objects to manipulate many different types of databases.

You can choose among several database object libraries. Microsoft's offerings are the best known, and include Data Access Objects (DAO) and ActiveX Data Objects (ADO). ADO is newer and is intended to be a one-size-fits-all solution for everything from single-PC programs to large-scale networked applications. At this point in time, however, ADO lacks some of DAO's features and is slower. Other companies have their own database object libraries. If you work exclusively with dBase files, for example, you should definitely consider CodeBase (Sequiter Software).

Both DAO and ADO are included with Office 2000, while DAO comes with Office 97 and various other VBA 5 applications. If you don't have them on your system you can download them from Microsoft's Web site — which may be a good idea anyway, to ensure that you get the latest versions.

Once the chosen database object library is installed you must add a reference to the library in your VBA project before you start using its objects. To do this, choose Tools⇨References and assign the reference in the resulting References dialog box, as detailed in the section "Exposing Themselves" earlier in this chapter. Unfortunately, I can't help you here with database programming — the specific techniques required depend on which object library you're working with, and to introduce any one library would require an entire chapter, at least.

Whichever object library you choose, you can cut your programming burden way down by using ActiveX controls that automatically display data from the specific database table or query you want to work with. When a user changes the data in one of these *bound* controls, the changes are automatically reflected in the underlying database without any coding on your part.

Controls that can be bound to data are a primary feature that sets Access apart from most other VBA applications. However, if you're using an application such as Word that doesn't include such controls, you can purchase them in ActiveX toolsets. One source is the Protoview components that are included in demo versions on the CD-ROM that comes with this book. The Developer Edition of Microsoft Office 2000 includes a variety of bound data controls for use in any Office application, as well as a raft of other tools and utilities for easing the development of custom database programs in VBA. See the "Adding ActiveX Controls" section later in this chapter for the techniques required to use "foreign" controls in VBA.

In Access, you can work with your data in either of two ways: via the properties and methods provided by the database object library (DAO or ADO), or using the DoCmd object. The DoCmd object encapsulates all the commands available from Access' menu system. With it, you can open tables, run queries or reports, display forms, fiddle with the user interface . . . in other words, anything a user can do sitting in front of the computer. Because Access forms aren't standard VBA forms, the Show method doesn't work — instead, to display forms in an Access VBA application, you must use the OpenForm method of the DoCmd object.

Working with Disk Files

Via an external object library, VBA lets you use object-oriented techniques to manage disk files, performing tasks such as reading directories and copying files. These techniques are discussed in the sections "Working with file properties" and "Copying, moving, and deleting files" later in this chapter. Alternatively, you can use VBA's older file-handling functions and statements, which are listed and briefly described in Table 11-9 in the section "Working with Files on Disk."

The time may come when you want your VBA program to store information in a disk file. Maybe you will want to keep track of some settings that the user has selected, or you'll want to keep the values of a few variables on hand for reuse the next time the program runs. Or maybe the program needs to save the results of many different calculations in a disk file or work with information stored in a text document.

Whether you need to access lots of information or just a little, VBA makes working with disk files as painless as you could hope. You don't have to know anything about how Windows keeps track of files. Instead, a few simple VBA objects and their methods handle all the details for you.

By way of clarification, I'm not talking here about reading and writing the disk files of the documents from the host VBA application. Of course, your VBA programs can work with the information those documents contain, and manipulate document files as a whole (typically with `Open` and `Save` methods).

Understanding how VBA handles files

As I point out in Chapter 11, VBA lets you work with files as objects, manipulating these file objects using their methods and properties. However, this capability isn't part of VBA proper;rather it relies on an external object library. As detailed in the next section, you must add a reference to that library before you can work with files as objects.

VBA has a built-in file handling scheme that does *not* treat files as objects. You use statements and functions, rather than object methods, to carry out file-related actions. These same techniques still work in VBA, but the file object is preferable for most tasks. However, Table 11-9 lists the relevant statements and functions, and the web site for this book (`www.seldenhouse.com/vba`) introduces their use.

Referencing the Scripting Runtime library

The basic tools you need for working with files as objects are supplied by the Microsoft Scripting Runtime object library. Before you write any file-related code, you must reference this library in your VBA project. And before you do that, you must make certain the library is present on your computer.

The Scripting Runtime library is contained in a file called SCRRUN.DLL located in the Windows\System folder. The library is installed automatically if you're running Windows 98 or Windows NT with the Option Pack, or if you have VBA 6 on your system. If you're working with VBA 5 in Windows 95, or if for any other reason you don't seem to have the Scripting Runtime, you can download it from Microsoft's developer Web site at `msdn.microsoft.com/scripting/`.

Once you've ensured that the Scripting Runtime library is present on your system, you must then add a reference to it in each VBA project in which you intend to use the library. Do so as follows:

1. **Select the target project in the Project Explorer**

2. **Choose Tools ⇨ References to open the References dialog box.**

3. **Scroll down to the Microsoft Scripting Runtime item and check its box.**

4. **Close the dialog box.**

   Ta-da! You're done.

Again, you must repeat these steps for each project that uses the Scripting Runtime no matter which version of VBA you're using. (Using external object libraries is discussed in detail in "Exposing Themselves" earlier in this chapter.)

VBA programs that rely on the Scripting Runtime should be distributed only to other users who have the required .DLL file installed on their computers. If you can't be sure, you can distribute the .DLL with your project (include installation instructions).

Accessing files

Once you've installed the Scripting Runtime and added a reference to it to your VBA project, you're ready to write object-oriented VBA code that manipulates any file on your disk. Working with an individual file as an object requires three simple coding steps:

1. **Create a** `FileSystemObject` **— the top-level object for accessing disk files.**

2. **Use a method of the** `FileSystemObject` **object to open the file in question, or to create the file from scratch.**

3. **Fiddle with the file object using its methods and properties.**

The following code fragment illustrates these steps. It creates a `File` object for a file called `lacewings.txt`, then copies that file to another location:

```
Dim objFileSystem As FileSystemObject
Dim objFile1 As File
Set objFileSystem = _
    CreateObject("Scripting.FileSystemObject")
Set objFile1 = _
    objFileSystem.GetFile("C:\bugs\lacewings.doc")
objFile1.Copy ("c:\my documents\buggy.doc")
```

Working with file properties

Once you have a File object to work with, you have easy access to all kinds of information about the file via its properties. For example, you can use the Size property to check the file's size on disk:

```
Dim lngFileSize as Long
lngFileSize = objFile1.Size
```

or see when the file was last modified using the DateLastModified property:

```
Dim dateFileDate as Date
lngFileSize = objFile1.DateLastModified
```

Copying, moving, and deleting files

File objects can be copied, moved, or deleted using the appropriate method, as in

```
objFile1.Copy "c:\weak efforts\"
objFile1.Move "c:\heroic measures\"
objFile1.Delete
```

Note that unless you're changing the file's name, there's no need to supply a name for the Copy and Move methods, just the destination path. If you don't include the file name, be sure to add a backslash at the end of the path. And by the way, the File object retains its association with the moved file.

To copy, move, or delete *groups* of files, use the CopyFile, MoveFile, and DeleteFile methods on a FileSystemObject object, not on an individual File object. You can use wildcards in the file name specifications of the FileSystemObject methods. The FileSystemObject also provides CopyFolder, MoveFolder, and DeleteFolder methods that act on entire folders, and any subfolders they contain.

Reading and writing data in files

Although it's important to be able to copy, move, and delete entire files, you may also be interested in the data stored within a file. This section introduces the object-oriented techniques you need to read and write that information.

Note that you can use only use file-related objects to access file contents as a continuous block of text. Of course, that text can contain numeric data, so you're not limited to storing and retrieving names, poetry, and prose. However, you have to access the data in sequence — you can't just jump to any location in the file.

But File objects don't provide a means for working with data in a structured format as you might with simple databases. In structured files, each record occupies a predetermined amount of space, allowing you to read or write any record by specifying its number. You can work with these random access files in VBA, but not via objects. Instead, use VBA's Open, Put, and Get statements.

Opening text stream objects

To read or write data in a file, you must first open the file as a *text stream*. As you might expect, you work with a text stream in your code as a TextStream object. You can accomplish this in one of three ways:

✔ Open an existing File object as a text stream.

✔ Create a new file and open it as a text stream in one step.

✔ Directly open an existing disk file as a text stream.

The following procedure opens three separate TextStream objects using each of these techniques, in the order listed above, writes data to one of them, and then closes them:

```
Sub TextStreamDemo()

Dim objFileSystem As FileSystemObject
Dim objFile1 As File
Dim objTextStream1 As TextStream
Dim objTextStream2 As TextStream
Dim objTextStream3 As TextStream

Set objFileSystem = _
   CreateObject("Scripting.FileSystemObject")

' Create a File object, then use it to create a
'    text stream object
Set objFile1 = _
   objFileSystem.GetFile ("C:\ExistingFile.txt")
Set objTextStream1 = _
   objFile1.OpenAsTextStream (ForReading)

' Create new file and open as text stream object
Set objTextStream2 = _
   objFileSystem.CreateTextFile ("C:\NewFile.txt")

' Open an existing file as a text stream
```

```
Set objTextStream3 = _
    objFileSystem.OpenTextFile ("C:\OldFile.txt")

' Write 2 lines of text to one of the streams
objTextStream2.WriteLine "In a cavern, in a canyon"
objTextStream2.WriteLine "Excavating for a mine"

' Close all 3 text streams
objTextStream1.Close
objTextStream2.Close
objTextStream3.Close

End Sub
```

Although all three techniques create TextStream objects, they aren't interchangeable. The particular technique you use determines how you access data in the underlying file. See the next section for more on this subject.

Choosing and using data access modes

A given TextStream object can let you read data from a file, write data to it, or both. Actually, a TextStream object allows one or more of *three* distinct *IO modes* (IO stands for "input-output"). One mode is reading, and then there are two separate modes for writing — ordinary writing (which starts writing characters at the beginning of the text stream) and appending (which starts writing at the end).

The IO mode, or modes, available for a particular TextStream object depend on which technique you use to create the text stream (of the three described in the previous section) and, in the case of the File object's OpenAsTextStream method, which mode you specify. Here's a breakdown:

Method	IO Modes Available in Resulting Text Stream Object
CreateTextFile (FileSystemObject object)	read and write
OpenTextFile (FileSystemObject object)	read and append
OpenAsTextStream (File object)	read, write or append (one IO mode only)

When you create a TextStream object from a File object, you specify the IO mode as an argument to the OpenAsTextStream method using one of three appropriately named constants: ForReading, ForWriting, and ForAppending. For example, if you wanted to add more text to the end of an existing file, you might open a text stream with the following statement:

```
Set objTS = _
    objFile.OpenAsTextStream (ForAppending)
```

Reading and writing file data

Once you've created a `TextStream` object with the IO mode or modes that suit your purposes, you can get down to business and start working with the file's contents. Several simple methods are at your disposal.

You can read and write data as individual characters or in lines. Unless each item of data occupies the same number of characters, I recommend the line-oriented technique. When you need to read a line of data, you don't have to know how long the line is, just which line number it occupies. And a "line" can consist of any number of data characters, from zero on up.

Anyway, to read data from a text stream, assign to a variable the value returned by one of the `TextStream` object's read methods. This sample code should give you the idea:

```
' reads the next line from the file into the variable
strSomeText = objTextStream.ReadLine
```

The available read methods are as follows:

Method (of `TextStream` *Object*)	What It Does
`Read(`*characters*`)`	Reads the specified number of characters starting from the current file position
`ReadLine`	Reads all the characters from the current file position up to the next newline character
`ReadAll`	Reads the entire file
`Skip(`*characters*`)`	Skips the specified number of characters when reading a file. The next read begins with the first character after the skip.
`SkipLine`	Skips the entire next line in the file. The next read begins with the first character after the skipped line.

To write data to a text stream, you simply supply the characters to be written as a string to the `Write` or `WriteLine` method, as in

```
' write a literal string
objTextStream.Write "Hello, Central."
' write a variable, followed by a newline character
objTextStream.WriteLine strMyTwoBits
```

Method (of TextStream Object)	What It Does
Write(*string*)	Writes the specified string to the text stream
WriteLine(*string*)	Writes the string plus a newline character to the text stream
WriteBlankLines(*lines*)	Writes the specified number of newline characters to the text stream

Closing text streams

After reading from or writing to a text stream, always close the TextStream object to free up system resources and memory, and so other programs or users can access the file. The Close method is simplicity itself:

```
objSomeTextStream.Close
```

Understanding text stream limitations

Text streams are fine for recording and retrieving relatively small amounts of data. The main problem is that you can't move freely around in them. The read methods start reading data from the beginning of the file and continue toward the end of the file. Although you can use the Skip and SkipLines methods while reading to jump ahead a specified number of characters or lines, respectively, you can't skip in reverse — a statement such as objTextStream.Skip(-10) causes an error.

Unfortunately, TextStream objects don't have a method or property for specifying the starting position for the next read directly. However, you can accomplish more or less the same thing. You must first close and reopen the text stream, and then Skip one fewer characters than the desired location. For example, if you want to start reading from the 5th character in the file, the following statements will do the trick:

```
objTextStream.Close
Set objTextStream = objFile.OpenAsTextStream(ForWriting)
objTextStream.Skip(4)
objTextStream.Read(25)
```

When you write data to text streams you're even more limited, because you can't skip around at all in the file. Each write action starts where the previous one left off, overwriting any text that might already be present in the file.

If you need a way to alter some data somewhere within a file without changing the information that comes before it, you must read in the entire file, make the changes in the resulting string variable or variables, and then rewrite all the data to the file.

Using Dictionary Objects

Dictionary objects are useful for storing simple 2-column tabular information. For each entry in the table, one column contains the item's name, or *key*, the other column the value you're interested in. Think of a dictionary — the words would be the keys, and the definitions their values. But Dictionary objects can store values of any data type.

You can work with Dictionary objects in both VBA 5 and VBA 6. However, they aren't a built-in feature of VBA itself. Instead, they are available through Microsoft's Scripting Runtime library, discussed in detail in the section "Working with Disk Files" earlier in this chapter. To use Dictionary objects in a VBA program you must follow the directions under the heading "Referencing the Scripting Runtime library."

Dictionary object basics

Use the techniques described in the "Exposing Themselves" section earlier in this chapter to declare a variable for your dictionary and then create the dictionary, as shown in this example:

```
Dim dictBigCats As Scripting.Dictionary
Set dictBigCats = CreateObject("Scripting.Dictionary")
```

Then go on to add keys and values to the dictionary using the Add method, as in:

```
dictBigCats.Add "Cheetah", "Fast and lean"
dictBigCats.Add "Lion", "Roaring and maned"
dictBigCats.Add "Panther", "Black, not pink"
```

Better than collections

Dictionary objects improve on VBA's similar Collection objects, covered in Chapter 13, in several simple but important ways:

✔ You don't need to know the keys to get at them, and the associated values. Instead, you can access the keys *en masse* with a `For Each...Next` loop as in:

```
For Each airplane in dictBiplanes
    MsgBox dictBiplanes(airplane)
Next
```

✔ You can change the value of an entry by directly assigning a new value using the key. In the following example

```
dictVacationDestinations("Number1") = "Fresno"
```

In collections, you have to delete the original entry, then add back a new one.

✔ You can delete all the entries in a dictionary using the `RemoveAll` method. To accomplish the same task with a collection, you must use a `For Each...Next` loop.

I don't have room to detail techniques for sorting dictionaries and selecting subsets of items that match your criteria. However, such basic database functionality is relatively simple to implement. You can find guidance and code samples in Bruce McKinney's article "Understanding the Dictionary Class" in the July, 1999 issue of *Visual Basic Programmer's Journal* (Fawcette Technical Publications), also available online at `www.vbpj.com`.

Do-It-Yourself Objects

Once you're comfortable using the built-in objects available in VBA and other object libraries, you may want to try your hand at building your own. Although you can perform great feats of legerdemain using standard `Sub` and `Function` procedures, compartmentalizing your code into objects can have real advantages, to wit:

✔ By keeping all the code that manipulates a set of data inside a single object, you reduce the opportunities for bugs to creep into your program when you make modifications.

✔ Your programs are easier to read and understand.

✔ You can create as many independent copies of an object as you want by writing two quick statements for each copy.

✔ Mentioning the benefits of *polymorphism* will probably get me into trouble, but . . . using the same properties and methods with different object classes can be handy. That's what polymorphism is all about. I don't have room to cover this topic here, but you should know that this powerful programming technique exists. Books on advanced VBA topics cover polymorphism.

As you know by now (especially if you read Chapter 10), an object consists of some data (the object's properties) and code that alters that data (its methods). Because properties are just variables and methods are just procedures, writing the actual code that defines an object is no big deal. But you do have to follow some rules so VBA can figure out what you're trying to do. The next few sections describe these rules.

Creating class modules

In VBA, a *class* is the pattern upon which an object is based. The class determines which properties, methods, and events the object has, and how each of those components behaves.

To create a class, you start by inserting a new class module in your VBA project (choose Insert⇨Class Module). A class module window looks and works exactly like a code window. Before going any further, name the new class using the (Name) item at the top of the Properties window.

Understanding the components of a class definition

The typical class has three main components:

- ✔ Private declarations for the variables used internally by the object
- ✔ Public property procedures that allow procedures in your standard modules to retrieve or alter current property settings
- ✔ Public method procedures that define the actions the object's methods will perform

The simple class definition shown here for a make-believe Thermostat class has all three of these elements. This example does nothing useful, but it does work and it's on the CD-ROM in case you want to try it out. If you want to enter the code yourself, name the class module Thermostat in the Properties window, then type in the following in its Code window:

```
Private sngDegrees As Single ' property variable
' Code for the Let Temperature property procedure:
Public Property Let Temperature(ByVal sngInput As Single)
    sngDegrees = sngInput
End Property
' Code for the Get Temperature property procedure:
Public Property Get Temperature() As Single
    Temperature = sngDegrees
End Property
```

```
' Code for the CalculateEnergyUse method:
Public Sub CalculateEnergyUse()
  Const cstConversionFactor = 2.45
  Dim dblResult
  dblResult = sngDegrees * 365 * cstConversionFactor
  MsgBox "Annual energy use for this thermostat" & _
    " setting is estimated at " & dblResult & " watts."
End Sub
```

Declaring class variables

Use the Declarations section at the top of the class module to declare any variables you plan to access in more than one property or method. Always declare them as Private. After all, the whole point of using objects is to ensure that your program can't access the data directly. Variables that you use only in one property or method should be declared there.

At a minimum, you need to declare a variable for each of the object's properties. The variable name should *not* be the name as the property (I show you how to define the property's name in a moment). But you can also declare other data that the object uses internally and that won't be accessible to other parts of your program.

Writing property procedures

The secret to endowing an object with a property is to write a pair of special procedures, the Let and Get *property procedures*. Both procedures in each pair should have the same name.

The name of a property is the name you choose for the property's Let and Get procedures. The name should describe the content or function of the property, of course.

Oh, one other point: If you're creating a property representing an object reference, you substitute a Property Set procedure for a Property Let procedure as half of the property procedure pair. Otherwise, such properties work the same as properties of other data types.

Setting object properties with Property Let procedures

A Property Let procedure sets the value of a property. In its simplest form, a Property Let procedure takes a value supplied as an argument, assigning that value to a variable that represents the property. To repeat the previous example:

```
Public Property Let Temperature (ByVal sngInput As Single)
  sngTemp = sngInput
End Property
```

When in the main part of your program you write a statement that sets the property, such as

```
Thermostat.Temperature = 75
```

VBA calls the `Let Temperature` procedure with 75 as the argument.

Of course, your property procedures aren't limited to one line of code. You can add statements that check the argument to ensure that it falls in a valid range before you assign it to the property. You can also perform other actions, depending on the particular argument.

Retrieving object properties with Property Get procedures

A `Property Get` procedure works like a `Function` procedure in that it returns a value — the value of the property, of course. As in a `Function` procedure, you assign the value you want it to return to the procedure name — which also happens to be the property name. Here's the example code again:

```
Public Property Get Temperature() As Single
   Temperature = sngTemp
End Property
```

Other parts of your program can call the `Get Temperature` procedure to assign its return value to a variable, or test the return value in conditional statements, as in these examples:

```
sngCurrentSetting = Thermostat.Temperature

If Thermostat.Temperature > 80
   MsgBox "Consider turning down the heater!"
EndIf
```

Writing methods

Methods are simply ordinary `Sub` and `Function` procedures that you happen to store in a class module. In most cases, of course, a method should do something directly related to the object itself, by manipulating the data stored in the object. But if you want, you can add a method that calculates the price of tofu in Tennessee to any class.

VBA automatically associates methods you write with the class you add them to. You can call your own methods from other parts of the program just as you would the methods of built-in objects.

Using your custom objects

You use an object based on one of your own classes in the same way you would work with the built-in objects of VBA and your application. The steps are:

1. **Declare a variable for the object, as in:**

```
Dim objCustomThermostat As Thermostat
```

2. **Use a** `Set` **statement to create the actual object you'll be working with.**

For example:

```
Set objCustomThermostat = New Thermostat
```

3. **Access the object's properties or trigger its methods using the standard VBA "dot" syntax.**

For example:

```
objCustomThermostat.Setting = 65
objCustomThermostat.CalculateEnergyUse
```

Adding ActiveX Controls

Despite its reputation for software imperialism, Microsoft has taken pains to make its development tools "open." Based on the ActiveX spec, anyone can create new controls that work with just about every Windows-based programming language — including C++, HTML, Visual Basic — and VBA. Of course, Microsoft defines the standards that govern how these plug-in software components work, so it hasn't actually given up any power.

Anyway, the benefit to you is that you can add new features by plugging in additional ActiveX controls that don't come in the standard VBA set. You can freely mix controls from any source to meet the needs of your programming projects. And all ActiveX controls work in fundamentally the same way as the built-in controls — which, by the way, are ActiveX controls too (see Chapters 15, 16, and the bonus chapter "Control Fetishes" on the Web at www.dummies.com/bonus/vba/ for details on the built-in controls).

Chapter 17 covers a smattering of the hundreds of commercial and shareware ActiveX controls you might find useful in your own work. In this chapter, I stick with the general techniques for using ActiveX controls and tips on accessing the common dialog box control that comes with Windows.

Some ActiveX controls don't work properly in every programming environ- ment. Before you plunk down money for a control, be sure to verify that it actually performs as promised in your version of VBA. Also, be aware that ActiveX controls written in Visual Basic may work in your VBA program, but are likely to require the large (approximately 2MB) Visual Basic runtime files.

Adding new controls to the Toolbox

Before you can use an ActiveX control in your VBA programs, you must do two things:

1. **Install the control software on your computer's hard disk.**

   I guess that makes sense.

2. **Register it as an available control in Windows.**

   You can register controls in various ways, and the installation process may have done it for you. If you have to do it yourself, the easiest way for VBA programmers is in the Visual Basic Editor.

3. **Select the control to activate it for use in VBA.**

Registering a control

To register a new control, make sure you know the name of the disk file that contains the control and where it's located on your hard disk. Then follow these steps:

1. **Choose Tools⇨References to display the ActiveX references available to your project.**

2. **Click Browse to display a standard-issue Windows dialog box for opening files.**

   In the Files of Type combo box, select ActiveX controls.

3. **Locate the file for the control and double-click it to open it.**

   Opening the file returns you to the References dialog box.

4. **Scroll to the item for the control in the list and make sure that its little check box is checked.**

5. **Close the dialog box.**

Putting the tool in your Toolbox

After a new control has been registered, the next step is to activate it by plac- ing its icon on the Toolbox. Here's how:

Controls, controls everywhere, but not a property to set

You may be in for a shock, or at least a mild arousal reaction, when you see how many ActiveX controls are already registered on your system. Every application that uses any ActiveX controls registers them automatically when the application is installed. (Note that the items in the list beginning with "Microsoft Forms 2.0" represent the standard VBA controls.)

You can use *any* registered control that appears in the Additional Controls dialog box in your programs. Feel free to experiment, but don't get too excited. Without the documentation or Help file that you get when you buy the control, it may be impossible to figure out how to make it work. You face legal restrictions as well — you certainly should not distribute a program containing a third-party ActiveX control without licensing the control from its author.

1. **Select any `UserForm` window active in the Visual Basic Editor so that the Toolbox is visible.**

2. **Either right-click the Toolbox and select Additional Controls or choose Tools⇨Additional Controls.**

3. **Scroll through the list of available controls to locate the one you want to activate. When you find it, check its little check box.**

4. **Close the dialog box.**

   The icon for the newly activated control appears on the Toolbox. Figure 17-2 shows the Toolbox with a bunch of new controls.

Figure 17-2:
A customized Toolbox with lots of additional ActiveX controls.

Some controls are invisible

Lots of really great ActiveX controls are invisible when your program runs. Rather than directly interacting with the user, such controls perform various actions for you so that you don't have to write your own procedures or create your own objects to get these jobs done.

Even though these invisible controls don't show up when your form is actually running, they do appear on the form during the design process. To use an invisible control in your program, you have to add it to a form just as you would any other control. Because the control will never be visible to the user, it doesn't really matter where you stick it on the form. Just put it somewhere where it doesn't overlap other controls.

If you use lots of third-party controls, you can organize them on separate pages of the Toolbox. To add new pages to the Toolbox, right-click over the tabbed area at the top and choose New Page (just like you would with a multipage control on a form, as discussed in the bonus chapter, "Control Fetishes" on the Web at www.dummies.com/bonus/vba/). The page that's showing when you activate a control is the one that receives the control's icon.

Using ActiveX controls in your programs

As soon as you have an ActiveX control on the Toolbox, you can add it to your forms just like the stock controls that come with VBA. However, to make the control do something useful, you need to know how its properties and methods work. For that, you need the documentation and Help files that come with the control. If the control was properly designed and installed, you should be able to get Help on any of its properties by pressing F1 when that property is selected in the VBA Properties window.

Chapter 18

Ten (Times Three) VBA Resources

. . . .

In This Chapter

▶ Getting more information on VBA from the software publishers

▶ Finding the prime printed periodicals pertaining to VBA

▶ Looking for VBA resources on the Web

▶ Getting cool ActiveX controls and add-on software tools

. . . .

*A*fter you can tread water comfortably at the deep end of the VBA pool, you're ready to start flailing around in style. This chapter points you in the direction of further information and key software tools that together can help make you an accomplished swimmer. (Disclaimer: The number mentioned in the chapter title may not agree with the actual count of VBA resources mentioned in this chapter — I never actually added them up.)

Your First Stop for More VBA Info

VBA programming is actually pretty simple, at least when it comes to working with variables, controlling program flow, and displaying forms. You're more likely to hit a sandbar with your VBA application's object model. You need to know which objects you need in your program, how to refer to them correctly, and which of their properties and methods to access, or you'll find yourself on frustrating bounces through the Help system. When you need guidance with a VBA application's objects, the first place to turn is the publisher who created the application in the first place.

Steal that source code

The maker of every VBA application offers help of one kind or another when it comes to using that application's features and object model in your programs. Remember to check the Help files supplied with your application for source code examples as well as more formal reference information. Beyond that, you can often find entire sample programs on the publisher's Web site. All of this material is fair game as a starting point for your own procedures and programs.

Look at what's available from Microsoft

What? After reading this book, you need *more* information on VBA? Well, consider buying a copy of Microsoft's Visual Basic documentation. Essentially, the documentation is simply a printed copy of the Help files, but many people find the information easier to refer to on paper rather than in electronic form.

You can find lots of other resources for VBA programmers on the Microsoft Developer Network Web site. The main VBA page is:

```
msdn.microsoft.com/vba/
```

You should also look at the Visual Basic site:

```
msdn.microsoft.com/vbasic/
```

Microsoft also has a special page for VBA development in Office. The address is:

```
msdn.microsoft.com/officedev/
```

The areas for the individual Office applications and the Microsoft Knowledge Base offer articles with programming tips and traps for the individual Microsoft VBA applications.

Magazines and Newsletters

The forests suffer for it, but the printed page is still the most convenient way to gain access to reference information. Visual Basic magazines and newsletters abound. The typical issue includes reviews of ActiveX controls and other software tools, tips, and secrets for handling difficult programming situations, and loads of source code. Most of these topics are directly applicable to VBA, and often, they even include VBA-specific articles.

Check out the following printed journals:

Visual Basic Programmer's Journal (Fawcette Technical Publications, 209 Hamilton Ave., Palo Alto, CA 94301; phone 650-833-7100)

```
www.windx.com
```

Inside Visual Basic (ZD Journals, 800-223-8720)

```
www.zdjournals.com/ivb/
```

Public VBA Web Sites

One way to convince your boss that you're working extremely hard without really straining is to spend hours of prep time on the Web. Tons of sites devote themselves to Visual Basic, and you can consume weeks tracking down obscure programming secrets and collecting ActiveX controls. You can assure the boss that eventually, when you finally get down to writing code, all your research will boost your productivity dramatically.

Programming pages on the Web are usually well endowed with links to other relevant sites. Starting with the following addresses, you should have no trouble finding enough to keep you busy:

```
www.download.com/PC/Activex/
```

```
www.geocities.com/WallStreet/9245/
```

```
www.vbapro.com/
```

```
www.apexsc.com/vb/index.html
```

```
www.outlookexchange.com
```

```
www.slipstick.com/dev (outlook development)
```

```
odyssey.apana.org.au/~abrowne/homepage.html (Access
        development)
```

Of course, you may also want to check out the Web sites maintained by the magazines, newsletters, and software tool vendors mentioned elsewhere in this chapter.

A Galaxy of ActiveX Controls

At last count, the number of ActiveX controls had already surpassed the count of stars in the known universe. If you can think of something you want your VBA program to do, chances are that somebody has already designed an ActiveX control to do it for you. You can choose from boatloads of commercially published ActiveX controls and more boatloads of shareware controls on the Web. And if you really can't find just the right control, maybe you've hit on a business opportunity — consider creating your own controls and marketing them to the masses.

Tool mania

Before you spend days assembling a collection of individual controls, consider buying a package deal. Many software publishers offer collections of ActiveX controls that cover the waterfront, or at least a few piers. Many such toolkits start with enhanced versions of the standard controls, with more formatting options and more control over data display. These are often supplemented with new kinds of controls such as gas gauges, meters, and knobs. You may also get grid controls for working with spreadsheet and database data, "tree" controls that let you display information in a Windows Explorer-like window, controls for faxing or printing, and invisible controls that perform timing or let you fiddle with the Windows registry.

As a starting point, consider the offerings of the following companies:

ProtoView Development Corp.
2540 Route 130, Cranbury, NJ 08512; phone 800-231-8588 or 609-655-5000

```
www.protoview.com
```

Sheridan Software Systems Inc.
35 Pinelawn Road Suite 206E., Melville, NY 11747; phone 800-823-4732 or 516-753-0985

```
www.shersoft.com
```

DameWare Development
1024 Live Oak Loop, Mandeville, LA 70448; phone 504-626-7545

```
www.dameware.com
```

Picturesque programming

Unaided, VBA does a pretty good job of importing pictures in various file formats and displaying them on your forms. But if your VBA program needs to work with a format that VBA doesn't recognize, or especially if you want to jazz up the images with special effects, you need an ActiveX graphics control set. One such product is:

Lead Tools

Available from: Lead Technologies Inc., 900 Baxter Street, Charlotte, NC 28204; phone 800-637-4699 or 704-332-5532

```
www.leadtools.com
```

Charts a la carte

Although it takes a sharp-thinking individual to comprehend the trends lying hidden in endless rows of numbers, anyone can understand a bar graph or pie chart, or at least claim to. VBA doesn't come with charting features, but you can add them easily with ActiveX controls such as:

Graphics Server

Available from: Pinnacle Publishing Inc., PO Box 72255, Marietta, GA 30007-2255; phone 800-788-1900 or 770-565-1763

```
www.pinpub.com
```

Olectra Chart

Available from: KL Group, 260 King Street East, Toronto, Ontario, Canada M5A 1K3; phone 800-709-2947 or 416-594-1026

```
www.klg.com
```

Word processing controls and spreadsheet grids

Text boxes are fine when you only need to collect a line or two of the user's input. If you expect your program to turn out complete, formatted documents, however, a text box obviously won't cut the mustard.

When it comes to presenting numbers and allowing the user to manipulate them, VBA is even more limited. You would have to be a card-carrying masochist — and have lots of time on your hands — to attempt building a spreadsheet-like grid for rows and columns of numbers using the VBA stock set of controls.

One very viable solution, if you have Word and Excel on your system, is to tap into their objects with VBA. No matter which VBA application your program runs inside, it can activate Word or Excel documents and extract their data using COM (see Chapter 17 for an overview of how this works).

Loading Word or Excel takes time though, and you don't have full control over the way they look on the screen. ActiveX controls offer nimbler, more customizable alternatives that you can integrate directly into your own forms. Try the following:

Spreadsheet control

Spread

Available from: FarPoint Technologies Inc., 133 Southcenter Court, Suite 1000, Morrisville, NC 27560; phone 919-460-7606

```
www.fpoint.com
```

Formula One

Available from: Tidestone Technologies Inc., 12980 Metcalf Avenue, Suite 300, Overland Park, KS 66213; phone 800-884-8665 or 913-851-2200

```
www.tidestone.com
```

Word processing control

TE Developer's Kit

Available from: Sub Systems Inc., 11 Tiger Row, Georgetown, MA 01833; phone 978-352-9020

```
www.subsystems.com
```

Hello, operator

With VBA and the right custom control, you can turn your computer into a sophisticated customized telephone switchboard, encompassing voice mail, order entry, paging, and faxing. Among several such products is Visual Voice.

Artisoft Inc.

5 Cambridge Center, Cambridge, MA 02142; phone 617-354-0600

```
www.artisoft.com
```

Take the money and run

Yet another of the many strangely wonderful things you can do with ActiveX controls is authorize credit card purchases via your modem or via direct Internet connections. If you're designing a custom system for order entry or retail point of sale, just plop the active-Charge control on a form. You can

then use its methods and properties to send the bank the credit card information from your customers and retrieve the bank's verdict on their
creditworthiness. Of course, using a custom form to process credit card
orders only makes sense if you're developing a full-scale database system. If
you're working in VBA instead of Visual Basic, you're most likely using
Access.

active-Charge

Go Software Inc., 42 W. Montgomery Crossroad, Suite O, Savannah, GA 31406;
phone 800-725-9264 or 912-925-4048

```
www.gosoftinc.com
```

Design your own controls

Microsoft isn't just allowing third-party developers to create ActiveX
controls — they're actively fomenting such efforts. Visual Basic 5 and 6 come
with the tools you need to create your own controls. Be aware that you may
need to include the Visual Basic run-time files when you distribute programs
containing controls built using VB. Don't forget to include installation instructions with the files.

Miscellaneous Stuff

Aside from ActiveX controls, a variety of other alluring software tools beckon
the harried VBA programmer, sweetly promising to make the development
cycle speedier and less painful — for a fee, of course.

Industrial strength calculations

VBA's strengths are in the areas of object-oriented programming and visual
forms design. When it comes to raw calculation speed, however, VBA falls
behind other programming languages. If you're writing programs for NASA
or the Census Bureau, consider the PowerBasic compiler. PowerBasic calculations run 4 to 20 times faster than the same code running in Visual Basic,
according to one extremely unbiased source (PowerBasic's publisher).

PowerBasic isn't a replacement for VBA but rather an add-on to it. You still
use VBA to get the program started, to communicate with objects in your
application, and to display forms. However, you compile the code for your

hard-core calculations with PowerBasic, which turns it into special DLL programs that VBA can activate when the time is right. Although it doesn't have VBA's object-oriented features, the core of the PowerBasic language is virtually identical to VBA, so you won't have much to learn.

PowerBASIC Inc.

316 Mid Valley Center, Carmel, CA 93923; phone 800-780-7707 or 831-659-8000

www.powerbasic.com

Help, help!

You won't have any trouble getting your VBA programs to display custom Help screens, but creating the Help files in the first place isn't so easy — unless *you* get help.

The official way to construct a Help file involves tiresome labor and lots of trial and error with a boring, inscrutable, non-visual programming language. Nobody does it that way. Instead, follow the crowd and get yourself a program that converts the output of your word processor into a Help file automatically. That way, you can set up your Help file visually, much like you create forms in VBA. Up-to-date tools that support both "classic" Windows Help and the newer HTML Help format include:

RoboHelp

Blue Sky Software, 7777 Fay Ave. Suite 201, La Jolla, CA 92037; phone 800-793-0364 or 858-551-2485

www.blue-sky.com

Check out *RoboHELP 7 For Dummies,* by Jim Meade, Ph.D. (IDG Books Worldwide, Inc.), for more details on Help authoring.

EasyHelp/Web and EasyHTML/Help

Eon Solutions Ltd, Eon House, 4 Hamble Way, Macclesfield, SK10 3RN, United Kingdom

www.eon-solutions.com

Appendix

About the CD

Here's some of what you can find on the *VBA For Dummies,* 2nd Edition CD-ROM:

- ✔ Source code files containing sample code from the book — for anyone who hates to type.
- ✔ A wide variety of shareware, freeware, and demo versions of ActiveX controls you can use to dress up your VBA forms.
- ✔ A trial version of ClipMate, an indispensable Windows Clipboard enhancement utility — great for programming VBA code, and for general use in Windows, too.
- ✔ Trial versions of EasyHTML/Help and EasyHelp/Web, easy-to-use tools that convert Microsoft Word documents into Windows Help files. They're perfect for creating online documentation for your custom VBA programs.
- ✔ Desktop.VBA lets you build utilities that run directly from the Windows Desktop by using a VBA-like programming language.
- ✔ CodeSmith (trial version) is a utility for neatly formatting your source code printouts.
- ✔ A demo version of SpeedFerret for Access 97, which performs search and replace operations on Access databases.

Be sure to check the CD itself for a complete list.

System Requirements

Make sure that your computer meets the minimum system requirements listed below. If your computer doesn't match up to most of these requirements, you may have problems in using the contents of the CD — but then, you probably wouldn't be able to run your VBA application either.

> ✔ A PC with a 486 or faster processor.
>
> ✔ Microsoft Windows 95 or later, or Microsoft NT 4 or later.
>
> ✔ At least 16MB of total RAM installed on your computer.
>
> ✔ At least of hard drive space available to install all the software from this CD. (You'll need less space if you don't install every program.)
>
> ✔ A CD-ROM drive.

If you need more information on the basics, check out *PCs For Dummies,* 6th Edition, by Dan Gookin, and the *Windows For Dummies* series (all published by IDG Books Worldwide, Inc.).

How to Use the CD

Follow these steps to get to the items on the CD:

1. **Insert the CD into your computer's CD-ROM drive.**

   Give your computer a moment to take a look at the CD.

2. **When the light on your CD-ROM drive goes out, double-click the My Computer icon (it's probably in the top-left corner of your desktop).**

   This action opens the My Computer window, which shows you all the drives attached to your computer, the Control Panel, and a couple of other handy things.

3. **Double-click the icon for your CD-ROM drive.**

   Another window opens, showing you all the folders and files on the CD.

4. **Double-click the file called License.txt.**

   This file contains the end-user license that you agree to by using the CD. When you are done reading the license, close the program (most likely Notepad) that displayed the file.

5. **Double-click the file called Readme.txt.**

   This file contains instructions about installing the software from this CD. It may be helpful to leave this text file open while you are using the CD.

6. **Double-click the folder for the software you are interested in.**

   Be sure to read the descriptions of the programs in the next section of this appendix (much of this information also shows up in the Readme.txt file). These descriptions give you more precise information about the programs' folder names and about finding and running the installer program.

7. **Find the file called Setup.exe or Install.exe (or something similar) and double-click that file.**

The program's installer walks you through the process of setting up your new software.

What You'll Find

Here's a summary of the software on this CD.

VBA For Dummies source code

In the *VBA For Dummies* source code folder on the CD-ROM, you'll find lots of VBA source code and UserForm files from the text. Because getting "real" results from VBA depends so much on the application you're using, these little programs don't do much of practical value. However, they do illustrate basic techniques of VBA programming, and you may prefer to use them in this pre-fab form instead of retyping the code from the book. When necessary, I enclosed code fragments in real procedures so they'll run correctly without additional work on your part.

The source code and UserForm files are organized by book chapter into subfolders. To use this material, fire up the Visual Basic Editor, open the VBA project in which you want to use it, and then choose File➪Import. In the resulting dialog box, select the module, form file, or class module you want to import, and then choose Open. The imported item appears in your project, where you can run it by pressing F5.

You're welcome to communicate questions or suggestions via my own Web page devoted to this book. I'll post any corrections or additions to the sample code there. Here's the address:

```
www.seldenhouse.com/vba
```

iGrafx Professional from Micrografx

This is a full-featured graphics application for creating sophisticated business diagrams such as organization charts and network or process diagrams. One of the first applications to adopt VBA 6, iGrafx' object model is rich, and a version called iGrafx Development offers additional tools to support the VBA programmer in creating specialized, custom programs. The demo version included on the CD-ROM includes iGrafx' entire functionality except that you can't save finished documents. Because it includes the complete version of VBA 6, you can use it to learn VBA programming, even if you don't have another VBA application. Micrografx' Web site is

```
www.micrografx.com
```

ActiveX Component Suite from ProtoView Development Corp.

The ActiveX Component Suite comprises three separate products, included on the CD-ROM as working demos:

- **WinX Component Library:** A set of enhanced ActiveX controls for data entry and display
- **DataTable:** A sophisticated "grid" control for displaying and manipulating information in row/column tables
- **DataExplorer:** A control for displaying and manipulating data in Windows Explorer "tree" format

You can find more information on these tools at ProtoView's Web site at

```
www.protoview.com
```

ActiveCandy by Edward Blake

This set of cool ActiveX controls is freeware. The only hitch is that you need to install the Visual Basic 6 runtime library files (MSVBVM60.DLL) on your system. The Web site for the controls is

```
members.xoom.com/eddyblake/actcandy
```

DameWare ActiveX controls from DameWare Development

This group of shareware ActiveX controls features interesting items such as a control that automatically dials your phone numbers under your program's control.

```
www.dameware.com
```

FSCompressFile by Fulvio Senore

This freeware ActiveX control allows you to compress single files for archival or backup purposes from within your programs. The Visual Basic 5 runtime library file must be installed on your system.

CodeSmith from Berkeley Software Associates

Use CodeSmith to print out your source code on neatly formatted pages, so that the code is easy to read. You can select a separate font for various code items, such as procedure declarations, comments, and the body of the code, and can print headers and footers that identify the source program. If you ask it to, CodeSmith will print brackets around structures such as If...Then statements and loops. Contact the publisher for a trial version at

```
www.bsaonline.com
```

SpeedFerret for Access 97 from Black Moshannon Systems

Access includes a find and replace feature, but it only works in code. If you rename an item that is referenced in queries and form properties, you must find and replace those references yourself — unless you have SpeedFerret. This demo version works with Access 97. You can contact the publisher at

```
www.moshannon.com
```

EasyHelp/Web and EasyHTML/Help from Eon Solutions, Ltd.

These two excellent shareware Help development tools let you use Microsoft Word to build custom Help files for your own VBA programs. EasyHelp/Web generates both WinHELP format and standard HTML files at the same time, while EasyHTML/Help produces Help files for Microsoft's HTML Help viewer.

```
www.eon-solutions.com
```

ClipMate from ThornSoft Development

ClipMate dramatically enhances the Windows clipboard. This great shareware utility is a necessity for anyone doing serious editing, whether you're working with code, text, or graphics. Find out more at

```
www.thornsoft.com
```

Desktop.VBA from ASM, Inc.

This clever utility — available in trial version — lets you write VBA-like programs to control the operations of Windows itself. Although the language behind the Desktop. VBA isn't actually Microsoft's VBA, it is a good facsimile, and your VBA programming skills should transfer readily.

WinZip 7.0 from Nico Mak Computing, Inc.

This shareware file-compression program "zips" several large files into a single, easy-to-transport file called a ZIP file. ZIP files are especially useful for sending files attached to e-mail messages — a common task for many Web publishers.

```
www.winzip.com
```

Time To Win (MCR Company)

Time To Win supplies a huge shareware set of useful functions, filling in many of the gaps in VBA's built-in function collection (see Chapter 11). The Time To Win menagerie covers inspection and manipulation of variable values, advanced math, file management, date and time calculations, and much more. You can read all about them in the Time To Win Help file. The author's Web site is

```
members.xoom.com/mcrcompany/
```

To use Time To Win functions in your programs, follow these steps:

1. **Install Time To Win by running the Setup program.**

2. **Check to see that the T2WIN-32.DLL file is in your Windows\System folder. If not, copy it there from the Time To Win installation folder (just in case you've forgotten, DLL stands for dynamic link library).**

3. **For each function you want to use, declare the function in the declarations section of your module by using the syntax indicated in the Time To Win Help file.**

Here's an example (the `cIsPalindrome` function determines whether the `Txt` string argument is a palindrome, of all things):

```
Declare Function cIsPalindrome Lib "t2win-32.dll" (Txt As
    _String) As Integer
```

You can copy the declaration for the chosen function directly from the Help file to your program, but be sure to change the library name from TIME2WIN.DLL to T2WIN-32.DLL, as shown in the preceding example.

4. **Call the declared function in any procedure in your program just as you would a built-in VBA function.**

Consult the Time To Win Help file for details as to each function's arguments and return values.

Sax Basic (Sax Software Corporation)

Sax Basic is a VBA-compatible programming language that software developers can build into stand-alone applications created with Visual Basic, C++, or Delphi. A demo version is included on the accompanying CD in the back of this book.

Like VBA, Sax Basic allows users to automate and customize applications to which it has been added. Although it doesn't benefit VBA applications, it's an interesting alternative to licensing VBA from Microsoft, if you want to add programmability to your standalone applications. The vendor's Web site address is

```
www.saxsoft.com
```

If You Have Problems (Of the CD Kind)

When you're working with complex software, you always face the possibility of glitches. If you can't get the items on the CD-ROM to work properly, the two likeliest problems are that you don't have enough memory (RAM) for the programs you want to use, or you have other programs running that are affecting installation or running of a program. If you get error messages such as Not enough memory or Setup cannot continue, try one or more of these methods and then try using the software again:

✔ Turn off any antivirus software that you have on your computer. Installers sometimes mimic virus activity and may make your computer incorrectly believe that it is being infected by a virus.

✔ Close all running programs. The more programs you're running, the less memory is available to other programs. Installers also typically update files and programs. So if you keep other programs running, installation may not work properly.

✔ Add more RAM to your computer. This is, admittedly, a drastic and somewhat expensive step. However, adding more memory can really help the speed of your computer and allow more programs to run at the same time.

If you still have trouble with installing the items from the CD, please call the IDG Books Worldwide Customer Service phone number: 800-762-2974 (outside the U.S.: 317-596-5430). If the installation process goes all right but the software itself doesn't seem to run, contact the manufacturers at the Web sites listed above, or via the phone numbers shown in the accompanying electronic documentation.

Index

• •

• **G** •

• *Q* •

• *R* •

• S •

IDG Books Worldwide, Inc., End-User License Agreement

5. **Limited Warranty.**

    (a) IDGB warrants that the Software and Software Media are free from defects in materials and workmanship under normal use for a period of sixty (60) days from the date of purchase of this Book. If IDGB receives notification within the warranty period of defects in materials or workmanship, IDGB will replace the defective Software Media.

    (b) **IDGB AND THE AUTHOR OF THE BOOK DISCLAIM ALL OTHER WARRANTIES, EXPRESS OR IMPLIED, INCLUDING WITHOUT LIMITATION IMPLIED WARRANTIES OF MERCHANTABILITY AND FITNESS FOR A PARTICULAR PURPOSE, WITH RESPECT TO THE SOFTWARE, THE PROGRAMS, THE SOURCE CODE CONTAINED THEREIN, AND/OR THE TECHNIQUES DESCRIBED IN THIS BOOK. IDGB DOES NOT WARRANT THAT THE FUNCTIONS CONTAINED IN THE SOFTWARE WILL MEET YOUR REQUIREMENTS OR THAT THE OPERATION OF THE SOFTWARE WILL BE ERROR FREE.**

    (c) This limited warranty gives you specific legal rights, and you may have other rights that vary from jurisdiction to jurisdiction.

6. **Remedies.**

    (a) IDGB's entire liability and your exclusive remedy for defects in materials and workmanship shall be limited to replacement of the Software Media, which may be returned to IDGB with a copy of your receipt at the following address: Software Media Fulfillment Department, Attn.: *VBA For Dummies,* 2nd Edition, IDG Books Worldwide, Inc., 7260 Shadeland Station, Ste. 100, Indianapolis, IN 46256, or call 800-762-2974. Please allow three to four weeks for delivery. This Limited Warranty is void if failure of the Software Media has resulted from accident, abuse, or misapplication. Any replacement Software Media will be warranted for the remainder of the original warranty period or thirty (30) days, whichever is longer.

    (b) In no event shall IDGB or the author be liable for any damages whatsoever (including without limitation damages for loss of business profits, business interruption, loss of business information, or any other pecuniary loss) arising from the use of or inability to use the Book or the Software, even if IDGB has been advised of the possibility of such damages.

    (c) Because some jurisdictions do not allow the exclusion or limitation of liability for consequential or incidental damages, the above limitation or exclusion may not apply to you.

7. **U.S. Government Restricted Rights.** Use, duplication, or disclosure of the Software by the U.S. Government is subject to restrictions stated in paragraph (c)(1)(ii) of the Rights in Technical Data and Computer Software clause of DFARS 252.227-7013, and in subparagraphs (a) through (d) of the Commercial Computer– Restricted Rights clause at FAR 52.227-19, and in similar clauses in the NASA FAR supplement, when applicable.

8. **General.** This Agreement constitutes the entire understanding of the parties and revokes and supersedes all prior agreements, oral or written, between them and may not be modified or amended except in a writing signed by both parties hereto that specifically refers to this Agreement. This Agreement shall take precedence over any other documents that may be in conflict herewith. If any one or more provisions contained in this Agreement are held by any court or tribunal to be invalid, illegal, or otherwise unenforceable, each and every other provision shall remain in full force and effect.

Installation Instructions

The *VBA For Dummies,* 2nd Edition CD offers valuable information that you won't want to miss. To install the items from the CD to your hard drive, follow these steps:

1. **Insert the CD into your computer's CD-ROM drive.**

   In a moment, an icon representing the CD you just inserted appears on your computer desktop. Chances are, the icon looks like a CD-ROM.

2. **Double-click the CD icon to show the CD's contents.**

3. **Double-click the Read Me First icon.**

   The Read Me First text file contains information about the CD's programs and any last-minute instructions you may need to correctly install them.

4. **To install most programs, just drag the program's folder from the CD window and drop it on your hard drive icon.**

5. **Other programs come with installer programs — with these, you simply open the program's folder on the CD and then double-click the icon with the words "Install" or "Installer."**

   Sometimes the installers are actually self extracting archives, which just means that the program files have been bundled up into an archive, and this self extractor unbundles the files and places them on your hard drive. This kind of program is often called a .sea. Double click anything with .sea in the title, and it will run just like an installer.

   After you have installed the programs you want, you can eject the CD. Carefully place it back in the plastic jacket of the book for safekeeping.

For more information, see the "About the CD-ROM" appendix.

IDG BOOKS WORLDWIDE
BOOK REGISTRATION

Register This Book and Win!

We want to hear from you!

Visit **http://my2cents.dummies.com** to register this book and tell us how you liked it!

✔ Get entered in our monthly prize giveaway.

✔ Give us feedback about this book — tell us what you like best, what you like least, or maybe what you'd like to ask the author and us to change!

✔ Let us know any other *...For Dummies*® topics that interest you.

Your feedback helps us determine what books to publish, tells us what coverage to add as we revise our books, and lets us know whether we're meeting your needs as a *...For Dummies* reader. You're our most valuable resource, and what you have to say is important to us!

Not on the Web yet? It's easy to get started with *Dummies 101*®: *The Internet For Windows*® *98* or *The Internet For Dummies*, 6th Edition, at local retailers everywhere.

Or let us know what you think by sending us a letter at the following address:

...For Dummies Book Registration
Dummies Press
7260 Shadeland Station, Suite 100
Indianapolis, IN 46256-3945
Fax 317-596-5498

BESTSELLING BOOK SERIES FROM IDG